ATLANTIC STUDIES
BROOKLYN COLLEGE STUDIES ON SOCIETY IN CHANGE
NO. 14

Editor-in-Chief Béla K. Király

War and Society in East Central Europe
Vol. V

DEDICATED TO BROOKLYN COLLEGE OF THE CITY UNIVERSITY OF NEW YORK UPON THE OCCASION OF ITS FIFTIETH ANNIVERSARY

Essays On World War I: Origins and Prisoners of War

Samuel R. Williamson, Jr.
and Peter Pastor, Editors

SOCIAL SCIENCE MONOGRAPHS, BROOKLYN COLLEGE PRESS
DISTRIBUTED BY COLUMBIA UNIVERSITY PRESS, NEW YORK

1983

EAST EUROPEAN MONOGRAPHS, N0. CXXVI

Library of Congress Card Catalogue Number 80-66798
ISBN 0-88033-015-5
Printed in the United States of America

TABLE OF CONTENTS

List of Maps

ACKNOWLEDGMENTS

This volume is the product of research shared at scholarly conferences conducted in the "Program on Society in Change" at Brooklyn College and at the Center for European Studies, Graduate School of the City University of New York. No serious academic work can be done except in the proper milieu. Brooklyn College and CUNY Graduate School offered such a milieu. Many substantial as well as smaller gestures of support were extended to those who worked on this project by President Robert L. Hess; Nathan Schmukler, Dean of the School of Social Science; Ann M. Burton, Chairman of the Department of History at Brooklyn College; and by Henry H. Wasser, Director of the Center for European Studies at the Graduate School and University Center, CUNY. The research and conferences were generously funded by Brooklyn College, CUNY, the National Endowment for the Humanities, the Joint Committee on Eastern Europe of the American Council of Learned Societies and the Social Science Research Council, the International Research and Exchanges Board and the Center for Byzantine and Modern Greek Studies, Queens College, CUNY. The cost of printing was granted by Brooklyn College, the Curriculum in Peace, War and Defense, the University of North Carolina at Chapel Hill, and Atlantic Research and Publications.

Publication was furthered by the Assistant to the Director, Jonathan Chanis. The greatest share of administrative work was done by Mrs. Dorothy Meyerson of the "Program on Society in Change," Brooklyn College. The map was prepared by Mrs. Ida Etelka Romann. The final preparation of this volume was assisted by the careful copy-editing of Mr. Peter Beales.

It is a pleasure and privilege to express warm thanks to all those colleagues, foundations, and institutions.

Béla K. Király
Editor-in-Chief
"Brooklyn College Studies on Society in Change"

PREFACE

The scope of the Brooklyn College Studies on Society in Change series is vast and varied. As President of Brooklyn College I am pleased that a number of the volumes deal with the immediate community of Brooklyn College and the borough of Brooklyn. As an historian with a strong commitment to international study, I recognize that Brooklyn College is honored to be associated with the current volume's scholarly examination of East Central Europe as it was affected by World War I. Brooklyn College is indebted to Professors Béla Király, Samuel R. Williamson, Jr., Peter Pastor and all the contributors to this volume.

Robert L. Hess
President
May 9, 1980

FOREWORD

The present volume is the second to appear in a series which, though not in chronological sequence, it is hoped, when completed, will offer a comprehensive survey of the many aspects of war and society in East Central Europe, including the World War I era.

The chapters of this and future volumes are selected from papers presented at a series of international, interdisciplinary, scholarly conferences sponsored by the Program on Society in Change, Brooklyn College, and the East European Section of the Center for European Studies, Graduate Center, City University of New York, and occasionally other institutions of higher learning.

These volumes deal with peoples whose homelands lie between the Germans to the west, the Russians to the east and north, and the Black, Adriatic, and Mediterranean Seas to the south. They constitute a particular civilization, an integral part of Europe, yet substantially distinct from west and east. Within the area there are intriguing variations in language, religion, and government; so, too, are there differences in concepts of national defense, in the characters of the armed forces, and in ways of waging war. Study of such a complex subject demands an interdisciplinary approach. The scholars involved therefore come from several disciplines, and from universities and other scholarly institutions in the USA, Canada, Western Europe, and the East Central European socialist states.

Investigations focus on comparative surveys of military behavior and organization in these various nations and ethnic groups, to see what is peculiar to them, what has been socially and culturally determined, and what in their conduct of war has been due to circumstances. Besides a historical survey, an attempt is made to define different patterns of military behavior, including the decision-making processes, the attitudes and actions of diverse social classes, and the restraints or lack of them shown in war.

We endeavor to present considerable material on the effects of social, economic, political, and technological changes, and of changes in the sciences applied to warfare and in international relationships, on the development of doctrines of national defense and practices in military organization, command, strategy, and tactics. We shall also present data on the social origins and mobility of the officer corps and the rank and file, on the differences between the officer corps of the various services, and above all on the civil-military relationship and on the origins of the East Central European brand of militarism. The studies will, it is hoped, result in a better understanding of the societies, governments and politics of East Central Europe, most of whose peoples now belong to the Warsaw Treaty Organization, although one Greece is a member of the North Atlantic Treaty Organization and three Albania, Austria and Yugoslavia are neutral countries.

The methodology takes into account that in the last three decades the study of war and national defense systems has moved away from the narrow concern with battles, campaigns, and leaders, and has come to concern itself with the evolution of the entire society. In fact, the interdependence of changes in society and changes in warfare, and the proposition that military institutions closely reflect the character of the society of which they are part have come to be accepted by historians, political scientists, sociologists, philosophers, and other students of war and national defense. Recognition of this fact constitutes one of the keystones of our approach to the subject.

Works in western languages adequately cover the diplomatic, political, intellectual, social and economic histories of these peoples and this area. In contrast, few substantial studies of their national defense systems have yet appeared in western languages. Similarly, though some substantial, comprehensive accounts of the nonmilitary aspects of the history of the whole region have been published in the West, nothing has yet appeared in any western language about the national defense systems of the area as a whole. Nor has there been any study of the mutual effects of the concepts and practices of national defense in East Central Europe. This comprehensive study on war and society in East Central Europe is a pioneering work.

The eighteenth and nineteenth centuries, the first period our efforts have concentrated upon, are crucial for all these nations, for they are the era of nation-building. Many of these peoples formed nation-states during the period, a development in which their armed forces played critical roles. Even in the case of the Poles, whose state was partitioned in the eighteenth century and was not to be reestablished until after the nineteenth century, insurrectionary armies played a vital part in consolidating national consciousness.

World War I wrought more change in East Central Europe than in any other part of the world. It brought to completion the process of creating nation-states, unifying nations, and partitioning Hungary. The war, at least during its last eighteen months, was already a total war: the massive application of armed force aimed to destroy the enemy's will and means to continue the belligerency. In total war not only armies but entire populations are engaged in the combat; battalion formations, farms, factories, mines, transportation systems all count equally in the war effort and all are equally legitimate targets of enemy action. Nothing is more exposed to concentrated enemy attack in total war than a people's will to produce and to fight. Psychological warfare, which aims to strengthen the will of one side and destroy that of the other, thus became a crucial element of the battle in the trenches as well as in the interior during World War I. It left the ugliest possible heritage: hatred, division and hostility among the East Central Europeans.

Set prior to the hostilities, the aims of the war were not adjusted to such warfare, as the essays in Part I of this book testify. The statesmen and military leaders had envisaged a conventional, limited, balance-of-power war of nineteenth-century vintage. They were in error. The various governments' policies toward the prisoners of war bore the stamp of total war. No international law, no principle, certainly no spirit of chivalry was involved. Both the policies toward the prisoners and the prisoners' fates typified total war.

The present volume, the first of several that will deal with World War I, considers two extremely important features of that war: the backward-looking war aims that reflected nineteenth-century thinking, and the governments' policies toward their prisoners of war, which reflected the brutality of total war and looked forward to warfare in the rest of the twentieth century, not least, World War II.

The character of World War I also illustrated the unpredictability of the outcome of total war. No one went to war to create Czechoslovakia, to create Yugoslavia, to enlarge Rumania, or for that matter, to resurrect Poland, with the presumable exception of the small, determined band of men whom Jozef Piłsudski led into Russia even before the declaration of war, and certain Serbian statesmen and conspirators. All those fundamental changes to the map of Europe came about unexpectedly. On the other hand, the realization of the Wilsonian principles of national self-determination for which more and more people came to yearn was finally achieved in some respect only at the cost of violation the principle in the case of Hungary. While the Rumanians encompassed 96 percent of all Rumanians within their enlarged Rumania, only 72 percent of the enlarged state were Rumanians. The new state of Yugoslavia included 93 percent of all South Slavs within its frontiers, but they amounted to only 79.8% of the state's population. Ninety-six percent of all Czechs and Slovaks were united within the new Czechoslovakia, but they accounted for only 66 percent of the state's inhabitants. Three multinational states were thus built on the ruins of other multinational states. By contrast, while 92 percent of the population of rump Hungary was Hungarian, they were only 74 percent of all Hungarians, the rest were excluded from their nation-state and became subjects instead of Czechoslovakia, Rumania or Yugoslavia.

The main results and repercussions of World War I were unexpected, and that is the pattern of total war. The present volume begins to examine the problems of World War I insofar as they affected East Central Europe. Further volumes will pursue these studies. We do not set out to revise the history of World War I *per se,* but, as the title of Dean Williamson's opening essay suggests, there are matters that need reconsideration. This is our intention.

Béla K. Király

I. THE ORIGINS OF WORLD WAR I RECONSIDERED

Samuel R. Williamson, Jr., Editor

INTRODUCTION

Samuel R. Williamson, Jr.

Historians frequently eschew the idea that their work is relevant to the contemporary situation. Not without reason, they contend that history does not repeat itself, that the "lessons" of history are complex and cautionary, and that each situation is different and unique. Yet these considerations should not obscure two important points: *first,* that basic historical problems, such as the causes of a war, are basic because of the continuing need to understand such phenomena; *second,* that certain geographical areas ebb and flow in historical importance, but the very fact of ebb and flow means that today's neglected issue may be tomorrow's area of greatest concern. If the historian's task is both to seek truth and to educate, then historians must continue to help the present understand the past—in all its complexity.

Few events are more central to understanding the present world—despite the passage of nearly seventy years—than the outbreak of war in 1914 and its bloody, protracted aftermath. And few events are more crucial to an understanding of developments in East Central Europe than the Great War. Now, at the start of the 1980s, when the specter of Yugoslavia without Josip Tito and the strategic tensions of yesteryear's imperialism—in Iran, Afghanistan, and the Northwest Frontier—loom large, a renewed appreciation of the events that brought the 1914 war may well be appropriate.

The debate over July 1914 and the origins of the crisis has long centered upon the role of Germany and the policy-makers in Berlin. Although the extreme revisionists of the 1920s sought to shift the attention (and the blame) to Russia and France, these themes gained no lasting acceptance. More moderate revisionists, such as Sidney B. Fay, were more evenhanded and spread responsibility (not guilt) more widely, ranking Austria-Hungary first, not Germany, and stressing the part played by Serbia. But Luigi Albertini's massive work and the two decades of controversy stirred by Fritz Fischer's work have riveted attention on German culpability.

Until late in the 1960s, Eastern Europe's participation in the coming of the war remained largely unexplored. Even then there were few exceptions. Vladimir Dedijer wrote about the conspiracy behind the assassinations, Anglo-American historians dissected specialized pieces of the story, and Hungarian and East German historians examined contextual issues behind the 1914 war. But for the most part historians did not focus on the Habsburg monarchy and the coming of the war, certainly not with the intensity of a Fritz Fischer. Nor were the domestic ramifications, apart from nationality or military issues, examined minutely.

Now, though Russia remains sadly neglected, the Balkans and the Habsburg monarchy on the eve of Sarajevo are being subjected anew (or often for the first time) to intensive research. The 1974 conference in Belgrade on Serbia and the Great Powers reflected this, as do the recent works by Friedrich Wurthle, Kurt Peball, Gunther Rothenberg, and the conferences and lectures sponsored by Brooklyn College on "Society in Change." The essays contained in the first half of this volume represent a further addition to this growing literature. They were presented on December 3, 1979, at the second conference on "War and Society in East Central Europe" sponsored by Brooklyn College. It is hoped that their appearance will stimulate further and renewed interest in this important topic.

* * * *

The essays in the first half of the volume reflect a wide variety of approaches to explaining the past, ranging from traditional diplomatic history based on a close reading of the archives to an incorporation of psychological and organizational behavior theories. In each, perception and misperception, whether of the individual decision-maker or of the small elite group at work in its society, receive new emphasis. Several continuing themes link the essays and their different approaches, and merit additional comment.

First, the papers reiterate the importance of alliances and ententes to the diplomatic history of the pre-1914 world. In an era accustomed to superpower dominance, the part played by alliances among nearly equal partners in the European state system must not be forgotten. In the pre-1914 world, alliances and ententes – with occasional duplicity by their members–were a familiar feature of the international landscape. If the French could always (but most insistently in July 1914) ask what Britain would do if war came, the Habsburg rulers could ask the question even more insistently of each of their alliance partners: Germany, Italy, and Rumania. Alliance politics and judgements drawn about what a partner would (or would not) do influenced the Habsburg decision-makers. Berlin's blank check, the defection of Rumania, and the mercurial behavior of Rome, each shaped the way the Habsburg apparatus reacted in 1914.

A second theme, linked to the first but individualized, is the place occupied by the central decision-makers and especially the senior military, diplomatic, and court officials. These essays stress how intimate was their association, how easy the chance of self-deception or misperception, and how important the individual is in making the decision for war or peace. The roots of such perceptions and explanations for this or that choice form the corpus of the four papers' efforts to show (in separate but neatly dovetailing fashion) that an individual's psychological makeup and perceptions can influence decisions. The unease of these decision-makers with a world in disarray (and in contrast to earlier, more complacent times) fused with their more recent perceptions about an ally's reliability, a commitment apparently made, or a government not to be trusted. This psychological approach serves to remind the reader of the complexity of decision-making and of the narrow line between one course of action and another.

A third current through the essays is the place that organizations–whether the army, the general staff, the foreign office, the Habsburg court, or the literary bureau of the *Kriegsarchiv* – have in the life of modern states. War planning and its implementation have long been recognized as the epitome of seeking to make a large bureaucracy function. What has been less emphasized but is no less important is the bureaucratization of other instruments of government–to include the foreign office, the office of the prime minister, and the parliamentary process – in addressing budget requests. Even the life of the Habsburg court grew more complex with the existence of the military chancellery of the Archduke Franz Ferdinand, the heir apparent, alongside that of Emperor Franz Joseph. The influence of bureaucracy on modern governments and their decision-making, admitted or not, had become increasingly important by 1914; its presence through succeeding decades – as bureaucracies rise to defeat the best intentions of politicians and statesman – remain pivotal.

A final theme is the intellectual in politics, either those dabbling at the fringes with ambitions for higher office such as Joseph Redlich, or a writer-intellectual such as Hugo von Hofmannsthal, seeking to do his patriotic duty during World War I. What the essays make clear is both the hope and the frustration of those who longed for a Habsburg monarchy at least as worthy as its monarchs. There was hope that reform, either before the war or as a result of a victorious war, might rescue the state; hope that the state and its people called to meet new challenges could revive the venerable monarchy. These hopes were repeatedly dashed. Frustration came first at Sarajevo when the heir apparent, judged to be best able to reorganize the edifice, disappeared; frustration continued as the war rendered increasingly bleak, then impossible, the revival of the monarchy. Thwarted, the intellectuals would then take different routes to cope with the new reality, but always with regret and greater nostalgia.

* * * *

Each of the essays addresses separate but related questions, each builds upon the other, each suggests new areas that require examination and reflection. The editor's contribution describes the increasingly abrupt diplomacy followed by the Habsburg foreign minister, Count Leopold Berchtold, as the Balkan Wars unfolded, and relates the mounting tendency among many Habsburg leaders to see the situation as requiring a military solution. So long as Archduke Franz Ferdinand lived, a braking device for peace existed. His disappearance catalyzed an already dangerous situation. Count Alexander Hoyos's mission, the conversion of the Hungarian Minister President, Count István Tisza, to aggressive action, the failure to estimate correctly Russia's reaction, the delay in the dispatch of the ultimatum, and then the decision to attack Serbia first are examined as examples of Habsburg decision-making.

Michael Palumbo's study returns to a scorned area: Austro-Italian relations. With careful attention to the memoir literature and new archival data, Palumbo argues that the improvement of Austro-Italian military and naval relations in the last months before July 1914 may have misled Gen. Franz Conrad von Hötzendorf about Italian reliability. Easing his customary cynicism, he came to believe and act as if Italy would be loyal to the Triple Alliance should Austria-Hungary attack Serbia. This perception would, Palumbo makes clear, help to convince the senior policy-makers in Vienna in July to proceed with their plans vis-à-vis Belgrade.

A similar, and more important misperception—what Russia would do—is the subject of Professor William Jannen's article. He addresses this basic issue by utilizing a series of recent hypotheses in the field of psychoanalytical theory and perceptions. Contrasting the careful attention paid to Russia's probable behavior during the Balkan Wars with almost "no attention" during the July crisis, Jannen continually asks: why this gap in the thinking of Habsburg officials? He concludes that individual frustration, the problem of personal adjustment to the jolts of industrialization, and differences in personality style converged to convince the Habsburg policy-makers that war with Serbia was the only solution. In 1914 the temptation to strike out became unendurable.

This level of frustration was not limited to government circles. It affected artists and intellectuals, a point that Professor Paula Sutter Fichtner stresses eloquently in her analysis of the artist-intellectual at work in the war effort. While seeking to explain the roots of the Conservative Revolution of the 1920s, Fichtner concentrates upon Hugo von Hofmannsthal and his activities on behalf of the state during the war. His propaganda work at the *Kriegsarchiv*, his attempts to stress and yet blur the connection between the intellectual and any government, are poignantly described. In the essay the illusions of intellectuals and the hardheaded realism of ministers (and monarchs) and their almost inevitable clash are etched with great clarity. One can conclude that the relationship is always likely to be fickle and uneasy in war, and especially in peace. The bewilderment and despair that led the monarchy's governing elite to misperceive, to err, and to go to war were shared by the intellectuals and the artists. That dissatisfaction with liberal or conventional politics would emerge in the 1920s is thus not surprising.

Taken together, these essays will introduce readers to new methodologies, possibly prompt renewed thought about old issues, and put the Habsburg monarchy's position in the events of 1914-1918 in a different context. They will, it is hoped, spark further historical discussion, and be subjected in turn to more refinement and precision. The essays, it is also hoped, may encourage other scholars—especially those in the whole of the old monarchy—to probe more deeply into some of the basic dimensions addressed by the conferences at Brooklyn College: war, society, their interconnection, and the risks that accompany their interaction. Only in this way can history hope to be of more than academic interest and serve a larger, more important role – making the past and the present more intelligible.

* * * *

The editor wishes to thank Professor Béla K. Király for his generous assistance, Professor James Leutze of the Curriculum in Peace, War, and Defense for assistance in publication, and his associates—Thomas Conner, Ronald Maner, Louise Dewar, and Mandy Hollowell—for their help in final preparation of the manuscript.

VIENNA AND JULY 1914: THE ORIGINS OF THE GREAT WAR ONCE MORE

Samuel R. Williamson, Jr.

For over three decades, and well into the 1950s, Austria-Hungary occupied a prominent place in historical assessments of the crisis of July 1914. But with the advent of Fritz Fischer and the Hamburg school, the Habsburg role faded. For many Vienna became only an enlarged version of Bucharest or Brussels, a pawn and virtual plaything of Germany's *Weltpolitik.*[1] Nor did any systematic study of Vienna's prewar policy emerge during the 1960s and 1970s to challenge this imbalance; indeed Austrian and Hungarian scholars were almost silent on the topic.[2] This essay attempts to rectify the situation. To that end, it seeks to reopen – once more – the debate over July 1914, and at the same time put Fischer's assessments in a less embracing context. Above all, it hopes to remind scholars of what the participants in 1914 readily perceived: that Vienna, though troubled and possibly anachronistic, was a great power capable of independent action and decision.

* * * *

In July 1914 the critical policy initiatives – after the deaths of Franz Ferdinand and Sophie at Sarajevo – were exercised by the Austro-Hungarian government: the decision for a showdown with Serbia, the approach to Berlin, the framing and timing of the ultimatum, the refusal to negotiate in any meaningful way, and the start of local war against Serbia. At every point Vienna, not Berlin, retained the initiative. Yet historians have often slighted this independence and determination, in part because of the dichotomy between long- and short-term causes, in part because of their fixation on Berlin, and in part because of their failure to appreciate how close Vienna had alreay come to war during the twenty months preceding Sarajevo. [3] In particular, three sets of developments after the start of the First Balkan War in October 1912 require attention: the progressive use of a diplomacy of abruptness and threat; a growing sense of desperation among senior Habsburg officials over the monarchy's long-term prospects; and the part played by Archduke Franz Ferdinand in the governmental process.

On three different occasions between September 1912 and July 1914 Vienna confronted war-peace decisions where one changed opinion by Kaiser Franz Joseph or Foreign Minister Count Leopold Berchtold would have ensured military action. Few governments ever have (or want) so many opportunities to analyze the costs and possible benefits of war. By comparison the celebrated war council *(Kriegsrat)* in Berlin on December 8, 1912, appears almost casual, isolated chatter.[4]

The first episode occurred in early December 1912. Reports reached Vienna that Serbian troops were leaving recently occupied Macedonia and moving northward into Serbia proper. The Habsburg military, making a "worst-case interpretation," concluded the Serbians would now attack the monarchy. The generals, backed by Archduke Franz Ferdinand, advocated—with some success—preventive countermeasures. On December 7 Franz Joseph agreed to put all of Bosnia-Herzegovina on a war footing *(Kriegsstand),* a measure only a slight step away from full mobilization. A total of 100,000 troops, increased from the usual 40,000, were now on duty in the south. But the military leadership, still backed by the heir apparent, wanted to launch a military operation against Serbia. In a climactic confrontation at Schönbrunn Palace on December 11, Franz Joseph and Berchtold rejected this demand. The old emperor refused to be stampeded unless the Serbian danger became more specific. Uncertainty about Berlin's attitude, the possibility of disrupting the impending London conference on the Balkans, and concern over winter weather—each played a part in the refusal to attack. The Habsburg monarchy came to the brink of war, only to veer away.[5]

The second occasion came in April-May 1913. This time in fact Vienna's decision-makers came closer to war than at any point before July 1914. The target was tiny Montenegro; the odds, 250,000 Montenegrins versus the 50 million citizens of the Habsburg holdings. The issues were straightforward: King Nikita refused to yield Skutari to the newly created principality of Albania. When an international fleet assembled off the minute Montenegrin coast, the king accused the great powers of violating Montenegrin territorial waters. The failure during April to dislodge Montenegro from Skutari thoroughly exasperated Habsburg policy-makers. A new war plan for Montenegro (Case M) was hastily prepared; German acquiescence in a limited campaign was secured. On May 2 the Common Cabinet agreed to mobilize within a matter of days along the Montenegrin frontier. This news quickly reached dusty Cetinje. King Nikita immediately abandoned his pretensions. The full mobilization scheduled for Bosnia-Herzegovina was canceled, though the 60,000 reservists called late in 1912 still remained on duty even after this crisis, and went home only after the Second Balkan War.[6]

The third war-peace crisis came in October. Again the issue involved Albania. For months Serbian troops had remained in territory along the Black Drin River assigned by the great powers to Albania. This caused friction, then fighting, between Serbian and Albanian military units. Repeatedly the powers, including Vienna, asked Belgrade to evacuate the area; repeatedly Nikola Pasić's government made promises, but did nothing. Finally, on October 18, Vienna took unilateral action. It dispatched a clear, unambiguous eight-day ultimatum to Belgrade: clear out of Albania or face the consequences. Again Berlin acquiesced, but virtually after the fact, Kaiser Wilhelm II with his customary impulsiveness, the Wilhelmstrasse more cautiously. This time Belgrade made good on its promises: all Serbian troops were off Albanian territory by October 25.[7]

From these crises there emerged in Vienna the conviction that forceful diplomacy worked. The European Concert had endorsed the creation of Albania, and accepted Berchtold's demand to forestall Serbian access to the Adriatic. But the concert was slow and clumsy, subject to delay and manipulation.[8] By contrast, stern, demanding diplomacy, reinforced by partial mobilization, threats, and even an ultimatum had won speedy compliance from Belgrade and Cetinje. Steadily, possibly without altogether realizing it, some policy-makers in the monarchy were militarizing their approach to the Serbian and South Slav issue. Berchtold, Austrian Minister President Count Karl Stürgkh, Common Finance Minister Leon von Bilinksi, senior officials at the Ballhausplatz such as Counts Alexander Hoyos and János Forgách, and (less consistently) Hungarian Minister President Count István Tisza were becoming more belligerent and less restrained. Each succeeding war-peace crisis had prompted an escalation of response. Soon the diplomatic arsenal would be exhausted.[9]

The confrontations, moreover, necessarily enhanced Habsburg military preparations. In October 1912, when the Balkan armies mobilized and Russia retained 375,000 troops on active duty (the rough equivalent of all Habsburg forces), Vienna did nothing despite pleas from Gen. Blasius Schemua, the then chief of the general staff. On the other hand, the diplomats and generals alike viewed the Russian action as not so subtle blackmail, designed to keep Vienna from intervening in the Balkan fighting. Yet for nearly six weeks Franz Joseph and Berchtold resisted military appeals to respond in some fashion to the apparent threats on the monarchy's northern and southern borders. Not until late October would several thousand troops be sent south. A few weeks later, in mid-November after the Delegations had recessed, reserves were progressively called to units in Galicia and later to units in the south. The strength of the Austro-Hungarian forces steadily increased from 400,000 to just over 620,000 men. Of those troops in the south, 60,000 reservists would remain on active duty from early December until August 1913 and the conclusion of the Peace of Bucharest.[10]

To pay for these military steps, including naval preparations and capital expenditures, the monarchy spent at least 309 million kronen ($62 million at 1912 rates, or almost three-quarters of its annual army budget) plus the regular defense budget as well.[11] Such abrupt financial demands forced both the Austrian and Hungarian governments to make hasty arrangements to borrow on the New York money markets in December 1912, the Austrians paying a substantial 6½ percent interest for a two-year loan (current bank rates were 5 percent).[12]

But the Habsburg military leaders not only wanted manpower increases and new equipment, they wanted action. They argued there could be no repeat of the 1909 crisis when the troops had been called up, only to go home unused—and alive. The major protagonist for action, though by no means the only voice urging an attack on Serbia, was Gen. Franz Conrad von Hötzendorf, chief of the general staff.

A complex, talented individual, Conrad von Hötzendorf is possibly the most intriguing of all the military and naval leaders of pre-1914 Europe. Born in 1852, the only son of a retired colonel who had fought against Napoleon and the revolutions of 1848, Conrad von Hötzendorf entered the army in 1863 at the age of eleven and continued on active duty until 1918. In 1906 Archduke Franz Ferdinand, acting with the cognizance of Franz Joseph, secured Conrad von Hötzendorf's appointment as chief of the general staff; he retained this position until late 1911 when his demands for a preventive war against Italy led to his ouster. But the possibility of war in December 1912 led to the heir apparent's insistence that Conrad von Hötzendorf be reinstated as chief, a position he then retained until March 1917. A painter, a military writer, an advocate of offensive warfare, a man who disdained parades and drill-ground exercises, Conrad von Hötzendorf had thoroughly inbibed the late nineteenth-century rhetoric of Friedrich Nietzsche and the social Darwinists. Life is a struggle. The fight for survival is everything. Individuals count for little. Nations fight for existence and exist to fight. Territorial expansion for conservative purposes is justified imperialism. Nationalism can be overcome by good government and dynastic loyalty. Toughness, combativeness, obedience: the military virtues were Conrad von Hötzendorf's dicta.[13]

Yet there was another Conrad von Hötzendorf, a general who enjoyed and even needed the company of women to whom he revealed insecurities, frustrations, and ambitions. With them the command mask slipped away, replaced by an ego needing comfort and psychological reinforcement. One who provided this nearly all his professional life was his mother, Barbara. After her daughter's death in 1884, Barbara lived with or near Conrad von Hötzendorf until her death in August 1915. The recently edited *Private Aufzeichnungen* of Conrad von Hötzendorf shed important new information on their relationship. Conrad von Hötzendorf's first wife, Wilma, also provided such company until her death from stomach cancer in April 1905. A devoted, loyal woman and the mother of four sons, Wilma's illness, and subsequent death were hard blows, not made easier by the responsibility for rearing the sons.[14]

But Gina von Reininghaus's appearance in Conrad von Hötzendorf's orbit in 1907 would help to assuage the grief. They first met at a party in Trieste in 1900, then not again until another party, this time in Vienna in 1907. The wife of a prominent Styrian businessman, Hans von Reininghaus, and mother of six children, Gina was an Italian beauty some twenty-eight years younger than Conrad von Hötzendorf. For the general it was love at first sight. He proposed; Gina refused to seek a divorce. The liaison continued. For eight years Conrad von Hötzendorf penned hundreds of letters of love and comment, while writing possibly another thousand that were not sent and which he later called "the diary of my suffering." Through more than one of these exchanges ran the theme: if only war will come, I can become a hero, return and marry Gina. In 1915, after his mother's death, Conrad von Hötzendorf finally did marry Gina following her adoption by a Hungarian Protestant general, the nullification of her first marriage, and Franz Joseph's reluctant consent to this charade. To the scandal of many, Gina was then to join Conrad von Hötzendorf at the general headquarters at Teschen. Conrad was no ordinary general, indeed no ordinary man.[15]

As chief of the general staff Conrad von Hötzendorf had long worried over the monarchy's vulnerable strategic position. For years Russia and Italy had ranked equally with Serbia as the foci of his fears. But by late 1912 the general was almost obsessed by the threat posed by Belgrade. For him Serbia had unquestionably become the monarchy's most dangerous problem; so long as Belgrade appealed to the Slavs in Bosnia and Herzegovina and talked of a Greater Serbia, Habsburg rule would never be secure. While Conrad von Hötzendorf suggested an economic association with Belgrade, or else Serbian membership (*à la* Bavaria) in a greater Habsburg monarchy, his preferred solution to the Serbia-South Slav problem was to defeat Serbia and then partition it.

As 1913 progressed Conrad von Hötzendorf's advocacy of war against Serbia began to sound like an elderly gramophone: high-pitched, scratchy, run-down.[16] The monarchy, he argued, had to act preemptively and without delay. As Conrad von Hötzendorf never failed to remind others (including Franz Joseph), he believed Vienna had missed its best chance for acting in 1909, when it was clear Russia would have stood aside. Now Russia was strong—and getting stronger. Vienna thus had to act before St. Petersburg became invincible. He wanted, moreover, to exploit German dependence and loyalty. Conrad von Hötzendorf insisted that Berlin, however much the Wilhelmstrasse might waver, would perforce support Austria-Hungary. Both allies needed each other. The Schlieffen Plan could not succeed without an Austro-Hungarian attack on Russia; Habsburg plans would not work without Germany helping to hold the ring in the east. And he would argue that Germany's mere affirmation of support might deter Russia altogether. These advantages, he insisted, had to be exploited, not frittered away.[17]

Conrad von Hötzendorf's military plans are well known. Plan R (Russia) involved total mobilization, with Habsburg armies on the offensive in Galicia, on the defensive in the south, and helped by a small German offensive from East Prussia against the Russians. Plan B (Balkan) involved partial mobilization, with a defensive force along the border in Galicia and Bukovina, and the major offensive against Serbia and Montenegro. The crucial strategic issue was Russia. Would St. Petersburg stand aside, decide to intervene immediately, or wait until Vienna was entrapped in the south? To meet these options, Conrad von Hötzendorf organized a "maneuver force" or "B echelon" of twelve divisions that could be sent either north or south at the last possible moment, their deployment determining the essential thrust of the Habsburg attack. In this way Conrad von Hötzendorf hoped to master his strategic dilemma, preserve his flexibility, and at the same time defer a final decision until the last possible moment.[18]

Throughout 1913 Conrad von Hötzendorf, joined by Gen. Baron von Krobatin, the common war minister, and Gen. Oskar Potiorek, the governor-general of Bosnia-Herzegovina, pressed for a preventive attack on Serbia. The forces were there; why not use them? Put another way, forces in being create a strategic opportunity. Or put still another way, available forces create temptation. It was in fact with the greatest reluctance that Conrad von Hötzendorf even consented in April 1913 to devise a Plan M (Montenegro), fearing any small-scale operation would jeopardize chances for wider war with Serbia. Nor would he even consider seizing Serbian territory as a hostage, or a halt-in-Belgrade scheme, because neither guaranteed a full military reckoning with Serbia.[19]

Because Conrad von Hötzendorf demanded "all or nothing," Foreign Minister Berchtold was able for the most part to resist his pressures. Yet the continual advocacy of the military option progressively acclimated even the political leadership to think in terms of a military solution of the South Slav problem. In May 1913 Berchtold wryly noted that even Count Karl Stürgkh, the Austrian minister president, and the most pacific of men, now demanded military action and had become a fire-breathing Austrian patriot. In the October 1913 crisis, Count István Tisza, his Hungarian counterpart, joined Stürgkh in urging a tough ultimatum to Serbia. Even the aging Franz Joseph increasingly veered toward military diplomacy. Possibly more important, Count Berchtold also came to share this view as he struggled to manage the monarchy's defensive diplomacy.[20]

* * * *

In February 1912 Count Leopold Berchtold had succeeded the dying Count Alois Lexa von Aehrenthal as Habsburg foreign minister. Emerging from a year's retirement on his Buchlau estates, Berchtold at forty-nine was the youngest foreign minister in Europe. He was also a relative newcomer to the monarchy's foreign service, with only nineteen years' experience and with many of his ambassadors a dozen years older than he. Yet he had served with competence, even distinction, as ambassador in St. Petersburg from 1906 to 1911. For that he enjoyed Franz Joseph's trust and gratitude. Treated harshly by interwar historians who castigated his love of horse-racing and fine clothes (Sir Edward Grey's passion for fly-fishing usually went unnoticed), Berchtold in fact performed adequately, occasionally ably, in the months before 1914.[21]

For example, Berchtold tried in vain in the late summer of 1912 to alert Europe to the danger of a Balkan eruption; his efforts met only suspicion and dismissal. And it was Berchtold in October 1912, seeking to limit the area of conflict, who agreed to partition the sanjak of Novi Pazar rather than make it a *cause célèbre* with Belgrade and Cetinje. Berchtold, moreover, early, clearly and unhesitatingly informed the other powers of Vienna's minimum conditions for any territorial changes in the Balkans: no Serbian access to the Adriatic and the creation of an independent Albania. In late 1912, he won the concert's grudging acceptance of these goals and its tacit consent to their imposition on Serbia and Montenegro. Especially sensitive to pressure from Berlin, the foreign minister had no intention of letting Habsburg foreign policy be shaped by German *Weltpolitik*. On more than one occasion, Germany found itself confronted by Berchtold's *faits accomplis*.[22]

Repeatedly during the Balkan fighting, Berchtold turned aside Conrad von Hötzendorf's demand for action while exploiting the situation to enhance Habsburg military preparedness. Indeed, as early as mid-1912 he recognized that a diplomatic policy without force was destined to be weak and timid.[23] Later, after reluctantly consenting in December 1912 to the war footing for Bosnia, he was the minister most responsible for keeping the extra 60,000 troops on extended duty in the south despite insistent pleas from Franz Joseph and Franz Ferdinand that they be released. Nor did Berchtold hesitate to use the presence of additional Habsburg forces in Galicia as a bargaining chip in negotiations with St. Petersburg in early 1913. Eventually in March he secured a profitable *quid pro quo:* 45,000 Habsburg and 375,000 Russian troops went home.[24]

By late 1913 Berchtold appears to have believed that, if the South Slav issue was ever to be resolved, a war with

Serbia was inevitable. What mattered would be the timing and circumstances of the conflict. As Gen. George Marshall once observed early in the Cold War, a political problem thought of in military terms eventually becomes a military problem.[25] By early 1914 Berchtold and his close associates at the Ballhausplatz, including Count Alexander Hoyos, his *chef de cabinet,* and Count János Forgách, the first section chief, were increasingly of this persuasion. Gone were the easy options in addressing the issue: bribery such as had been tried before 1903 with the Obrenović dynasty; economic sanctions as in the Pig War; economic concessions as in the 1909 trade treaty; pledges by Belgrade to end subversive propaganda as had been elicited in 1909; even surrender on the sanjak issue. Nor did a repeat of the partial mobilization of late 1912, with its high cost and disruptive impact on civilian morale, appear an option any longer. While diplomacy was not yet abandoned, force loomed as a compelling last resort, however distasteful or poor the odds. That this was a dangerous, self-fulfilling attitude for a foreign minister and foreign ministry needs little stress.[26]

Berchtold's despair over the South Slav issue found no solace in his evaluation of the monarchy's long-term situation, domestic or international. If the monarchy's overall economic prospects, at least with hindsight, appeared promising, the problems of state finances and of the economic dislocation caused by the Balkan Wars pressed hard on government policymakers.[27] So too did the political stalemate in the two halves of the monarchy. In Austria the *Reichsrat* adjourned on March 16, 1914; it did not reconvene until May 1917. In Hungary Tisza dominated the political scene but with increasing difficulty.[28]

Nor were foreign-policy prospects attractive either. Perhaps most importantly, the Triple Alliance appeared less an alliance and more a sparring association. By early 1914 the fruitful cooperation between Rome and Vienna in creating Albania and thwarting Greek and Serbian ambitions had given way to open rivalry over the new principality. Italian nationalism, fanned by the ineptness of Habsburg local government in Trieste, had also flared anew. And the two governments were equally at odds over Vienna's belated demands, should Turkey actually collapse, for a share of

Anatolia already coveted by both Germany and Italy. To be sure, there were renewed and detailed military and naval talks that settled Italian help in case of European war. Conrad von Hötzendorf, who remained dubious about Italian reliability but liked General Alberto Pollio, hoped the chief of the Italian general staff could sway his government in the hour of crisis. Ironically, Pollio died of a heart attack on June 28.[29]

With Berlin relations were uneven, occasionally fractious, and mainly ambivalent. Contact between the dynasties remained close, too close some of Franz Joseph's advisers thought, given the frequent contacts between Kaiser Wilhelm and Archduke Franz Ferdinand.[30] The military associations were likewise frequent, if carefully circumspect and occasionally taciturn.[31] Political and diplomatic relations were less harmonious, the product of almost continuous differences over how to assess and meet the rapidly evolving situation in the Balkans. Berlin's *Weltpolitik* concerns inevitably differed from those of Vienna's *Balkanpolitik.* Berlin wanted a Habsburg rapprochement with Rumania and the inclusion of Greece in the alliance system (King Constantine I was Wilhelm's brother-in-law); Vienna favored Bulgaria, and thought Wilhelm's talk of a partnership with Serbia cavalier and fatuous. Economic competition in the Balkans between the allies did not help either. The two political apparatus had unmistakably drifted apart, a drift not helped by the less than warm personal relations between Gottlieb von Jagow, the German foreign secretary, and Berchtold after Jagow's appointment in January 1913. Austro-Hungarian-German relations had seen better days.[32]

Relations with Rumania, long the silent partner of the Triple Alliance, were virtually beyond repair. Although the Hohenzollern King Carol had renewed his secret ties in February 1913, relations between Rumania and Austria-Hungary had thereafter plummeted. Bucharest accused Vienna of flirting with Bulgaria in June 1913, and then of seeking to undo Carol's diplomatic success of August—the Treaty of Bucharest. Renewed unrest among the three million Rumanians living under less than benevolent Magyar rule in Transylvania exacerbated Habsburg-Rumanian relations. Foreign Minister Berchtold, anxious to keep the Rumanians in the alliance, continually pressed Budapest to be more conciliatory in Transylvania. In a move with a number of motives, Berchtold sent Ottokar Czernin, Franz Ferdinand's sometime confidant, to Bucharest as minister in December 1913 in a last-ditch bid to improve ties. He was not a shining success. By April 1914 Habsburg policymakers could, at best, expect only neutrality from Rumania if war came. Conrad von Hötzendorf now had to face the prospect of war on four fronts.[33]

On the Russian front, relations between St. Petersburg and Vienna were correct and formal in early 1914. At the Ballhausplatz distrust of Sergey Sazonov, the Russian foreign minister, festered. Russia's role, first in creating the Balkan League, and then in blatantly exploiting the ambassadorial conferences in London, was not easily forgotton. Nor did the subversive activity of Pan-Slavic groups in Galicia and the bombast of Russia's minister to Belgrade, N.H. Hartwig, about a final reckoning with the Habsburgs generate optimism in Vienna. Berchtold for his part reciprocated. In late 1913 Berchtold eased Aehrenthal's pro-Russian appointee, Count Thurn, out, installing instead a hardliner on Russian issues, Count Friedrich Szapáry, as Habsburg ambassador to Russia. Austro-Russian relations, whatever Franz Ferdinand's wistful hopes about a renewed *Dreikaiserbund,* were correct and no more in June 1914.[34]

By that month, surprisingly, relations with Belgrade were no worse than in the preceding October. In May both states had agreed to release a small number of convicted spies. And negotiations continued in an effort to resolve the economic legacies of the Balkan wars: Serbian compensation to Vienna for its former commercial concessions in Macedonia, commercial access for Serbia to the Adriatic Sea, and the legal status of the Oriental Railway Company in the now conquered Turkish territories.[35] While progress was scant, at least the two governments remained in contact. At the same time, as May gave way to June, Vienna watched with fascination (though not much alarm) as Nikola Pasíc struggled to keep power and to curb the ambitious Serbian military.[36]

Even in Bosnia-Herzegovina, target of continuing Serbian propaganda activity, the political situation almost appeared promising. The Bosnian *Landtag* was hard at work; a massive new railway program offered potential economic rewards.

Despite reports of students' agitation and travel to and from Serbia, the imperial colony looked stable, even calm. Indeed, the apparent passivity may have misled Gen. Potiorek and his civilian superior, Leon Ritter von Bilinski, in assessing the security risks of a visit by Franz Ferdinand to Sarajevo.[37]

Whether with allies, possible foes, or erstwhile friends, the Ballhausplatz found the longer international perspective discouraging. There were moments of optimism, but far more of pessimism and despair. The alliance with Germany was shaky; Italy and Rumania were dubious associates; the Serbs, once they had absorbed their new gains, would doubtless again be troublesome; the Russians showed no signs of wanting "détente"; and Habsburg financial resources appeared weak and getting weaker. It was in this mood that Vienna in mid-June 1914 prepared for a new set of diplomatic initiatives aimed at resolving the threat posed by Serbia. Drafted by Ballhausplatz officials and then carefully polished by Berchtold, the proposed program urged one last try for a Rumanian accord that would publicly align Bucharest with the Triple Alliance. If that failed, the monarchy would then launch a deliberate policy of isolating Serbia and Montenegro through new alliance ties with Bulgaria and Turkey. At the same time such an alignment would put new pressure on Rumania and allow Vienna to fortify the Rumanian frontier. And the new alliance ties might also strengthen the Austro-German position vis-à-vis Franco-Russian intrigue in the Balkans. If this diplomatic approach failed to intimidate Belgrade and St. Petersburg, then the entire problem would be reconsidered. Thus, already on the eve of Sarajevo, the policymakers in Vienna were considering a new, assertive, and high-risk diplomatic initiative.[38]

* * * *

By mid-1914 senior Habsburg officials had become progressively more alarmed about the deterioration of the Balkan situation. Aggressive diplomacy could easily veer into militant action. Only one person remained profoundly skeptical of a military solution: Archduke Franz Ferdinand. While foreign observers tabbed him the leader of the monarchy's military party and Tsar Nicholas claimed that he wished to lead an invasion of Russia, the archduke's dispositions were far different. To be sure, in November-December 1912 he had backed military action against Serbia. But this was an aberration, not seen before or repeated after. As in the Bosnian crisis of 1909, so throughout 1913, the heir apparent opposed precipitate military action. He consented with great reluctance to any move against Montenegro in May 1913, and may have been deliberately bypassed by Berchtold in October 1913. His opposition sprang less from his own pacificism, of which there were few signs, than from considerations of *raison d'état.* He feared Russia, worried about becoming dependent on Germany, and recognized that war would almost certainly prevent constitutional change should the old emperor finally die while it was under way.[39]

Also, as 1913 progressed, Franz Ferdinand came to have serious reservations about the judgment of his former protégé, Conrad von Hötzendorf. Rankled by the latter's handling of the Redl spy case (to chastise the general he made him stand at attention for thirty minutes) and possibly aware of the general's increasingly open relationship with Gina von Reininghaus, the archduke warned Berchtold at one point that Conrad von Hötzendorf sought war merely to cover up his own mistakes. The festering situation erupted at the Bohemian maneuvers in September 1913, when Conrad von Hötzendorf resigned in protest at the archduke's childish treatment of him. The heir apparent, recently appointed Inspector General of the Common Armed Forces, refused to accept the resignation, correctly concerned that three separate chiefs of the general staff within ten months would damage army morale. But Conrad von Hötzendorf's days were clearly numbered; he would have been out as chief by the end of 1914.[40] As it was, Conrad von Hötzendorf and the military regarded their future emperor (along with the German emperor) as the major obstacles to belligerent action.

How Franz Ferdinand would have responded had the victims at Sarajevo been his wife and Gen. Potiorek, or just one of them, can only be conjecture. But almost certainly he would have forced a more thorough discussion of the consequences of a military adventure and made Berchtold more cautious. As it was, his death had three important consequences. First, it removed the quasi-institutional presence of the heir apparent and his staff as part of the decision-making process. No longer did Ernest von Koerber's remark: "We not only have two parliaments, we also have two emperors," hold true. Second, the archduke's death removed an opponent of military action, a person who would pose the question: What about Russia? And third, and most dramatically, his death supplied the pretext for a final solution of the South Slav problem.[41]

* * * *

The events in Sarajevo convinced Berchtold, Stürgkh, and Bilinski, almost without discussion, that this time Belgrade had gone too far. The senior military commanders—Conrad von Hötzendrof, War Minister Krobatin, and the culpable Potiorek in Sarajevo—were, of course, eager to settle accounts with Belgrade. Even the old kaiser turned bellicose and inclined to action. István Tisza raised immediate doubts about a belligerent response, reservations prompted in part by concern that a possible victory might bring territorial acquisitions that would affect Magyar power. By July 3 the senior policymakers, Tisza excepted, were ready for a military confrontation. The psychological step from the tough, abrupt diplomacy of 1913 to war in 1914 was a small one, too easily made and with few second thoughts. All other options had been tried and found wanting.[42]

This belligerency was reinforced, moreover, by Potiorek's alarming (and possibly distorted) reports of widespread disorder in Bosnia-Herzegovina. Attacks upon Serbs and the burning and looting of Serbian property by loyal Habsburg citizens suggested unchecked chaos. Potiorek argued that only military measures, including martial law in the two provinces, could restore the situation. Quite rightly, no policymaker doubted that the assassins had connections with Belgrade. As the Sarajevo investigations of the conspiracy progressed, allegations of other subversive activities also surfaced. Fears about political disruption, conspiracy, and terrorism reinforced each other, further alarming officials in Vienna. [43] Faced with what later generations called "wars of national liberation," Franz Joseph's government resolved to protect its one imperial acquisition of the late nineteenth century. Serbia would be punished and Russia, it was hoped, would be prudent enough to stand aside.

Once Berchtold, the key swing man, resolved to fight Serbia, he and Conrad von Hötzendorf faced a set of interlocking problems of implementation: discovering how Berlin would react, convincing Tisza, assessing Russia's intentions, dispatching the ultimatum, and initiating the offensive action.

The first and most celebrated problem was the approach to Berlin. An essential first step in keeping the war with Serbia localized was to deter Russian intervention. Berchtold and Conrad von Hötzendorf believed that unequivocal German support would act as a deterrent to Russian intervention. But this had to be unambiguous support, not the mercurial ups and downs of 1912 and 1913 when Berlin had tilted first in one direction, then in another. Experience also suggested that gaining Germany's consent to the idea of action was easier than winning approval for its tactical implementation. This time Vienna would seek assurances early rather than late.

The man selected to win German support was Berchtold's belligerent, impulsive *chef de cabinet,* Count Hoyos. On July 3 he traveled to Berlin with an amended version of the June memorandum, a letter from Franz Joseph to the German kaiser, and with oral instructions, all of which left no doubt that Vienna would attack Serbia.[44] Berlin, as Fritz Fischer and others have exhaustively shown, had its own reasons for readily giving the Habsburgs a "blank check." But it was Vienna that first resolved for war, that sought German assurances, and that exploited them once received. In the critical early days of July the initiative rested with the Danubian leadership, not vice versa. Sidney Fay's earlier assessment retains much validity: "The Kaiser and his advisors on July 5 and 6 were not criminals plotting the World War; they were simpletons putting 'a noose about their necks' and handing the other end of the rope to a stupid and clumsy adventurer who now felt free to go as far as he liked."[45] What happened was a fateful meshing of aggressive German *Weltpolitik* with an even more aggressive, irresponsible Habsburg *Balkanpolitik.*

How Berchtold would have responded had Theobald von Bethmann-Hollweg, the German chancellor, and Wilhelm II reacted ambiguously or negatively to Vienna's request remains a central (and unanswerable) question about July 1914. It is clear, however, that Vienna would not have easily abandoned its intentions. In the recent past German ambivalence had merely prompted Berchtold to redouble efforts to secure Berlin's support. Certainly he would have done the same on this occasion. And in the October 1913 demarche against Belgrade there was a hint (and no more)—in a situation far less electric—of Habsburg determination to act unilaterally. Had Berlin hesitated in early July, this possibility might have recurred. Beyond these conjectures, available evidence permits little. In any case, once Berchtold had his "blank check," he became progressively less cooperative with Berlin. Ambassador Heinrich von Tschirschky had easy access to Berchtold in early July, indeed even participated in Count Hoyos's briefing of the foreign minister and other ministers on July 7. Thereafter he followed the efforts to convince Tisza to endorse an openly belligerent course and duly reported Vienna's apparently dilatory posture. While subsequently not directly involved, he reported on the pace of Habsburg action, the framing of the ultimatum, and the stage-managing of Habsburg tactics before July 23, such as Conrad von Hötzendorf's decision to go on vacation. After July 7 the Habsburg apparatus released minimal information to its German ally. Possibly Berchtold appreciated, from past experience, that too high a profile might prompt a change of heart in Berlin. This time he took no chances. Thus throughout July he set the pace (however much the Germans disliked its tempo), defined the moves, and closed off the options.[46]

The Hoyos mission had another crucial ramification as well. It furnished Berchtold with added leverage in dealing with István Tisza's reluctance for a military solution. An advocate of caution, the Magyar leader preferred a slower pace. Instead Berchtold outmaneuvered him, first by dispatching Hoyos to Berlin, and then by getting a surprisingly strong answer of apparently limitless German support. Outflanked, the minister president found himself the only holdout in the Common Cabinet against Berchtold's desire to plunge ahead. In the cabinet meeting on July 7 Tisza argued against the idea of a local war, but convinced no one else. And by the end of the session even his opposition had weakened. Yet Tisza continued to argue the diplomatic case, sending a new memorandum to Franz Joseph on July 8 in which he advocated hesitation and prudence. But the old kaiser, now also ready for quick, decisive action, remained unmoved. Berchtold and others continued to remind Tisza of their German support. Under this pressure Tisza slowly altered his position. On July 14, when he went back to Vienna, he finally approved a military course. A day later, on July 15, he told the Hungarian House of Delegates that, while a state might prefer peace and work for it, sometimes it was forced in the last resort simply to remain a state and nation. Hoyos's trip to Berlin and Tisza's subsequent isolation helped to eliminate the most important constitutional barrier to military action against Serbia.[47]

Tisza's obstinacy gained one apparent concession for Budapest. Berchtold, then later the Common Cabinet on July 19 when it met to approve the ultimatum, agreed that the monarchy would seek no substantial territorial gains from a defeated Serbia. Or put another way, no more Slavs would be added to the monarchy and so further endanger Magyar rule. Yet this concession had a hollow ring, best illustrated by Conrad von Hötzendorf's alleged comment when the July 19 meeting broke up: "Well, we shall see. Before the Balkan War, the powers talked about the *status quo.* After the war, nobody bothered about it any more." And in August, well before Bethmann-Hollweg's famous September memorandum, planners in the Ballhausplatz were developing territorial ambitions toward Poland that clearly betokened what Tisza feared most: some form of trialism involving the Slavs instead of German-Magyar dualism. At most Tisza won only a Pyrrhic victory in his struggle with Berchtold during the July crisis.[48]

Berchtold's third problem was Russia: what would it do? It was not a new problem: it had had to be considered in 1912 and 1913. At that time two contradictory analyses had emerged. The pessimistic one held that Russia, in contrast to its pacific behavior of 1909, would not again stand aside; an attack on Belgrade would launch a European war. Even Conrad von Hötzendorf occasionally subscribed to this estimate. The optimistic assessment argued that Russia was not yet ready to intervene, its military recovery from its Japanese defeat not yet complete. To this some added that Russia would not intervene because war would once more pose the threat of revolution. For these reasons some policymakers believed St. Petersburg would fulminate—but no more—if Vienna moved against Belgrade. And they contended that, if Berlin stood resolutely beside the monarchy, the Russians would be deterred altogether. Throughout the successive war-peace crises of 1912 and 1913, these visions of Russia's probable behavior had vied with each other, usually in approximate cautionary balance.[49]

Possibly the most striking feature of the Habsburg decision-making process in July 1914 was its failure to think seriously anew about Russia's position and its possible intervention. The policymakers acted as if Russia did not exist. Possibly they were overconfident about the deterrent affect of Berlin's "blank check"; possibly they exaggerated Romanov adherence to the principle of monarchical solidarity and the need to avenge the Sarajevo murders. Certainly they failed to pay even elementary attention to the danger signals of Russian military response. Until late in the whole process, the senior leadership blissfully directed its attention only southward. In almost classic, cybernetic fashion, Berchtold, Conrad von Hötzendorf and the others, now programmed for action against Serbia, disregarded any information that might require them to modify their plans—and ambitions. They would do what they wanted and, of course, preferred to do: fight Serbia.[50]

Berchtold's fourth problem centered around the dispatch of an unacceptable ultimatum to Belgrade. Commentators have frequently asserted that, had Vienna moved more quickly in July 1914, it might have exploited a reservoir of European sympathy and been allowed to punish Belgrade. Moreover, swift action would have eliminated the later accusation that Vienna lulled Europe into somnolence, only to precipitate a crisis. These assessments merit two observations. First, the Habsburg armies were incapable of a quick, decisive strike against Serbia, or even the speedy seizure of, say, Belgrade. Conrad von Hötzendorf's insistence on a total attack had eliminated such possibilities, leaving Plan B (fourteen to sixteen days for mobilization) as the only alternative. A swift surprise move was neither programmatically nor temperamentally an option for Vienna.

Second, a fundamental organizational arrangement virtually ruled out immediate action that would contain any element of surprise. On July 6 half the military strength of Agram (Zagreb), Innsbruck, Kaschau (Kosice), Temesvar (Timisoara), Budapest, Pressburg (Bratislava) and Graz was away on "harvest leave." If these troops were recalled to their units, their return would immediately be detected. This in turn would deprive the Habsburg decisionmakers of any chance for even modest surprise, alarm the other powers, probably disrupt the mobilization process, and–not without grave consequences–leave the crops unharvested. Instead of recalling these troops, it was better, from Conrad von Hötzendorf's viewpoint, quietly to cancel all remaining leaves and let the others expire on schedule between July 19 and July 25. It is this consideration that helps explain Conrad von Hötzendorf's relative lack of concern over the timing of military action against Serbia, that accounts for Berchtold's leisurely pace in his treatment of Tisza, and that explains the ultimatum's clash with the French state visit to St. Petersburg. An innocuous organizational measure, taken years earlier by Conrad von Hötzendorf to help to bring in the harvest, paradoxically handicapped the Austro-Hungarian generals and diplomats alike in the moment of supreme crisis.[51]

The final problem in launching a local war was Conrad von Hötzendorf's own: which offensive scheme to implement–Plan B or Plan R? In actuality, he drew from both and failed with each. Prematurely ordering Plan B into effect and thereby committing his "swing force," Conrad von Hötzendorf allowed the troop movements to continue southward despite evidence that Russia would not stand aside. Then, on August 4, he reversed himself and ordered a version of Plan R. This required those troops moving south to continue, then to be remustered onto trains again and sent north toward Galicia. A bevy of historians (and generations of war-college students) have examined this strategic error. One view holds that Conrad von Hötzendorf actually thought he could deal Serbia a knockout blow, then turn and defeat Russia. A second, related to the first, argues that Berlin's failure in early August to launch a modest but prompt offensive from East Prussia forced Conrad von Hötzendorf to divide his forces earlier than he had anticipated. Still another analysis argues that Conrad von Hötzendorf compounded his error by failing to exploit the inadequate but still valuable rail resources of the Habsburg empire. And another critique, not yet adequately examined, focuses on Vienna's failure to evaluate early enough, and correctly, the signs, unmistakable in retrospect, of Russian involvement.[52]

A simpler, if more Machiavellian, analysis may possibly explain Conrad von Hötzendorf's decision more accurately. By going south, Conrad von Hötzendorf would have the war he wanted, earlier and less ambiguously. Had he opted for Plan R, he would have been on the defensive in the south, with no guarantee of an Austro-Hungarian offensive attack on Serbia. If he adopted Plan R and planned for the offensive in the north, the actual fighting would not begin for almost three weeks, a week longer than Plan B. This additional week, he may have concluded, would allow more time for diplomatic intrusions and the possibility of peace. By launching the attack on Serbia, even if it was later to be reduced, he was at war more quickly. And Conrad von Hötzendorf knew that any war, once under way, is not easily stopped by political intervention. In addition, not reckoning on Russia's accelerated mobilization, he almost certainly believed he would still have time to transport his "swing force" north in time for the first battles. By moving south Conrad von Hötzendorf, whatever his later comments, ensured the military denouement that he so passionately believed was essential to the survival of the Habsburg state. The strategic blunder was part of a calculated risk to open war—and it worked.[53]

* * * *

In 1914 Austria-Hungary was not an innocent, middle-level government pressured into war by its more aggressive, ambitious northern ally. Rather those in power in Vienna were determined to control and fulfill the only international mission left to the Habsburgs: benevolent supervision of the Balkans. To do so, effectively and without interruption, required, so they believed, the reduction or elimination of the most potent internal danger to the monarchy—the South Slav problem. Serbia's continued appeals to the South Slavs, even a Serbia backed by Russia, could no longer be tolerated if the monarchy were to survive. After the Balkan Wars began in October 1912, Berchtold worked desperately, and with some success, to protect Habsburg interests. He blocked Serbia's access to the Adriatic and created Albania as a potential counterbalance. At each step the foreign minister faced the temptation to abandon diplomacy in favor of force. He rejected it, yet gradually he grew convinced that Serbia understood only threats. Lesser options appeared inappropriate, even self-defeating. Prestige, monarchical self-esteem, exhaustion of patience and imagination—all lured Vienna into a military campaign. Military values, mixed with illusions about Russia and the nature of modern war, acquired an unassailable position. Even Tisza, once he became convinced of the need for military action, became its most ardent proponent. In 1914 the Habsburg decisionmakers, like their German counterparts, were in a *Kriegslust* frame of mind. All that was needed was a pretext.

If viewed from this perspective, the interaction between Berlin and Vienna assumes a different balance and proportion. Certainly it is incorrect to focus all attention on Berlin, or to suggest that Vienna was merely a marionette in the July crisis. It must be remembered that Berchtold eventually joined Conrad von Hötzendorf and the military in pressing for military action. Ironically the most assertive phase of Berchtold's diplomacy was also its most dangerous. In July 1914 peace gave way to war; desperation, hope, blind faith, illusion, exhaustion, and a mix of military ambition overcame the prudence and caution of the earlier Balkan crises. The monarchy at length opted for a draconian solution; the results were equally draconian and devastating. War brought not victory and a solution to the Slav problem, but defeat and dissolution. From that result momentous consequences still flow.

NOTES

Previous versions of this paper were presented at the University of East Anglia; the University of Sussex; King's College, London; and Oxford University. Research for it was made possible by the National Endowment for the Humanities, the University of North Carolina at Chapel Hill, and Churchill College, Cambridge. The author is especially grateful for comments from Paul Kennedy, John Röhl, Zara Steiner, Jonathan Steinberg, Lamer Cecil, Gerhard Weinberg, John Leslie, Tom Conner, Ron Maner and for archival assistance from Dr. Kurt Peball, Archivoberrat, Kriegsarchiv, Vienna.

1. The literature on Fritz Fischer and his work is already voluminous. His three major summations *(Griff nach der Weltmacht* [3rd ed.; Düsseldorf, 1964], *Weltmacht oder Niedergang* [Frankfurt a/M., 1965], and *Krieg der Illusionen* [Düsseldorf, 1969] — all available in English) merit repeated examination. On the controversy, see Wolfgang Mommsen, "Domestic Factors in German Foreign Policy before 1914," *Central European History,* March, 1973, pp.3-43; John A. Moses, *The Fischer Controversy in German Historiography* (New York, 1975); and Erwin Hölzle, *Die Selbstentmachtung Europas* (Frankfurt a/M., 1975) Chaps. 2 and 3.

2. F. R. Bridge, *From Sadowa to Sarajevo* (London, 1972) opens no new ground on 1914. For provocative suggestions on the topic, see Joachim Remak, "1914 - The Third Balkan War: Origins Reconsidered," *Journal of Modern History* (hereafter *JMH*), Sept., 1971, pp. 353-366, and *idem,* "The Healthy Invalid: How Doomed the Habsburg Empire?" *JMH,* June, 1969, pp. 127-143.

3. Sidney B. Fay, *The Origins of the World War* (New York, 1928) popularized the dichotomy between long- and short-term causes; Fischer, *Krieg der Illusionen* continues it with his limited analysis of July 1914. By contrast, the monumental Luigi Albertini, *The Origins of the War of 1914* (London, 1952-57) generally avoids this distinction.

4. Cf. Fischer, *Krieg der Illusionen,* pp. 231-241; John Röhl, "Admiral von Muller and the Approach of War, 1911-1914," *The Historical Journal,* XII (1969), pp. 651-673; and his "An der Schwell zum Weltkrieg; Eine Dokumentation über den 'Kriegsrat' vom 8. Dezember 1912," *Militärgeschichtliche Mitteilungen,* XXI, No. 1 (1977), pp. 77-134.

5. Hugo Hantsch, *Leopold Graf Berchtold* (Vienna, 1963), I, 349-379; Samuel R. Williamson, Jr., "Influence, Power, and the Policy Process: The Case of Franz Ferdinand, 1906-1914," *The Historical Journal,* XVII (1974), pp. 417-434; Ernst C. Helmreich, *The Diplomacy of the Balkan Wars, 1912-1913* (Cambridge, Mass. 1938), pp. 224-230, 237-248.

6. Hantsch, *op. cit.,* I, 405-417; Franz Conrad von Hötzendorf, *Aus meiner Dienstzeit, 1906-1918* (Vienna, 1921-25), III, 231-308, *passim.*

7. Cf. Albertini, *op. cit.,* I, 471-487; Fischer, *Krieg der Illusionen,* pp. 306-317. Berlin learned of the ultimatum only hours before its delivery, Stolberg to Auswärtiges Amt, Oct. 17 (tel.), 1913, in Johannes Lepsius *et al.* (eds.), *Die grosse Politik der europäischen Kabinette 1871-1914* (hereafter *G.P.*) (Berlin, 1922-27), XXXIV (1), 394-395. The ultimatum was telegraphed to Belgrade, very late on the 17th (actually encoded, 12:10 a.m. on the 18th). Ludwig Bittner and Hans Uebersberger (eds.), *Österreich-Ungarns Aussenpolitik von der bosnischen Krise 1908 bis zum Kriegsausbruch 1914* (hereafter *Ö-U.A.)* (Vienna, 1930), VII, 453.

8. On Berchtold and the Concert, see Richard J. Crampton, "The Decline of the Concert of Europe in the Balkans, 1913-1914," *The Slavonic and East European Review,* LII (1974), pp. 393-419.

9. For glimpses at attitudes, the diaries of Joseph Redlich are indispensible. See Fritz Fellner (ed.), *Schicksaljahre Österreichs, 1908-1919: Das politische Tagebuch Joseph Redlichs* (Graz, 1953-54), I, 209-238, *passim;* also the entries in Berchtold's diaries for late 1913 and early 1914, "Memoiren des Grafen Leopold Berchtold," Politisches Archiv (hereafter P.A.), Haus-, Hof-, und Staatsarchiv, Vienna, carton I/524b.

10. See the valuable "after action" report on the mobilization steps, "Darstellung der Anlässlich der Balkancrise 1912/13 getroffen militärischen Massnahmem," Generalstab: Operations Bureau, Kriegsarchiv, Vienna, fasc. 61; also Wilhelm Deutschmann, "Die militärischen Massnahmen in Österriech-Ungarn während der Balkankriege, 1912/13," (Ph.D. diss., Vienna, 1966); Helmreich, *op. cit.,* pp. 461-462.

11. Originally the army budget for 1913 was 403,557,769 kronen (in 1912 1 kronen = 20¢). The official 309,093,000 figure cited in the text as the costs of the Balkan episodes probably represents a low estimate, since the 1914 budget contained requests for 353,628,500 kronen to cover the Balkan expenses. The added naval costs ran to 40,443,000. On the expenses, see *Parlamentarische Chronik, 1913* (Vienna, 1913), pp. 48-552; Helmreich cites the official army estimate, *op. cit.,* p. 462.

12. On the Austrian negotiations for this loan, see files Nos. 91178, 92041, 93426 of Department 14, Österreichisches Finanz-Ministerium, Finanzarchiv, Vienna. Interest on the bonds was 4½%, but they were discounted to 96 (on a 100) for sale, thus making the effective interest rate 6½% over a two-year period. See E. Rosenbaum and A.J. Sherman, *Das Bankhaus M.M. Warburg Co., 1798-1938* (Hamburg, 1976), pp. 135-136; Bernard Michel, *Banques & banquiers en Autriche au début du 20e siècle* (Paris, 1976), p. 260. On bank rates, see *The Economist,* Dec. 7, 1912.

13. There is no adequate biography of Conrad von Hötzendorf, but Oskar Regele, *Feldmarschall Conrad: Auftrag und Erfüllung, 1906-1918* (Vienna, 1955) and August von Urbanski, *Conrad von Hötzendorf* (Graz, 1955) provide valuable biographical information. Conrad's own memoirs are indespensible for understanding him, to which must be added his *Private Aufzeichnungen,* ed. Kurt Peball (Vienna, 1977). For an analysis of his imperial conceptions, see Hans Angermeier, "Der österreichische Imperialismus des Generalfeldmarschalls Conrad von Hötzendorf," *Festschrift für Max Spindler,* ed. Dieter Albrecht *et al.* (Munich, 1969), pp. 777-792; on his strategic views see Gunther Rothenberg's valuable *The Army of Francis Joseph* (West Lafayette, Ind., 1976), pp. 143-145, 169-170.

14. Conrad von Hötzendorf, *Private Aufzeichnungen,* pp. 32-49, *passim.* On his relationship with his wife, see his letters to Frau Wally von Sonnleithner, quoted in Kurt Peball, "Briefe an eine Freundin: Zu den Briefen der Feldmarschall Conrad von Hötzendorf an Frau Walburga von Sonnleithner während der Jahre 1905 bis 1918," *Mitteilungen der Österreichischen Staatsarchivs,* XXV (1972), pp. 492-403.

15. Gina Conrad's indiscrete *Mein Leben mit Conrad von Hötzendorf* (Leipzig, 1935) has not received the attention it deserves; private information and interviews with Baron Curt de Reininghaus (one of her surviving children), May 14 and June 17, 1971, April 1, 1977, and with Franz Joseph Mayer-Gunthoff, May 1971. Also see, e.g., the diary entries for Aug. 26 and Sept. 9, 1914, in Fellner (ed.), *op. cit.,* I, 253-254, 270.

16. On his thoughts, see Horst Brettner-Messler, "Die Balkanpolitik Conrad v. Hötzendorfs von seiner Wiederernennung zum Chef des Generalstabes bis zum Oktober-Ultimatum 1913," *Mitteilungen des Österreichischen Statts-archivs,* XX (1967), pp. 180-276. See also Conrad von Hötzendorf to Berchtold, March 27, 1913, quoted in Conrad von Hötzendorf, *Dienstzeit,* III, 190-191; Conrad von Hötzendorf to Berchtold, Oct. 8, 1913, *ibid.*, 463.

17. See, e.g., Conrad von Hötzendorf's "Denkschrift," Jan. 20, 1913, quoted in *ibid.*, III, 12-16; Conrad von Hötzendorf to Berchtold, Jan. 27, 1913, *ibid.*, 52-53; *ibid.*, 194-195, 213, 268-270.

18. See Rothenberg, *op. cit.*, pp. 158-160; Norman Stone, *The Eastern Front, 1914-1917* (London, 1975), pp. 70-73; also *Österreich-Ungarns letzter Krieg 1914-1918* (Vienna, 1930-38), I, 10-15.

19. See, e.g., his refusal in Sept. 1913; Conrad von Hötzendorf, *Dienstzeit,* III, 443.

20. See Berchtold's full diary entry, May 2, 1914, in "Memoiren des Berchtold," P.A.I/524b; also Hantsch, *op. cit.*, I, 417-447; and the minutes of May 2, 1913, Common Cabinet, *Ö-U.A.*, VI, 324-337. See also Robert A. Kann, *Kaiser Franz Joseph und der Ausbruch des Weltkriegs* (Vienna, 1971).

21. See Hantsch's general effort to rehabilitate, and also G. P. Gooch, *Before the War: Studies in Diplomacy* (London, 1936-38), II, 373-447. F. R. Bridge adopts a harsher line, *op. cit.*, 340 ff. Also see Robert A. Kann, "Erzherzog Franz Ferdinand und Graf Berchtold als Aussenminister, 1912-1914" reprinted in his *Erzherzog Franz Ferdinand Studien* (Vienna, 1976), pp. 206-240.

22. On Kiderlen's annoyance at Berchtold, see his memorandum of Aug. 15, 1912, *G. P.*, XXXIII, 92-94; also Kiderlen to Tschirschky, Nov. 15, 1912, *ibid.*, 402; Hantsch, *op. cit.*, I, 349-353.

23. In July 1912 he strongly supported (in contrast to Aehrenthal) the military and naval demands for higher budgets. See, e.g., Berchtold to Franz Joseph, July 11, 1912, Kabinetts Archiv, Direktionsakten, Haus-, Hof-, und Staatsarchiv, carton 18; also the full minutes of the Common Cabinet, July 8-9, 1912, *ibid.*, P.A. XL/310.

24. Helmreich, *op. cit.*, pp. 281-290; Deutschmann, *op. cit.*, pp. 137-151.

25. Cited in Adam Yarmolinsky, *The Military Establishment* (New York, 1971). p. 133.

26. Berchtold's changed attitude is easily followed in his diary entries. See, e.g., October 12, 13, 16, 17, 20, 1913 in "Memoiren des Berchtold," P.A. I/524b.

27. The economic impact was almost certainly more psychological than real, but nonetheless crucial, in shaping attitudes toward the future. Michel, *op. cit.*, pp. 363-369; Richard L. Rudolph, *Banking and Industrialization in Austria-Hungary* (Cambridge, 1976), pp. 37-38. The two finance ministers, especially the Hungarian one, fretted constantly over the financial situation. See, e.g., the records of the Common Cabinet discussion of October 3, 1913, P.A. XL/311.

28. On the Austrian parliamentary scene, see Alexander Fussek, "Ministerpräsident Karl Graf Stürgkh und die Parliamentarische Frage," *Mitteilungen der Österreichischen Staatsarchiv,* XVII-XVIII (1964-65), pp. 337-358. On the Hungarian side, which is much less well served, see the survey in C.A. Macartney, *The Habsburg Monarchy, 1790-1918* (London, 1968), pp. 763-770. Cf. Arno J. Mayer, "Internal Causes and Purpose of War in Europe, 1870-1956: A Research Assignment," *JMH,* Sept. 1969, pp. 291-303.

29. For an example of the 1914 friction, see Berchtold's report of his talk with Ambassador Avarna, March 30, 1914, *Ö-U.A.*, VII, 1017-1018; on Anatolia, see F. R. Bridge, "*Tarde venientibus ossa:* Austro-Hungarian Colonial Aspirations in Asia Minor 1913-14," *Middle Eastern Studies,* Oct., 1970, pp. 319-330; on the military and naval talks, see Horst Brettner-Messler, "Die militärischen Absprachen zwischen der Generalstaben Österreich-Ungarns und Italiens vom Dezember 1912 bis Juni 1914," *Mitteilungen des Österreichischen Staatsarchiv,* XXIII (1970), pp. 225-249; Paul Halpern, *The Mediterranean Naval Situation, 1908-1914* (Cambridge, Mass., 1971), Chap. 8. The essay by Michael Palumbo in this volume takes a different view of the prospects of Italian military assistance.

30. Prince Montenuovo, no friend of Franz Ferdinand, held this view. See diary entry, Sept. 26, 1913, "Memoiren des Berchtold," P.A. I/524b. On the earlier Wilhelm-Franz Ferdinand relationship, see Robert A. Kann, "Kaiser Willhelm II und der Thronfolger Erzherzog Franz Ferdinand in ihrer Korrespondez," reprinted in *op. cit.*, pp. 47-85.

31. Norman Stone's article is the best recent summary, "Moltke-Conrad: Relations between the Austro-Hungarian and German General Staffs 1909-14," *The Historical Journal,* IX (1966), pp. 201-228; also see Georg Waldersee, "Über die Beziehungen des deutschen zum österreichische-ungarischen Generalstabe vor dem Weltkriege," *Berliner Monatsheft,* Feb., 1930, pp. 103-142.

32. Berchtold found Jagow no "übermässig austrophil," and feared that his years in Rome as embassy secretary and later as ambassador (1901-06, 1909-12) meant that he knew about Austria-Hungary chiefly from the Italian press. Also Jagow was a Protestant, a point that Berchtold duly noted. See entry Sept. 27, 1913, "Memoiren des Berchtold," P.A. I/524b; Fischer, *Krieg der Illusionen,* pp. 310-317, 586-612. On German economic competition, also see Willibald Gutsche, "Mitteleuropaplanungen in der Aussenpolitik des deutschen Imperialismus vor 1918," *Zeitschrift für Geschichtswissenschaft,* XX (1972), No. 5, pp. 533-549; Dörte Löding, *Deutschlands und Österreich-Ungarns Balkanpolitik von 1912-1914 unter besonderer Berücksichtigung ihrer Wirtschaftsinteressen* (Hamburg, 1969), pp. 236-262; R. J. Crampton, "The Balkans as a Factor in German Foreign Policy," *Slavonic and East European Review,* July, 1977, pp. 370-390.

33. Williamson, *op. cit.*, pp. 431-433; Conrad von Hötzendorf, *Dienstzeit,* III, 549-563.

34. See, e.g., Szápáry to Berchtold, April 12, 1914, *Ö-U.A.*, VII, 1048-1050; also Tisza's memorandum, March 15, 1914, *ibid.*, 974-979. A minor press feud in March and April, though not so bitter as the parallel German-Russian one, also drew close attention. For a sample of the exchanges, see "Die russische Probemobilisierung," *Danzer's Armee-Zeitung,* March 12, 1914; "Die Aufteilung Oesterreich-Ungarns oder Russlands?", *ibid.*, March 26, 1914; Z.A.B. Zeman, *The Break-up of the Habsburg Empire, 1914-1918* (London, 1961), pp. 3-13, 31-32; Hans Uebersberger, *Österreich zwischen Russland und Serbien* (Graz, 1958), pp. 187-225.

35. On the exchange of spies, see e.g., Giesl to Berchtold, June 1, 1914, Belgrad: Gesandschaftsarchiv, Haus-, Hof-, und Staatsarchiv, carton 21. On the economic and rail negotiations, the discussions in the Common Cabinet provide valuable summaries; see the minutes for the meeting of May 24, 1914 (held in

Budapest) P.A. XL/311; also the memorandum, Bardolff to Franz Ferdinand, May 15, 1914, Militärkanzlei des Generalinspektors des gesamten bewaffneten Macht (Franz Ferdinand) 39-8/2-4ex 1914, Kriegsarchiv. Still useful on the rail question generally is Herbert Feis, *Europe: The World's Banker, 1870-1914* (New Haven, 1930) pp. 298-312.

36. The reports to Vienna were numerous, detailed, and well informed. See, for example, Giesl to Berchtold, May 16, June 6, 12, 1914, *Ö-U.A.*, VIII, 41-42, 118-120, 130-131.

37. On reports of student movements and hints of conspiracy, see Foreign Ministry to Bilinski, May 19, 1914, *Ö-U.A.*, VIII, 53-54; Giesl to Berchtold, May 31, 1914, *ibid.*, 100-102. Potiorek's monthly summaries, entitled "Persönliche Vormerkungen," are invaluable for insights into his thinking; in a postscript, written July 1, 1914, on the summary for June 1-June 30, he states that his optimism was misplaced; Nachlass Potiorek, Kriegsarchiv. Also see Albertini, *op. cit.*, II, 111-115; Vladimir Dedijer, *The Road to Sarajevo* (New York, 1966), pp. 405-417. Friedrich Würthle, *Die Spur führt nach Belgrad* (Vienna, 1975) does not address the issue, but his newspaper article, "Die Schuldigen und die Verantwortlichen," *Die Furche,* 29 (1964), does.

38. The first draft of the memorandum, dated June 24, 1914, is in *Ö-U.A.*, VIII, 186-195; the revised draft, dated July 1, 1914, and sent to Berlin, is in *ibid.*, 253-261. It is partially reprinted in Bridge, *op. cit.*, pp. 443-448. On the origins of the memorandum, see *ibid.*, pp. 363-368; Hantsch, *op. cit.*, II, 544-555.

39. Kann, *op. cit.*, pp. 26-46, 206-240; Williamson, *op. cit.*, pp. 417-434; Stephan Verosta, *Theorie und Realität von Bundnissen* (Vienna, 1971), pp. 407-432, 488.

40. On their relationship, see, e.g., Conrad von Hötzendorf, *Dienstzeit,* II, 434-442; Rudolph Kiszling, *Erzherzog Franz Ferdinand* (Graz, 1953), pp. 264-269; Redlich's diary entry, April 25, 1914, in Fellner (ed.), *op. cit.*, I, 226.

41. Quoted in Maurice Muret, *L'archiduc Francois-Ferdinand* (Paris, 1932), p. 172; Fay, *op. cit.*, II, 15; Samuel R. Williamson, Jr., "Theories of Organizational Process and Foreign Policy Outcomes," in *Diplomacy: New Approaches in History, Theory, and Policy,* ed. Paul G. Lauren (New York, 1979), pp. 137-161.

42. For participants' views, see, e.g., Conrad von Hötzendorf, *Dienstzeit,* IV, 13-36; Hantsch, *op. cit.*, II, 557-569; Tisza to Franz Joseph, July 1, 1914, *Ö-U.A.*, VIII, 248-249; Franz Joseph to Wilhelm II, July 2, 1914, *ibid.*, 250-252; Leon von Bilinski, *Wspominienia i dokumenty, 1846-1922* [Memoirs and Documents, 1846-1922] (Warsaw, 1924-25), I, 274-278. Also see Count István Burián's reactions, diary entries, June 28-July 3, 1914, in István Diószegi, "Aussenminister Stephan Graf Burian: Biographie und Tagebuchstelle," *Annales: Universitatis Scientiarum Budapestinensis, Sectio Historica,* VIII (Budapest, 1966), 204-205. Also Heinrich von Lützow, *Im diplomatischen Dienst der k.u.k. Monarchie* (Vienna, 1971), pp. 218-228; Albertini, *op. cit.*, II, 120-133.

43. The reports from Potiorek were, understandably, defensive; see, e.g., his telegraphic reports of June 29, June 30, and July 1, 1914, *Ö-U.A.*, VIII, 213-218, 225-226, 240-246; cf. Bilinski to Potiorek, June 30, 1914, *ibid.*, 227-231. These records ought to be compared to Potiorek's direct reports to the

War Ministry, Nachlass Potiorek. Also see Würthle's detailed discussion, *op. cit.*, pp. 118-140.

44. For a recent thorough discussion based on the Hoyos papers, see Fritz Fellner, "Die 'Mission Hoyos' ", *Recueil des travaux aux assises scientifiques internationales: Les grandes puissances et la Serbie à la veille de la Première guerre mondiale,* IV, No. 1 (Belgrade, 1976), 387-418; Williamson, "Organizational Theories," pp. 146-151; Albertini, *op. cit.*, II, 133-150.

45. Fay, *op. cit.*, II, 223; cf. Fischer, *War of Illusions,* pp. 473-478; Hantsch, *op. cit.*, II, 558-576; Verosta, *op. cit.*, pp. 461-490.

46. Cf. Albertini, *op. cit.*, II, 150-159, 162. The exchanges between Berlin and Vienna can be followed most conveniently in Imanuel Geiss (ed.), *Julikrise und Kriegsausbruch 1914: Eine Dokumentensammlung* (Hannover, 1963-64), I, 119-323, *passim*.

47. On Tisza's shift, see József Galánti, "István Tisza und der Erste Weltkrieg," *Annales: Universitatis Scientiarum Budapestinensis, Sectio Historica,* V (Budapest, 1963), 199-204; see also Burián's diary entries, July 7-14, 1914, quoted in Diószegi, *op. cit.*, pp. 205-206; Redlich's diary entry, July 15, 1914, Fellner (ed.), *Tagebuch,* I, 237-238; Norman Stone, "Hungary and the Crisis of July 1914," *Journal of Contemporary History* (July, 1966), pp. 153-170; *Fremdenblatt,* July 16, 1914.

48. On Tisza and the territorial issue, see Berchtold to Franz Joseph July 14, 1914, *Ö-U.A.*, VIII, 447-448; Jagow to Tschirschky, July 17, 1914, Geiss, *op. cit.*, I, 197; Conrad von Hötzendorf, *Dienstzeit,* IV, 91. On Habsburg territorial and political ambitions, see Wolfdieter Bihl, "Zu den österreichisch-ungarischen Kriegszielen 1914," *Jahrbücher für Geschichte Osteuropas,* XVI (1968), pp. 505-530.

49. In Jan. 1913 the clash between the views of Generals Krobatin and Conrad von Hötzendorf and of two diplomats, Count Thurn (ambassador to St. Petersburg) and Gyula Szilássy (Berchtold's new political advisor), were especially sharp; see, e.g., Julius Szilássy, *Der Untergang der Donau-Monarchie* (Berlin, 1921), pp. 209-210, 222-250; Conrad von Hötzendorf, *Dienstzeit,* II, 82-83; Hantsch, *op. cit.*, I, 381; Uebersberger, *op. cit.*, pp. 111-118.

50. On Habsburg military views through German eyes, see Kageneck to Waldersee, July 15 and July 18, 1914, Geiss, *op. cit.*, I, 179-181, 211-212; also Conrad von Hötzendorf, *Dienstzeit,* IV, 114-165, *passim;* Stone, *op. cit.*, pp. 70-79. On the broader assessments of Russian military power, see Risto Ropponen, *Die Kraft Russlands* (Helsinki, 1968), pp. 235-274. On the use of cybernetic theory to explain perceptual misjudgments, see John Steinbruner, *The Cybernetic Theory of Decision Making* (Princeton, 1974), pp. 47-87; Robert Jervis's discussion of "wishful thinking," *Perception and Misperception in International Politics* (Princeton, 1976), pp. 356-372; and the essay by William Jannen included in this volume.

51. For a full discussion, see Williamson, "Theories of Organizational Process," pp. 151-154.

52. Norman Stone has surveyed this issue in detail, "Die Mobilmachung der österreichisch-ungarischen Armée 1914," *Militärgeschichtliche Mitteilungen,* II (1974), 67-95; also Rothenberg, *Army of Francis Joseph,* pp. 176-184.

53. On his mood later, see Conrad von Hötzendorf, *Private Aufzeichnung,* pp. 65-66.

ITALIAN-AUSTRO-HUNGARIAN MILITARY RELATIONS BEFORE WORLD WAR I

Michael Palumbo

The Habsburg Monarchy's military relations with Italy before World War I have received relatively little attention in most studies on the origins of the great conflict. But the attitude of Italy was a key concern of the Vienna policy-makers in the period immediately preceding the outbreak of World War I. In particular there is strong evidence that the military agreements negotiated between Italy and the Central Powers just prior to the Sarajevo crisis influenced the actions of the Habsburg government during the crucial days when the decision for war or peace hung in the balance.

Italian-Habsburg military relations were a part of the Triple Alliance war planning and must be discussed in this context. Germany participated in most of the military negotiations that involved Italy and Austria-Hungary. As in diplomatic matters, Germany acted as a catalyst to bring its two antagonistic allies together. Although the distinct Austro-Italian military relationship over the years was not as close as the bond between the Rome and Berlin general staffs, Rome and Vienna also tended to draw together just before the world war.

The first military convention between Italy and the Central Powers came in January 1888, following the first renewal of the Triple Alliance. The agreement provided that six Italian army corps and three cavalry divisions would travel through the Habsburg Monarchy en route to aid the Germans on the Rhine. In February 1889 the technical arrangements for transporting these troops through Habsburg territory were completed[1] Soon after, however, relations between Italy and the Dual Monarchy deteriorated. By the turn of the century Vienna and Rome could hardly be considered allies. Count Alfred von Schlieffen, then German chief of staff, was particularly concerned about the possible attitude of Italy in the event of an Austro-Russian war.[2] Italy had drifted away from the Central Powers and closer to France; and in 1902 Rome and Paris signed a secret agreement.

The Italians soon began to spend large sums on their border defenses facing Austria-Hungary. There were even reports of the Italian military attaché in Belgrade working on plans for supporting Serbia against the Dual Monarchy. In November 1908, the French ambassador in Rome, Camille Barrère, was informed that the Triple Alliance was dead.[3] The most persistent factor contributing to Italian resentment against the Dual Monarchy was the border dispute over the Trentino, a dispute aggravated by periodic incidents of irredentist agitation. Friction in the Balkans compounded this issue. In reality the union with Austria-Hungary, never popular in Italy, had only been tolerated in order to secure an alliance with Germany.

In the Habsburg Monarchy the Italian alliance was equally unpopular. High-ranking Austrian officials doubted Italy's loyalty. One man who wished to do something about it was Gen. Franz Conrad von Hötzendorf, chief of the Austro-Hungarian general staff, who was bitterly anti-Italian and who consistently urged a preventive war against the Dual Monarchy's neighbor. Conrad von Hötzendorf, appointed chief of staff in 1906 after years of troop duty along the Italian frontier, may have been influenced by this service to see Italy as Austria's real enemy.[4] He allowed few opportunities to go unpassed without expressing distrust of Italy. In May 1907, Conrad von Hötzendorf met Helmuth von Moltke, the chief of the German general staff, for the first time. When the Austrian general expressed his skepticism about the southern ally, Moltke deprecated Conrad von Hötzendorf's apprehensions. Consistently the Germans wished to downplay the Austro-Italian antagonism. They did not wish to see the Habsburg Monarchy expend its efforts against Italy and not have enough troops for use against Russia. Nor could the Germans ignore that a war against Italy would be more popular in Austria-Hungary than a war against Russia, particularly among the Slavic and clerical elements in the empire.[5]

On February 1, 1910, Conrad von Hötzendorf submitted a memorandum to Emperor Franz Josef in which he described Italy as Austria's congenital foe. He urged the "earliest reckoning" with Italy to gain a free hand for the Dual Monarchy in the Balkans.[6] During the war over Tripoli, Conrad von Hötzendorf urged an attack on Italy while it was engaged against Turkey. On this occasion the chief of staff was opposed by the equally strong-willed foreign minister, Count Alois Lexa von Aehrenthal. Aehrenthal summarized Conrad von Hötzendorf's position for a visiting Rumanian political leader: "They say that Italy would never fight on our side in any case and that it would have been better to square accounts now."[7] A deep split existed over the issue between the military and political leadership, with Conrad von Hötzendorf supported by Archduke Franz Ferdinand, who had a deep hatred of the Italians, and wished to replace Rome by St. Petersburg in the Triple Alliance. Emperor Franz Josef, who did not want a war on his southern frontier, opposed the anti-Italian faction. Conrad von Hötzendorf was dismissed, the emperor stating, "My policy is a policy of peace."[8]

But the fiery general was ultimately reappointed in December 1912. This came at a time when Italian policy was drifting away from France and toward the Central Powers. This was particularly true after 1910, when the Marquess di San Giuliano become Italian foreign minister. Under his direction, Italian policy slowly began to lean toward Germany and Austria-Hungary. In December 1912, in keeping with this policy, the Triple Alliance was renewed. To German Chancellor Theobald von Bethmann-Hollweg the alliance had gained new life. Italy and Austria-Hungary cooperated, moreover, on such questions as preventing Serbia from acquiring a foothold on the Adriatic. At the same time, Italy's relations with France, friendly since 1902, grew less cordial. The chief cause of the estrangement was the Libyan war; and indeed relations between the two countries grew so bad that the British ambassador in Rome believed that he saw "the grip of the Triple Alliance closing around Italy more tightly than before. The position which France commanded in the country . . . has been lost."[9] And the French were startled to learn that the Italians were suggesting that, in case of a war arising from a Balkan dispute, Italy would probably side with the Central Powers.[10]

An important reason for this change of policy was Gen. Alberto Pollio, who became chief of the Italian general staff in 1908. A former military attache in Vienna and a noted military historian, he is usually described as a good organizer. He is especially credited for his work in the Libyan war under difficult circumstances.[11] Pollio, a great advocate in the desirability of the offensive, was almost as fanatic a believer in the Triple Alliance.

Pollio believed that the Triple Alliance must act in unison, and that in case of war Italian troops should serve wherever they were needed without regard to political considerations. He even suggested sending Italian troops to help the Habsburgs against Russia or Serbia. Such sentiments were music to the ears of the military staffs of the Central Powers. The German attaché in Rome, Kleist, claims that he "almost fell off his chair" when he heard of Pollio's offer to send Italian troops to the Eastern and Balkan fronts.[12]

With such an Italian chief of staff, it was possible for the Triple Alliance to negotiate new and detailed military conventions on the eve of World War I. These agreements integrated the Italian army and navy into the military plans of the Central Powers, and had a profound influence on the Sarajevo crisis in the summer of 1914.

The negotiations for new Triple Alliance military conventions opened in December 1912 when contracts were initiated between Rome and Berlin. In January 1913, Gen. Alfred von Waldersee, the quartermaster general of the German staff, traveled to Vienna and Rome to further the alliance's military cooperation. In Rome, Waldersee received a very favorable impression of Gen. Pollio and other Italian military leaders.

From Rome Waldersee went to Vienna for talks with Conrad von Hötzendorf, chief of the Austro-Hungarian general staff. The Austrian chief had already been notified by the

Italian attaché that the Third Italian Army was not being sent to the Rhine. Conrad von Hötzendorf not surprisingly saw this as another sign of the ally's unreliability. But upon his arrival in Vienna, Waldersee explained to the incredulous army chief that the Italians stood quite honorably and loyally by the side of the Central Powers. Conrad von Hötzendorf openly argued this point, and revealed his firmly held belief that the Italians could not be trusted. When Waldersee hinted that Austria should supply Italy with war materials, the Habsburg general brushed aside the possibility of such aid to so undependable an ally.[13] At this stage it was obvious that Waldersee had done little to promote Italian-Austrian cooperation.

But gradually Vienna, and Conrad von Hötzendorf in particular, became more receptive to the idea of military cooperation with Italy. An important step in that process came at the German maneuvers in Silesia later in 1913 when Pollio, Conrad von Hötzendorf, and Moltke discussed the strategic situation. Conrad von Hötzendorf and Pollio got along well, and the Italian chief agreed to ask his monarch for permission to send at least five infantry divisions to the Rhine in case of war. But for the time being, he could promise only two divisions of cavalry. Other topics at the Silesian maneuvers included the possibility of using Italian cavalry in East Prussia against the Russians. Pollio agreed in principle to this ambitious proposal. Later the three military leaders dropped the scheme because of the technical difficulties involved. In these talks Pollio stressed that the Triple Alliance must act as a single entity with a common goal and unity of command. This view proved popular with both the Austro-Hungarian and German chiefs. Gen. Waldersee had the impression that everyone left the Silesia meeting satisfied. Indeed, Conrad von Hötzendorf, the old enemy of Italy, returned much encouraged after his discussions with Pollio. In a letter dated October 6, 1913, Conrad von Hötzendorf expressed the hope that Italian troops could be put into the Triple Alliance's military calculations for 1914-1915.[14]

In December 1913, Gen. Waldersee made his second trip to Rome and Vienna. In Rome, Pollio told him of his desire to send as many troops as possible to Germany in case of war. He had already pledged some cavalry units. He promised

Waldersee to try to convince the Italian government to add a large force of infantry to the promised cavalry units. From Rome Waldersee went to Vienna where he participated in preliminary negotiations for the shipment of the Italian cavalry through the Tyrol to the Rhine front.[15] The Germans hoped that this token force of cavalry would prompt an Italian pledge of large infantry units.

In early February 1914, the Italian general staff sent Lt. Col. Fiastri to Vienna to arrange for the transportation of the cavalry divisions through Habsburg territory. In the agreement he made, it was specified that the two principal routes would be via Innsbruck and Villach, and that Italian officers would be in charge of a mixed commission at the railroad stations and transfer points.[16] Shortly after, the Italian military attaché notified Berlin that Pollio agreed to send three Italian army corps to Germany in case of war. Pollio further promised to look into the possibility of even larger troop commitments in the near future. Similar notification went to the general staff in Vienna at the same time.

In March representatives of the Triple Alliance met in Vienna to work out details of the movement of an Italian army corps to Germany through Austria.[17] During Easter week in April 1914, representatives of the railroad sections of the Italian and German general staffs met their Austro-Hungarian counterpart in Vienna to work out the transfer of the infantry corps. The convention agreed upon paralleled that made in February for the transportation of the cavalry divisions. Moreover, the new agreement called for a meeting in Berlin in October 1914 to resolve any remaining problems for transport of the Italian troops to the Rhine by way of the Tyrol.[18]

Also during April 1914 Pollio notified Kleist, the German military attaché, that he would like to send more troops to Germany; at the same time he indicated that he hoped to put Italian forces at the disposal of the Triple Alliance for use against Russia and even Serbia. And Berlin, once the negotiations had begun, became convinced of the feasibility of using Italian troops in the east to assist Austria-Hungary. Conrad von Hötzendorf who had now changed his attitude toward the Italians, later asserted that in May 1914 Pollio had offered to put the three allies' oral agreement to send Italian troops to the east into a written convention. But the Italian general apparently never prepared any staff memorandum that revealed a pledge to send two Italian army corps against Russia. Of course, the absence of a written record does not disprove Conrad von Hötzendorf's assertion that an oral agreement was made. Besides his claim is believable in view of Pollio's repeated demonstrations of loyalty to the Triple Alliance.[19]

In addition to the army commitments, Italy and Austria-Hungary also negotiated a comprehensive naval agreement during 1913. This agreement was particularly important in the light of Franco-Italian friction in the Mediterranean. From Vienna's perspective, a convention was necessary because without such an agreement its fleet could not use Italian bases in the Mediterranean. The French fleet was superior to either the Italian or the Austrian squadron, but together the two might gain control of the Mediterranean. The Germans, moreover, were especially concerned about the French Third Army Corps in North Africa, not wishing to see it on the Western front in case of war.[20] The Germans also hinted that, if these North African troops could be prevented or delayed from landing in France, Berlin would possibly be able to send more troops east – which the Austrians greatly desired. Finally, although the Triple Alliance was still operating under a 1900 naval convention that provided for separate zones of operations, the convention was effectively a dead letter. An updated agreement was needed.

In January 1913, on his first trip to Rome, Waldersee spoke to Gen. Pollio about naval matters. The Italian chief favored a new naval agreement. Pollio seemed unconcerned about the British squadron in the Mediterranean, and shared the prevailing consensus that the French fleet was in poor condition. In Vienna, Waldersee spoke to Conrad von Hötzendorf and Adm. Raimondo Montecuccoli, head of the Austro-Hungarian navy. He found both agreeable to a new naval agreement despite doubts about Italian loyalty.[21]

In February, Pollio informed Conrad von Hötzendorf that Italian naval officers would be coming to Vienna to work out a naval treaty, and stressed the importance of Habsburg-Italian cooperation in gaining control of the Mediterranean. On February 24 Adm. Haus replaced Montecuccoli as commander of the Austro-Hungarian navy: he was still more sympathetic to a naval accord with Italy.[22] In April 1913, the negotiations began in Vienna. Many problems, such as the nationality of the supreme commander, codes, and Habsburg use of Italian bases were gradually resolved. The Italians displayed a spirit of cooperation and compromise. On May 14, 1913, at a Common Minister's Conference, Adm. Haus stated:

> France aimed at hegemony in the Mediterranean. This has driven Italy into our arms and has led to the renewal of the Triple Alliance. All Italy is inclined to cooperate with us at sea, because our fleet can protect Italy against a landing attempt and prevent the transportation of 100,000 French troops from North Africa.[23]

The German naval attaché in Rome noted widespread support in Italy for increased naval expenditures and for closer cooperation with Austria-Hungary to prevent French domination of the Mediterranean. [24] Leopold von Berchtold, the Habsburg foreign minister, was very encouraged by the negotiations for a naval convention, calling them "a very pleasant business."[25]

The naval convention was signed on June 23, 1913. It provided that at the outbreak of war there would be a united command under Adm. Haus. The combined fleets were expected to rendezvous off Messina immediately after the *casus foederis* was established. A principle mission of the allied fleet was the interdiction of French troop ships sailing from North Africa to metropolitan France, a matter of continuing concern to Berlin. [26] The convention also contained numerous technical provisions for cooperation among the three allies.

Habsburg-Italian chances for gaining control of the Mediterranean were good. British battle cruisers could not stand up to heavy shellfire, and the French fleet in all categories left much to be desired.[27] On the other hand, the Italian navy had strong points. The ideas of the Italian naval engineer Cuniberti had influenced the original "Dreadnought"; the battle cruiser concept also owed much to Italian design.

As to the sailors, the British *Naval Annual 1913* states: "The personnel of the Italian Navy is well organized and trained . . . the seamen are excellent fighting material."[28] During this period the Habsburg navy was engaged in an expansion program which was producing a squadron of well-designed dreadnoughts. And the Germans were committed to keeping a small force in the Middle Sea. Thus the naval forces of the Triple Alliance could expect at the very least to delay the transportation of French troops from North Africa long enough to keep them out of the crucial opening battles on the Western front. This would greatly aid the Germans in their western campaign. Without Italian bases and the assistance of the *Regina Marina,* the Habsburg fleet would be bottled up in the Adriatic—which is, of course, what happened in August 1914.

There was another key area of possible Italian military cooperation in the event of a European war. The Italians had close diplomatic and military links with Rumania. This strategically placed Balkan state was rated by Conrad von Hötzendorf and others as an important balance of power on the Eastern front.[29] In 1912 the Italians and Rumanians signed an agreement stipulating that in the event of a European war Italy would send two army corps to support the Rumanians against the Russians.[30] It was generally assumed that Bucharest would be influenced by Rome in any European confrontation. Thus effective Italian support of the Triple Alliance could have meant the addition of the Rumanian army to the forces of Austria-Hungary and Germany on the Eastern front. Conrad von Hötzendorf also considered the possibility of direct Italian support in the east; in fact, in May 1914 he ordered a study of using Italian troops in Galicia against Russia.[31]

The key question remains: how much faith did Conrad von Hötzendorf and Vienna have in Italian support of the Triple Alliance in case of war? There is evidence that Conrad von Hötzendorf had altered his earlier skepticism toward Italy by the time of Sarajevo. The principal reasons for this change were the military and naval agreements and Gen. Pollio. Thus on the very eve of the war Conrad von Hötzendorf, the old enemy of Italy, had mellowed in his antagonism toward the monarchy's southern neighbor. Even Moltke congratulated

Conrad von Hötzendorf on the Austrio-Hungarian military rapprochement with Italy. A further indication of Conrad von Hötzendorf's faith in Italian help, despite Pollio's sudden death on June 28, was reflected in a memorandum he drew up on July 2, 1914. In this document, the Austro-Hungarian chief expressed regret that Italy could not put its full force into the field. But he still believed Italy would give significant aid to the Dual Monarchy if war came. In a table attached to this memorandum, the Habsburg army chief calculated the opposing sides in case of a European war. Italy's 34 divisions are clearly placed in the column of the Triple Alliance along with Germany's 78 divisions and Austria-Hungary's own 48.[32]

Nor were Conrad von Hötzendorf's hopes entirely based on shadows. There were, in fact, influential groups in Italy that supported the Alliance with Austria-Hungary. Some highly placed people in the country were expected to support the Dual Monarchy in a moment of crisis. Most "responsible" Italians favored the Triple Alliance. This was particularly true of the diplomatic corps and, of course, the military. It should be noted that such groups as the clergy and elements of the nobility particularly favored the link with conservative Catholic Austria. For obvious reasons, to them such an agreement was even more desirable than the connection with Germany. Thus although the general public in Italy disliked the hereditary enemy, Vienna had a basis for hope that its interests would be defended by a sizable portion of the influential circles in Rome. The Austrians could believe that, under normal circumstances, no Italian government would openly break an alliance that had served the country's interests for over thirty years.

In retrospect Vienna clearly overestimated the extent of Italian friendship. Typical was the attitude of the aged Habsburg emperor. Franz Josef had long since mellowed in the animosity toward Italy that had characterized the early years of his reign. On July 2, the monarch told German Ambassador Heinrich von Tschirschky that the "Marquess di San Giuliano was in every way worthy, and fortunately, things were going decidedly better in connection with relations with Rome."[33] According to Baron Albert von Margutti, the emperor's military aide, Franz Josef had high hopes for the southern ally. Margutti states that Franz Josef's "greatest desire was to be able to regard Italy as an effective member of the Triple Alliance." According to the aide, the Habsburg monarch respected the Italian emissaries to his court, including the ambassador, the Duke d'Avarna, and the military attaché, Lt. Col. Albricci.[34] And Franz Josef was particularly fond of Gen. Pollio; it was even alleged that the emperor displayed more grief over the death of Gen. Pollio than over Franz Ferdinand's. The German ambassador reported that the emperor bemoaned how "the sudden death of Gen. Pollio was a great blow to Italy and also for us. 'Everyone is dying around me,' said His Majesty."[35]

The death of Gen. Pollio was indeed an unfortunate development for the Dual Monarchy. The new chief of staff, Gen. Luigi Cadorna, had little authority. In addition, the Italian foreign minister was gravely ill during the crisis so that affairs were handled by the pro-Entente prime minister, Antonio Salandra. His policy during the Sarajevo crisis was to demand territory for Italy under Article VII of the Triple Alliance Treaty, which provided for compensation to Italy if Austria-Hungary gained territory in the Balkans. This policy caused considerable apprehension in Vienna.

As early as July 5, Conrad von Hötzendorf had urged mobilization against Serbia. But on July 23, when Foreign Minister Berchtold told Conrad von Hötzendorf about his misgivings over Italy's position, the general replied, "If we have to fear Italy as well, let us not mobilize." Then he added, "We could not fight a war on three fronts."[36] Conrad von Hötzendorf realized that he needed Italy's 34 divisions, and could not possibly hope to win in a struggle in which Italy was added to the enemy coalition. And indeed Conrad von Hötzendorf had never contemplated a general war with Italy estranged. It is significant that no plans existed for simultaneous mobilization against Russia, Serbia, and Italy. A war against these three countries was completely beyond the power of the Dual Monarchy.[37]

Yet on July 25, Austria-Hungary did in fact mobilize against Serbia, despite Conrad von Hötzendorf's statement only two days earlier. Why? The answer possibly lies in the encouragement given Vienna by the Italian ambassador, the Duke d'Avarna, who like Ambassador Bollati in Berlin made a number of reassuring comments during the crisis. On July 23 Avarna saw the Habsburg foreign minister. After stressing the danger of a war between Austria-Hungary and Serbia, Berchtold concluded his remarks by saying, "The Royal and Imperial Government had made allowances for the benevolent attitude of its allies."[38] This remark was not lost on Avarna, who was always ready to accommodate his Austro-Hungarian hosts.

On July 25, Avarna returned to the Vienna foreign office and stated among other things:

> The Royal Italian government begs to say that it will adopt a friendly attitude consonant with the duties of an ally, in the eventuality of an armed conflict between Austria-Hungary and Serbia.[39]

This statement clearly suggests the probability of Italian aid to Austria-Hungary in case of European complications arising from the Austro-Hungarian-Serbian conflict. Count István Burián states that on July 25 he gained the impression that "the Italian government still assured us of its friendly attitude and one that was consonant with the duties of the alliance."[40] It is not clear whether the assurances given by Avarna were on his own initiative or were the result of instructions from Rome. But no matter what the cause, the effect of Avarna's demarche in Vienna was devastating. For on the very day when mobilization against Serbia was being decided, Vienna was receiving assurances of Italian loyalty to an alliance that stipulated common action in the event Russia supported its small Balkan ally. It is obvious that no effort was made by the Rome government to restrain Austria-Hungary, or to make it clear that Italy would not recognize the *casus foederis* arising from an Austro-Hungarian-Serbian conflict.

It is easy to see why Berchtold lost all fear about Italy's attitude, and on July 25 wrote to his envoy in Rome:

> Convey to San Giuliano that the announcement of a friendly attitude on the part of Italy corresponding to the obligations of the alliance has made a most agreeable impression with me.[41]

Unlike two days previous, the Austrian foreign minister raised no objection to mobilization against Serbia because of concern about Italy. Indeed Avarna's actions were of such a nature that Vienna was more sure of Italian loyalty after the ultimatum was delivered to Belgrade than immediately prior to it.[42] But it is equally clear that this dangerous situation could have been avoided. Rome could have notified Vienna at this point that it refused to take part in a war of aggression against Serbia. This had been done in 1913 when there had been a danger that Austria-Hungary would attack Serbia.[43] On that occasion San Giuliano had spoken quite bluntly to the Austrians. But in the summer of 1914, he and Salandra chose to give Vienna the appearance of support in the hope of gaining concessions for Italy under Article VII of the Triple Alliance Treaty.

The Italian efforts to acquire compensation were supported by the Germans, who urged Vienna to accommodate Rome. These efforts, especially Moltke's pressure on Conrad von Hötzendorf, were not without results. In the words of Salandra: "The Austrian chief, in deference to the solicitations of his German colleague to whom Italy's cooperation was not a matter of indifference, urged that we should be given some scrap or other."[44]

During this same period, military measures were taken in Italy which gave the impression that the Triple Alliance would enter a general conflict united. On July 13, just two weeks after the murder of the archduke, the Italian government called up the 1891 class for active service. This step had nothing to do with the international situation; rather it resulted from domestic problems arising out of a railroad strike. But the press portrayed it as a war measure and the action caused apprehension in some European capitals. When added to the military actions taken by Austria-Hungary and Germany, it created concern in Paris and St. Petersburg. Not unnaturally, the troop movements had the effect in Vienna of helping to create a false sense of confidence at this decisive juncture.

Somewhat later, when news of the Austro-Hungarian ultimatum to Serbia was received in Rome, Italian forces began to concentrate in the general direction of the French frontier. Throughout the last week of July military measures, which included the concentration of the fleet, took place in Italy. On July 29, the new Italian chief of staff, Cadorna, ordered emergency military measures.

These measures were quite inclusive, leaving the frontier with Austria practically undefended.[45] It is obvious how such actions would be perceived in light of the close cooperation of the preceding two years between the Italian general staff and the high commands of the three powers. Although there obviously was not sufficient time for Cadorna's orders to be completely carried out, enough were initiated to give Berlin and Vienna an impression of Italy's likely friendly attitude in the event of a general war.

On July 29, Szeptycki, the Habsburg military attaché, sent a telegram to Vienna in which he stated:

> I have gathered in conversation that Italy seriously thinks of cooperation in the event of a European conflict. . . . I have noticed that for the last two days the official and unofficial attitude of Italy toward Austria-Hungary has changed and that there is willingness to do everything to help us.[46]

We know that this information was passed on to Berlin because on August 1, in a memorandum to the foreign office, Moltke stated, "Imperial Austrian military attaché gives assurances that Italy will faithfully perform her alliance obligations."[47]

These reports from Rome of military movements in addition to the assurances of the Italian diplomats gave the Austro-Hungarian leaders reason to believe that the military conventions negotiated over the previous eighteen months would be honored. Avarna's demarche and the military steps taken by Rome created a situation where Conrad von Hötzendorf, like so many others in Berlin and Vienna, completely misjudged his southern ally. Ironically, he was more certain of Italian assistance in the last few days before the conflict erupted than at any other time in his career. On July 31, in a report to Emperor Franz Josef, Berchtold could write, "Baron Conrad hopes to induce Italy besides fulfilling its obligations with respect to France also to place troops at his disposal for Galicia."[48] This was a great change from only the week before when Conrad von Hötzendorf openly contemplated canceling mobilization against Serbia because of his apprehensions about Italy. Now with a general war possibly at hand, Conrad von Hötzendorf advanced into the abyss, his better judgment clouded by the illusion that his Italian ally would honor its alliance obligations.

The Austro-Hungarian navy shared Conrad von Hötzendorf's delusions about Italy in the last few days before the outbreak of war. Then on August 1, Adm. Haus, commander of the fleet, was notified that, if Italy failed to perform its duty as an ally, he was to restrict his operations to the Adriatic. Adm. Miklos Horthy, not surprisingly, states in his memoirs, "Italy's declaration of neutrality upset the plans of the [Austro-Hungarian] naval staff." [49]

In Vienna the general population held out hope for Italian help even longer. During the crucial days when the European states were one by one becoming involved, almost in a chain reaction, the Italian national anthem was played in Vienna along with those of Germany and Austria.[50] It was not until August 3, when news of the Rome government's declaration of neutrality was received in Vienna, that pro-Italian demonstrations were halted by the police.

Vienna could only be shocked when, in reply to Conrad von Hötzendorf's request for a meeting to determine Italian assistance to the Habsburg effort, Cadorna answered: "Conference purposeless. . . . If Austria-Hungary refrains from . . . disturbing the balance of power in the Adriatic, Italy will never march against it."[51] Within a few days the question had turned from the amount of Italian aid to Austria-Hungary to what the Dual Monarchy must do to avoid being attacked by its erstwhile ally. The Habsburg leadership had never imagined such a turn of events, such a total disappointment of their policy. Clearly the negotiations for a military and naval convention on the eve of World War I had given Vienna a misleading impression about Italy's attitude. Had Conrad von Hötzendorf, Berchtold, and the other Habsburg officials known that—at the moment of crisis—the military conventions would be a dead letter, it is doubtful that they would have been so willing to risk a European war in the summer of 1914.

NOTES

1. For the texts of the 1888 and 1889 agreements, see ML-684 [Italian records seized after World War II] folder 29 U.S. National Archives (cited as N.A.), Washington, D.C. For a discussion of the military negotiations between Rome and Berlin see Michael Palumbo, "German-Italian Military Relations on the Eve of World War I" in *Central European History,* Vol. 12 (May 1979), p. 343-371.

2. Alfred von Waldersee, "Von Deutschlands Militarpolitischen Beziehungen zu Italien," *Berliner Monatschefte,* July, 1929, p. 640.

3. *Documents Diplomatiques Français, 1871-1914* (hereafter cited as *D.D.F.),* (Paris, 1930-55), XI, 260, 262, 574, 576.

4. Angelo Gatti, *Nel tempo della tormenta* (Rome, 1923), p. 232. For examples of Conrad von Hötzendorf's violently anti-Italian attitudes, see Franz Conrad von Hötzendorf, *Private Aufzeichnungen,* ed. Kurt Peball (Vienna, 1977), pp. 91, 115, 137, 210, 299.

5. Franz Conrad von Hötzendorf, *Aus meiner Dienstzeit, 1906-1918* (Vienna, 1921-25), I, 69.

6. Gstb. Op. Fasz 89 (A), 1910-4, Kriegsarchiv, Vienna (hereafter cited as KAW).

7. Take Jonescu, *Some Personal Impressions* (London, 1919), p. 84.

8. Conrad von Hötzendorf, *Dienstzeit,* II, 282.

9. *British Documents on the Origins of the War, 1898-1914* (London, 1926-38), X (2), 620.

10. *D.D.F.,* 2nd ser., IV, 520.

11. Luigi Susani, "Nel 50 anniversario della morte del Generale Alberto Pollio," *Rivista Militare,* XX (1964), 528; Adriano Alberti, *L'opera di S.E. il generale Pollio e l'esercito* (Rome, 1923), p. 5. See also *D.D.F.,* 3rd ser. (Paris, 1929-36), III, 236.

12. Wolfgang Foerster, "Die deutsche-italienische Militärkonvention," *Kriegsschuldfrage,* May, 1927, p. 402.

13. Conrad von Hötzendorf, *Dienstzeit,* III, 87-88; Ludwig Bittner and Hans Uebersberger (eds.), *Österreich-Ungarns Aussenpolitik von der Bosnischen Krise 1908 bis zum Kriegsausbruch 1914* (hereafter *Ö.-U.A.),* (Vienna, 1930), p. 176.

14. Waldersee, *op. cit.,* p. 655; Wolfgang Foerster, *Aus der Gedankenwerkstalt des deutschen Generalstabes* (Berlin, 1931), p. 96; Helmuth von Noltke, *Erinnerungen, Briefe, Dokumente* (Stuttgart, 1922), p. 375; Italien No. 83, Vol. 2, No. 4, Politisches Archiv des Auswartigen Amt, Bonn.

15. KAW: Gstb. Op. Fasz 89 (A), 1913-11.

16. NA: ML-684, Folder 29, doc. 5.

17. NA: ML-684, Folder 29, doc. 4.

18. NA: ML-684, Folder 29, doc. 6.

19. Waldersee, *op. cit.,* p. 660; Conrad von Hötzendorf, *Dienstzeit,* III, 671; *I Documenti diplomatici italiani* (hereafter cited as *D.D.I.),* 5th ser. (Rome, 1954), I, No. 207.

20. *Ö.-U.A.,* V, 418-420.

21. Waldersee, *op. cit.,* pp. 643-649; Conrad von Hötzendorf, *Dienstzeit,* III, 86-88, 92, 153; Report by Conrad von Hötzendorf, 24 Jan. 1913, KAW: MKFF No. 652 (1913). On the negotiations, see Paul Halpern, *The Mediterranean Naval Situation, 1908-1914* (Cambridge, Mass., 1971).

22. Conrad von Hötzendorf, *Dienstzeit,* III, 89.

23. Sitzungsprotokolle des Gemeinsamen Ministerrats, No. 507, May 14, 1913, Politisches Archiv XL, Haus-, Hof- und Staatsarchiv, Vienna.

24. Report of German naval attaché in Rome, March 13, 1913, NA:T-1022/503/A5444.

25. *Ö.-U.A.*, VIII, 65.

26. Report of the Austro-Hungarian naval attaché, Jan. 11, 1913, KAW: MKSM-20-2/1 (1913).

27. Jean L. Couhat, *French Warships of World War I* (London, 1974), pp. 30, 46, 81; Anthony Preston, *Battleships of World War I* (Harrisburg, 1972), pp. 28, 45, 119, 129, 168; Viscount Hythe (ed.), *Naval Annual 1912* (London, 1912), pp. 152, 174.

28. Hythe (ed.), *op. cit.*, p. 152.

29. Conrad von Hötzendorf, *Aufzeichnungen,* p. 92.

30. Carlo Cialdea, *L'intervento rumeno nella guerra* (Rome, 1927), p. 43. For an indication of the important role played by this military agreement in Italian-Rumanian relations during the Sarajevo crisis, see *D.D.I.*, 4 ser., XIII, Nos. 472, 573, 856, 885.

31. Conrad von Hötzendorf, *Dienstzeit*, III, 670 673.

32. *Ö.-U.A.*, VIII, 268.270.

33. Max Monteglas and Walter Schucking (eds.), *Outbreak of the World War* [German documents collected by Karl Kautsky] (hereafter cited as *KD*) (New York, 1924), p. 65.

34. Albert Margutti, *The Emperor Franz Josef and His Times* (New York, 1921), pp. 246-247.

35. *KD,* p. 66.

36. Conrad von Hötzendorf, *Dienstzeit,* IV, 108.

37. Margutti, *op. cit.*, pp. 302-303.

38. *D.D.I.*, 4 ser., XII, No. 448.

39. *Austrian Red Book (Diplomatische Aktenstücke zur Vorgeschicte)* (hereafter cited as *RB*) (London, 1920), XX, No. 46.

40. Stephan Burian von Rajecz, *Austria in Dissolution* (New York, 1925), p. 25.

41. Berchtold to Merey, July 25, 1914. *Ö.-U.A.*, VIII, 752.

42. As late as July 31, Berchtold still seemed to believe that if the Rome government were satisfied under Article VII, Italy would join the Central Powers in the oncoming conflict. *D.D.I.*, 4 ser. XII, No. 797.

43. Giovanni Giolitti, *Memorie della mia vita* (Milan, 1922), II, 502-503.

44. Antonio Salandra, *Italy and the Great War* (London, 1932), p. 63.

45. Giorgio Rochat, "L'esercito italiano nell-estate 1914," *Nuova Rivista Storica,* XLIV (1961), 324-325.

46. *Ö.-U.A.*, VIII, 892-893.

47. *KD,* No. 609.

48. *ARB,* III, No. 80.

49. Miklos Horthy, *Memoirs* (London, 1956), p. 70.

50. Luigi Aldrovandi-Marescotti, *Guerra diplomatica* (Milan, 1937), p. 35.

51. Albertini denies that this message was sent by Cadorna but admits that similar statements were made by Cadorna to Colonel Szeptycki, the Habsburg military attaché in Rome. Luigi Albertini, *The Origins of the War of 1914,* (London, 1957), III, 309-310. Conrad von Hötzendorf, *Dienstzeit,* IV, 176.

THE AUSTRO-HUNGARIAN DECISION FOR WAR IN JULY 1914

William Jannen, Jr.

Why did Austro-Hungarian statesmen virtually ignore the possibility of Russian intervention and a Great Power war in July 1914? Prior to the assassination of Archduke Franz Ferdinand on June 28 these twin dangers had always been among their major concerns. The emperor, the archduke, Foreign Minister Count Leopold Berchtold and his predecessor Count Alois Lexa von Aehrenthal, and numerous imperial ambassadors had all warned that a Great Power war was a danger to the thrones of Germany, Russia, and Austria-Hungary.[1] Even a victorious war with Russia was regarded as dangerous because defeat would topple the tsarist monarchy and open the way to revolutionary forces that would be far more dangerous to the Habsburg monarchy than tsarist Russia had ever been.[2]

After Sarajevo this line of analysis virtually disappeared. Within forty-eight hours of the assassination almost everyone in a position of responsibility had agreed to attack Serbia regardless of the consequences. No example has been found of anyone who initially wanted to attack Serbia, and then later changed his mind as the Russian danger became clearer. Indeed, the only major example of hesitation is in the opposite direction. Hungarian Minister President István Tisza was initially skeptical of an unprovoked attack upon Serbia and insisted upon prior diplomatic demands, but once those steps had been taken, no one was more determined than he to press the war upon Serbia.[3]

This single-minded determination to attack Serbia has puzzled historians for decades. A prompt response in the heat of anger would have been reasonably explicable, but to adhere rigidly through five long weeks to a course that was almost certain to provoke war with Russia is another matter entirely. This essay will reexamine the decision to attack Serbia, utilizing some of the insights and behavioral hypotheses that have been developed in the study of international crisis management.[5]

Since the essay will be dealing largely with various psychological explanations of behavior, it should be made clear at the outset that I regard the Austro-Hungarian statesmen to have been facing real dangers and real problems, not fantasies rooted in the psychological traumas of infancy and childhood.[6] Serb irredentism and Russian support of that irredentism posed grave threats to the monarchy, ones that required resolution. The structure of the July crisis, when it came, was shaped by the evolution of the European balance of power in the preceding decades, and the freedom of action of the monarchy's leaders was constrained both by the institutional machinery within which they operated and by their experiences in the international arena in the immediately preceding years.[7] The concern in this paper is to find a psychological explanation that will relate the decisions of the Austro-Hungarian statesmen to the historical context.

* * * *

Even before the assassination of the archduke, an increasing number of the monarchy's leaders were arguing that war with Serbia was the only way out. What was required was a successful war with Serbia. The problem was to achieve it without fighting Russia as well. It was the fear of a Russian war that caused the emperor, the archduke, Berchtold, and Tisza to impose restraint upon those who insisted upon preventive war with Serbia, men such as the chief of the general staff, Gen. Franz Conrad von Hötzendorf, the governor of Bosnia-Herzogovina, Gen. Oskar Potiorek, the common war minister, Gen. Baron von Krobatin, the common finance minister, Leo von Bilinski, and even the elderly bureaucrat with failing eyesight, Austrian Minister President Count Karl Stürgkh.[8]

But on the eve of the assassination the policy of restraint still prevailed. After months of debate and after assessing all the baleful consequences of the two Balkan Wars, the foreign ministry still concluded that there were viable, peaceful options. A renewed approach to Rumania was proposed. If that failed, the monarchy should seek new ties with Turkey and Bulgaria. Those in hand, and with internal growth and consolidation, the monarchy might emerge stronger than ever. These views were shared by a number of influential people. Archduke Franz Ferdinand had always argued: "First one must have order at home . . . . then one can make *hurrahpolitik*." Count Gyula Szápáry, the new ambassador in St. Petersburg, wrote in January 1914 that the way to compel Russia to respect the monarchy's interests in the Balkans was to strengthen the monarchy at home. "In this sense, the future of our relations with Russia may in no small measure take on the character of a problem of internal policy."[9]

After the assassination, the options, the flexibility, the concern with Russia, disappeared from view. In 1912, for example, when the Austro-Hungarian leadership became aware that the Balkan states might ally to attack Turkey, the then chief of the general staff, Gen. Blasius Schemua, urged an attack on Serbia the moment it initiated war with Turkey. But the general wanted assurances against Russian intervention or Italian intervention. Berchtold and his chief aide, Count Alexander Hoyos, rejected Schemua's proposal because such assurances were unobtainable. In July 1914, however, Berchtold and Hoyos refused to regard the Russian threat as decisive while others simply denied that Russia would come in.

The minutes of the Council of Ministers of July 7 do not reflect a debate over whether or not the empire should go to war with Serbia. That had apparently been settled. The question was whether the empire should mobilize and attack without warning, or first make demands upon Serbia which, if rejected, would bring war. It was only the former course to which Tisza objected because, in his view, the only hope of localizing the war with Serbia would be to make demands which, if rejected, would justify the monarchy's war with Serbia in the eyes of Europe.[10] Berchtold had opened the meeting by announcing that they should decide whether or not the time had come for action against Serbia. He conceded that "a clash of arms with Serbia could have war with Russia as a consequence," but he met that objection by saying that they would have to fight Russia sooner or later, and that their position would only be worse later on.

Apart from that brief statement and Krobatin's and Conrad von Hötzendorf's outline of mobilization procedures (with or without Russian intervention), the minutes show no serious discussion of what war with Russia might mean. Only Tisza asked them again and again to consider "the terrible calamity of a European war." Berchtold, Bilinski, Krobatin, and Stürgkh all responded to Tisza's warnings by arguing that failure to act would be regarded as weakness, and that it would undermine the loyalty of the monarchy's South Slavs. Their obsession with Serbia is well illustrated by Stürgkh's response to Tisza's arguments. Tisza's whole point had been that time was not necessarily against the monarchy. If it won a major diplomatic victory by forcing Serbia to accept its severe demands, new alliances and firm internal measures might considerably improve the monarchy's position. If Serbia rejected its demands, he was prepared to fight, but then the war would begin in a far more hopeful diplomatic position. Stürgkh ignored these points, saying merely that "how the conflict should be begun is a question of detail" compared to the principal question of war or peace. As long as the empire attacked Serbia, Stürgkh did not care how it began.[11]

The Russian danger that had loomed so menacingly for years was simply dismissed. Even at the July 19 Council of Ministers, after the long delay had sharply reduced the chances of localization, there was no discussion of the possible consequences of Russian intervention; even Tisza suggested only that it would be more likely that Russia would stay out if they disclaimed any intention of annexing Serb territory.[12]

The dismissal of the Russian danger became spectacularly manifest when a stop-in-Belgrade proposal came up for discussion on July 30-31. By July 30 the British foreign secretary, Sir Edward Grey, had accepted a German suggestion that Austria-Hungary occupy Belgrade as security for an adequate settlement, and there was some hope that Russia would go along. On the afternoon of July 30 the German ambassador delivered an urgent message from Berlin that Vienna should accept Grey's proposal, cease hostilities, occupy Belgrade, and agree to Great Power mediation. The German note added that to refuse the British proposal would risk world war.[13] The German message was discussed shortly after it was received on July 30, first among Berchtold, Count János Forgach (Berchtold's first section chief) and Krobatin, and then a little later between Berchtold, Conrad von Hötzendorf, Krobatin and the emperor. Virtually the first thing every man said was that they could not stop the war with Serbia. The heart of the stop-in-Belgrade proposal—a cessation of hostilities—was simply not considered.

The council meeting called for the next morning to review the matter could not have lasted more than two hours. At least half the time was spent discussing Italian claims to compensation in the Balkans. Russia was barely mentioned. Everyone, including Tisza, agreed that the war against Serbia had to go ahead.[14] No one acknowledged any alternative to war with Serbia nor considered the possible consequences of such a war.

The peculiarly blinkered approach of the Austro-Hungarian decision-makers is reflected in the results of content analyses performed upon the published documents of the European powers for the six weeks between the assassination and the outbreak of war.[15] An analysis of the perceptions of available options showed that European leaders repeatedly perceived themselves as having no choice but to issue an ultimatum, or to mobilize, or to fight, while they saw their opponents as free to back down, to compromise, or to pursue some alternative line of action. But while such perceptions on the part of England, France, Germany, and Russia reflected a significant concern with the options available to other countries, statements of Austro-Hungarian leaders "reveal a virtual absence of attention to any other country." Similarly, a content analysis of perceptions of comparative capability and perceptions of threat concluded that "despite these moments of anxiety, the Austro-

Hungarian leaders were far more concerned with the 'perceived threat' to the Dual Monarchy than with the consequences of their actions."[16] The monarchy's leaders appear to have paid virtually no attention to the likely response of other powers or to the monarchy's ability to sustain a Great Power war. When the monarchy's leaders did consider comparative military capability, they tended to measure themselves against Serbia and Bulgaria rather than against France and Russia.[17]

How is such extraordinary behavior to be accounted for?

* * * *

What crisis studies suggest is that the Austro-Hungarian leadership was displaying all the signs of behavior under stress. Severe stress impairs the judgmental abilities required for effective policy-making: the correct perception of reality, a creative awareness of the options available, the ability to think out the possibilities in a period of uncertainty, the willingness to accept information that contradicts policy, the ability to see events with the eyes of one's opponent.[18] Moreover, prolonged stress and the combination of threat and uncertainty which usually accompanies a crisis can lead to such acute discomfort that decision-makers develop an urgent sense that they must act quickly to resolve the crisis and to relieve the tension. This is often reflected in statements like "the worst is better than this," or, as in Austria-Hungary, "better a frightful end than frightfulness without end," or Joseph Redlich's "better war than this uncertainty."[19]

This urgency is directly related to another aspect of crisis behavior, and that is a serious overestimation of how fast time is passing and a mounting sense that there is simply not enought time to consider all the possibilities. If fear, anxiety or the perception of threat are intense enough, decision-makers will disregard their nation's insufficiencies or inferior capabilities, and act "regardless of the consequences."[20] The tendency will be to reach a solution early and to force a consensus around that solution. A final decision, even when it means war, reduces tension and comes as a relief. Virtually all of the Austro-Hungarian memoir literature emphasizes the exultation and relief that greeted the news that war had been decided upon.[21]

Having reduced tension and relieved stress by coming to a decision, the decision-makers are often reluctant to reopen the question. The dynamics of small-group behavior may operate to bring critics and dissenters into line. Expressions of doubt will be regarded as disloyal, unrealistic or weak, not consistent with being part of the team. A number of factors entered into Tisza's evolution from relative caution and skepticism early in the crisis to a determination to prosecute the war at all costs after Serbia rejected the note. But his isolation and the pressure of his colleagues could not have been the least of them.[22]

If the decision is one that had hitherto been avoided because of its high risks, as was certainly the case in Austria-Hungary, considerable cognitive dissonance may be generated, that is, an awareness that the line of action chosen may lead to disaster. There is then intense emotional pressure to escape that dissonance. This is consistent with the finding that intense threat may lead decision-makers to disregard their country's weaknesses. Rather than return to the stress and anxiety which have just been relieved by coming to a decision, they simply ignore information indicating that their decision is disastrous.[23] When the possibility of disaster—in the present case Russian intervention—can no longer be disguised, the decision-maker may absolve himself from responsibility by arguing that he had no choice, that his opponents were forcing him into action. In the extreme case, the actor perceives only one course of action open to him and policy is reduced to resignation to the inevitable.[24]

The three top officials of the Austro-Hungarian foreign ministry—Berchtold, Forgách, and Hoyos—all argued at one time or another that they had no choice, that even if Russia came in nothing much would be risked, or that they would have to face Russia sooner or later. Berchtold, for example, wrote Mérey, his ambassador in Rome, on July 21 that the responsibility for deciding to take action against Serbia was no light one. But, he added:

> The responsibility for doing nothing, for letting things take their course till the waves engulf us, seems

> to me still more grave – if momentarily less trying – than to offer resistance and accept its consequences.

Berchtold did not want to go into the consequences, because to do so would be to "enter into a labyrinth." He again resorted to fatalism: "At the moment I have the feeling of having been chosen by Providence to be among those ministers who wanted peace, but had to make war." Mérey, who had suffered seriously from strain and overwork, who was bedridden during most of the July crisis, and who suffered a nervous breakdown when the Italian alliance came apart, replied:

> I would regard it as a genuine stroke of luck if war with Serbia does come about. Supposing a European conflagration does result, that would seem to me to prove that it was in the air and would have come sooner or later . . . and there is no doubt . . . the present moment is more favorable than a later one.[25]

The emperor reportedly told Krobatin: "I can do nothing else." Over and over again, Austrian memorialists wrote that they acted as they did because they had no choice. A highly charged imagery of burial, imprisoning webs and engulfing seas combined with an ever more violent rhetoric of breaking out: "ruthless disregard of the consequences," "bath of steel," "*le saigner à blanc.*" Many memorialists recall people in the streets saying, "War is being forced upon us."[26] Outsiders and those not involved in the dealings with Serbia could not understand what was happening. Gyula Szilassy in Athens thought it was "madness"; Count Ottokar Czernin reported from Bucharest that everyone there was saying, "Austria had gone mad." The memoirs of men like Joseph Baernreither, Count Heinrich Lützow, Rudolf Sieghart and Gyula Szilassy, all of whom repeatedly warned of Russian intervention, are full of bewilderment that their colleagues, sane men all, acted as they did.

* * * *

Granted that the Austro-Hungarian leadership acted irrationally and granted that the irrationality was due to stress, what was the source of the stress? Most of the literature on domestic disasters or international crises assumes that the stress arises from the immediate problem being confronted. This is reflected in the definition of crisis often used in international studies: "a situation of unanticipated threat to important values and restricted decision time."[27] That is satisfactory as far as it goes, but something more is required if the crisis is exacerbated, or caused by overperceptions or by misperceptions of threat and hostility arising out of forces and events antecedent to, or unrelated to, the immediate foreign-policy crisis.

Some analysts have focused on precisely this problem when they question the assumption that powers behave rationally in crises, an assumption that underlies the arms race and deterrence policies of the United States and the Soviet Union. Dieter Senghaas, for example, notes that history is full of examples in which elites intellectually and emotionally deceive themselves and remain prisoners in a self-induced inner world until catastrophic defeat forces them to restore a realistic relationship to actuality. Moreover, in situations of hostility or threat, such as an international confrontation, aggressive feelings rooted in a variety of sources, such as the background and upbringing of the decision-maker, his work situation, his family structure, or domestic social concerns, can easily be projected by him upon his opponents.[28] Since virtually all perception analyses agree that the most significant cause of hostile action by one nation is the perceived hostility of another, such projection may be a major source of international tension.[29] Where, in addition, complexity and incomprehensibility are so great that even realistic analysis cannot encompass them, there is a real danger that decision-makers will seek to escape from uncertainty through illusory solutions. The result is "a desire to rush the decision in order to reduce the mounting tension."[30] That decision, unfortunately, is often one to "clarify" the situation once and for all by prompt, aggressive action.

In applying this analysis to Wilhelmine Germany, V. R. Berghahn has argued that Germany's elites fell prey to just such compulsions under the pressures of trying to maintain their position in a rapidly industrializing society during a period of recurrent international crises. He therefore rejects Fritz Fischer's argument that the German leadership consciously provoked a world war in 1914, arguing instead that internal difficulties and foreign failures put the German leadership under such stress that they stumbled into war by stress-induced irrationality and errors of judgment amounting, in some instances, to virtually autistic behavior.[31]

Central to the argument of historians like Fischer, Berghahn, Dieter Groh, and Hans Wehler is the observation that a period of great and rapid change makes great demands upon the human personality. If the change is great enough and rapid enough, "important aspects of the personality become dysfunctional" because "changes and strains create in effect a revolutionary situation from the standpoint of psychic structure."[32] Values internalized during youth may become irrelevant. Traditional roles are no longer socially rewarded. People are no longer sure about what is expected of them. Elites may become uncomfortable with what they perceive as a decline in the traditional respect and deference due them. The uncertainty and ambiguity brought about by rapid change will be perceived as threatening. As political leaders attempt to cope with what they perceive as threat, disorder and decline, and fail to stem the tide of change, they will become frustrated by what they regard as persistent failure. Persistent failure to cope with threat can induce high levels of anxiety; both leaders and the populace may come to feel that they are facing a "life or death" situation. This sense of crisis, in turn, can lead to rigid, irrational responses in both domestic and international affairs.[33]

The present argument is that the generation in power in Europe in 1914 was in precisely the position described in the preceding paragraphs. Between 1850 and 1914 the major European powers were undergoing massive and unprecedented transformations of industrialization. Men in positions of responsibility in 1914 were usually in their fifties and sixties, which meant that they had been born in the rural, largely pre-industrial Europe of the 1840s and 1850s. They came to power in a world radically different from that of their youth and radically different from that which they had been trained to rule. They were educated in schools that inculcated traditional and often aristocratic values. English public schools, for example, found it necessary to remove themselves from the new urban world by acquiring protective greenbelts or by moving to estates outside of town. This move began in the 1870s so that this generation experienced the threat of urban sprawl in their earliest school days. The French university rejected the daily world of industrial society through the cult of antiquity and the great classics.[34]

A number of studies illustrate the anxiety, alienation and antimodern malaise that resulted from the rapid and massive changes engendered by European industrialization. Among the more obvious examples are the despair of traditional artisans at the destruction of their ancient guild society and its protective monopolies and welfare institutions, the alienation of rural nobles in Austria at the loss of their traditional political functions to the centralizing, bureaucratic state, the inability of the high aristocracy to adjust to bourgeois society, and the despair of conservative intellectuals at what they regarded as the rapacious values of the new industrial Mammon.[35]

The leaders of the monarchy could not have been immune from all this. Many of them were of the old nobility of birth (*Uradel*) like Berchtold, Forgach, Hoyos, Czernin in Bucharest, Szögyény in Berlin and Szapáry in St. Petersburg, or service nobles (*Briefadel*) like Conrad, Krobatin and Giesl, the envoy in Belgrade. Even those not formally ennobled, like the young foreign ministry officials Musulin and Urbas, shared the prevailing aristocratic ethos. These men judged the dislocations of industrialization as a breakdown of the social and moral order. Count Hoyos regarded the rise of industrial bourgeois society as pernicious and subversive. Urbas considered modern society crass and immoral. Count Lützow could not find a comfortable niche in the modern world once he retired from government service.[36] Such men could hardly avoid bringing to their political decisions the anxieties induced by the massive changes they had seen in their lifetimes.

Nor were their anxieties diminished by the fact that they headed a multinational, dynastic conglomeration that they knew was widely regarded as an anachronism. Industrial society, socialist revolution, nationalist dissolution, the collapse of the moral order—all seemed more or less threatening and inevitable, depending upon the individual. If there was anything like a consensus in the empire, it was that things could not go on as they were. Indeed, a truly status quo conservatism was almost out of the question. A whole series of reforming initiatives were undertaken in the prewar years, and ruling circles endlessly discussed proposals for restructuring imperial institutions. Nowhere in Europe were fundamental institutions so widely questioned as in the monarchy.[37] The difficulty was that most initiatives and reforms had had disappointing results.

In these circumstances many of the empire's leaders became obsessed by the threat of Great Serb irredentism. They regarded the monarchy as facing a life or death situation, and feared that it would become the "second sick man of Europe." They viewed their attempts at reform as being frustrated by Serbian agitation. They repeatedly made, and were subject to, demands for a "final reckoning." Their internal and diplomatic documents reveal a Serbia that had become the focus of a whole range of political and social fears. Serbia was a "Slavic nest," a hotbed of radical democracy, of anarchism, and of regicides, that "introduces revolutionary terror" into the life of nations. It was an "anarchistic socialist polity that calls itself a monarchy," the eventual union of which with Montenegro would result in a Great Serb state that might eventually adopt a republican form of government.[38] This intense and growing desire to settle with Serbia was frustrated by an almost equal dread of war with Russia. The pressure to escape the stress of such unpalatable alternatives could and did lead to a tendency to seek an illusory way out, for example, to destroy Serbia without war with Russia.[39]

****

If the intensity of the desire to settle with Serbia once and for all was a function, at least in part, of more generalized fears and anxieties, then one would expect those who confronted politics and life with relative confidence and calm to be more restrained in their response to Serb irredentism than those who despaired for the empire and feared the collapse of "civilization" and "the social order." That, generally, was the case.

Those who had some confidence in the dualist status quo, like Berchtold and the emperor, or who felt no great urgency about reform, like Lützow, or who retained confidence in internal measures and consolidation as a way out of the monarchy's difficulties, like Archduke Franz Ferdinand, Tisza, or the political diarist Baernreither, were much less likely to see themselves facing a fateful either/or. Those, on the other hand, who felt that the empire was tottering towards dissolution, who urgently felt the need for radical reform, whether trialism (German, Magyar and Slavic parity under the emperor) or federalization by nationalities, were far more likely to be exasperated by the faltering pace of reform and were almost always more threatened by Serb irredentism. Stürgkh, Hoyos, the foreign ministry confidant and political diarist Redlich, foreign ministry officials such as Musulin and Urbas—all shared this peculiar juxtaposition of fearfulness and aggressiveness. They therefore found themselves in the paradoxical position of urging an empire whose imminent dissolution they feared to go to war. [40]

Tisza and Stürgkh illustrate the contrasting modes of response. Each came from old gentry families and each was deeply worried about the future stability of the empire. Tisza was something of a pessimist on human affairs, but he never despaired. He and his Magyar nationalists won a sweeping electoral victory in 1910 that sharply reduced the representation of national minorities in the Hungarian parliament. By 1912, as president of the Hungarian lower house, Tisza had revised the rules of procedure to gag nationalist obstruction. When Magyar separatist extremists continued to disrupt the proceedings, Tisza had them removed by force. With parliament in hand, money increases for the imperial armed forces were voted for the first time in years, and constructive, if modest, laws on labor welfare, social insurance, and salary increases for civil servants were adopted. In 1913, after minor concessions to Croatian moderates, Tisza felt secure enough to restore local elections and constitutional government to Croatia.

While Tisza was restoring effective government in Hungary, Stürgkh was giving up all hope of effective parliamentary rule in the Austrian half of the empire. Negotiations for electoral reform for the Galician diet broke down in April 1913. In the same year, Stürgkh dissolved the Bohemian diet and installed an imperial committee. In March 1914 he adjourned the Austrian parliament. By the eve of the war, the Austrian parliament and provincial assemblies were no longer sitting, and the Austrian half of the empire was being ruled by emergency decrees.[41] In late 1913 Stürgkh was convinced that something would have to be done about Serbia, and during July 1914 he was unshakable in his determination to make war upon that country. Tisza, on the other hand, rarely abandoned his powers of analysis and always seemed to be able to find a workable line of action. Until well into July 1914, he was a force for restraint in Austro-Hungarian policy.

Stürgkh was a traditional autocrat from an old, if impoverished, gentry family. But Joseph Redlich, a Jew and an intellectual, showed exactly the same pattern of response, and Redlich was active with the left liberal Austrian Fabians who wanted to make "feudal" Austria into a modern, secular bourgeois state with manhood suffrage, parliamentary government, and an intelligent social policy to forestall socialist revolution and nationalist disintegration.[42] Redlich repeatedly lamented the failure of aggressive action. He feared Serbia's irredentist appeal, and had been calling for war upon that country since 1908. On one level, Redlich understood the Russian danger. Then an assassination attempt, or a nationalist brawl in Prague, or food riots in Budapest would bring on an outburst of rage and a call for action. On the food riots in Budapest, and the related question of worker-management relations, on the other hand, Tisza merely commented: "Struggle is, after all, the father of things."[43] Redlich, in April 1913, saw revolution "lurking" in Dalmatia, Croatia and Bosnia, and regretted not having publicly urged the monarchy to go to war. In July 1913 he regarded the empire as "in full, open decomposition." He reacted to the assassination in July 1914 with that peculiar combination of enthusiasm and foreboding that was so prevalent that summer. He did not know how the empire would come out of the war, but it was impossible not to see the necessity of war with Serbia, and as the certainty of such a war mounted, he barely contained his joy.[44]

Redlich's friend Hoyos, scion of the old aristocracy, also despaired of the existing dualism and of what he perceived as

Magyar dominance. He was constantly drafting reform proposals along federal lines that would provide some autonomy for the empire's nationalities. But where Redlich wanted a modern bourgeois society and parliamentary government, Hoyos detested the "revolutionary movement of the bourgeois intellectuals" and their striving for democracy. He felt that Wilhelmine Germany had erred in abandoning the principles of landed society, and had no doubt that the entry of Italy and the United States into the ranks of the monarchy's enemies was due to Masonic propaganda and the spread of antimonarchial principles. In July 1914 he insisted on the necessity of attacking Serbia. It would be better to see the empire collapse than to have it become the "sick man" of Europe. When war broke out, he rejoiced with Joseph Redlich and regaled him with the reforms that would follow upon its successful conclusion.[45]

Neither the aristocratic Magyar nationalist Tisza, nor the conservative, bourgeois Bohemian German nationalist Baernreither saw any internal need for war. Tisza was committed to dualism and saw nothing wrong in Bosnia-Herzogovina that firm administration would not cure. Baernreither's detailed studies of Habsburg administration, schooling, tax and trade policies, and his contacts with the nationalities had convinced him that reform in these areas would restore the monarchy without war.[46]

It was, in short, the emotional posture of the actor, not the substance of his politics, that was decisive.[47] The pattern of relative confidence and restraint on the one hand, and fear and aggressiveness on the other, also appears in the policy debates in the Council of Ministers. Austrian governing circles felt the need for reform far more urgently than did the Magyars. With the Balkan Wars of 1912 and 1913 the fear grew that the rising tide of nationalist aspiration might not allow the empire sufficient time for gradual reform.[48] By 1912 and 1914 people as politically diverse as Bardolff and Brosch, military advisors to the archduke, the Czech noble and industrialist Count Heinrich Clam-Martinic, Austrian Railway Minister Forster, Krobatin, Conrad von Hötzendorf, the diplomat and high aristocrat George Franckenstein, the left liberal Austrian Fabian Michael Hainisch, and the historian Alfred Pribram agreed on the need for a final reckoning with Serbia followed by constitutional reform and trialism.

In the spring of 1913 Berchtold and the Hungarians contemplated an ultimatum to Montenegro followed by a limited thrust at Skutari to force the Montenegrins out of the city. Bilinski, Sturgkh, and Austrian Finance Minister Zaleski – all of whom had opposed major military initiatives the previous September–now wanted to extend the war to Serbia so that the South Slav menace could finally be resolved. Financial weakness persuaded Berchtold and the Magyars that only a limited action was feasible, but Bilinski and Stürgkh insisted that aggressive action was necessary if they were to maintain the loyalty of their South Slavs. They also insisted that Russia would not intervene. The Hungarian finance minister, Teleszky, objected that the Russians would certainly intervene once they saw the monarchy's financial weakness. The monarchy needed four or five years of peace and economic recovery to regain its strength. By that time, Bilinsky retorted, they would have lost Bosnia and Dalmatia. Hungarian Minister President Laszló Lukács was almost contemptuous. They were tougher in Hungary and had fewer intellectuals among their South Slavs, so that the latter were quieter.[49]

Up to the assassination, Berchtold, Tisza, the emperor and the archduke were able to impose a policy of restraint and maneuver. By June 24, 1914, a lengthy policy debate had come to the relatively pacific conclusion that while the situation was bad, it was not hopeless. The June 24 statement made no mention of hostile action against Serbia. On the contrary, if Rumania insisted upon it as the price for continuing in the Triple Alliance, the monarchy was prepared to improve relations with Serbia by offering economic and political concessions.[50]

* * * *

The assassination of June 28, 1914, shattered the political and psychological basis for such a policy. A thoroughly dynastic elite saw an essential symbol of the monarchy's coherence and continuity assassinated by what they regarded as tools of a fanatically destructive nationalism. Literature on the emotional force which can attach to political and national symbols is very suggestive. Where the values symbolized have become an essential part of the self-identity of those who accept the symbol, an assault upon the symbol such as the desecration of a flag, or, as in this case, the assassination of the heir to the throne, can provoke an overwhelming emotional response.[51] Brosch, a former and devoted military aide to the archduke, described himself as "half mad with pain and outrage." Conrad von Hötzendorf described the assassination as a direct assault upon the monarchy. For those already overwhelmed by anxiety and fear of imminent dissolution, the assassination unleashed an irresistible desire to have the empire at long last act. For those who regarded the archduke as the monarchy's "last great hope," like Bardolff, Brosch, Conrad von Hötzendorf, Czernin, Krobatin and Urbas, many of whom were already convinced of the need to reduce Serbia in order to further reform, there was nothing left but the desperation of a military solution. Emotions were so intense after the assassination, Szilassy wrote afterwards, that even high officials who earlier had thought otherwise, now argued that Russia, out of regard for dynastic principles, would not intervene. Even Tisza eventually bowed before the storm.[52]

Berchtold was particularly hard hit. Even before the assassination the strain of continuous confrontation abroad and criticism at home was beginning to tell. His diary complains repeatedly of headaches, nightmares and sleepness nights:

> At home I am pressed to action, forcefulness, armaments. Abroad I am admonished to peace, reasonableness and disarmament. Yesterday an attack from within, today another from without, and tomorrow?

With the Peace of Bucharest that ended the Second Balkan War in 1913, his despondence deepened:

> The peace bells of Bucharest have a gloomy tone. They toll no festive joy. Sometimes they sound like funeral bells, an undertone of mourning for all those who have been done violence and whose hopes are now covered by cool earth.[53]

Tisza, typically, wrote of the Peace of Bucharest that they would come through "this unfortunate transition period" if they made policy with cool detachment and waited until "a realistic assessment of each state's own interests gains the upper hand."[54]

The assassination seems to have snapped Berchtold's ability to continue a policy of maneuver and restraint. From the time he learned that the assassins were Bosnian Serbs, he became the strong man of the government, grimly determined to attack Serbia. Nowhere is this more dramatically revealed than in the differences between the June 24 statement and the memorandum delivered to the Germans on July 5. The memorandum dropped the emphasis upon retaining Rumania for the Triple Alliance, and argued instead for an alliance with Bulgaria and a final reckoning with Serbia. The new memorandum gave up all hope of reconciliation with Serbia, "the monarchy's bitterest enemy in the Balkans." The June 24 statement made no mention of action against Serbia; on the contrary, it had accepted the possibility of conciliation. The new memorandum declared the differences between Serbia and the monarchy to be "unbridgeable," and concluded by declaring the "imperative . . . need for the monarchy to sever with a firm hand the threads which its enemies seek to draw into a net over its head." Hoyos' covering letter for the emperor's signature made it clear that Austria-Hungary would try to reduce and isolate Serbia. The June 24 statement dealt entirely with foreign-policy analysis. Hoyos' letter turned upon the internal consequences of the Pan-Slav threat and concluded that after the assassination reconciliation with Serbia "was no longer to be thought of."[55]

There is no evidence whatever that Berchtold's change of front was the result of German pressure. Nor do the detailed accounts of Austro-Hungarian actions in July 1914 portray a Berchtold swept along by more aggressive members of the government. After the assassination, Berchtold led the war party.[56] If the assassination acted as an important triggering event that released a host of fears and anxieties which Berchtold had hitherto kept under control, and if these unleashed fears and anxieties led him to identify Serbia as the external enemy that had to be destroyed so that he could master his fears and anxieties, that might explain how a temporizing moderate became an unyielding hawk during the month of July 1914.[57]

* * * *

The leaders of the monarchy shared a European experience that made the war something more than the diverting of domestic pressures through foreign adventures, or the kind of conservative restoration through war that Fritz Fischer and Arno Mayer seem to have in mind. The war was at least partially an escape from intolerable tension and anxiety, tension and anxiety that were not entirely due to the immediate foreign-policy problem at hand.

If this is what happened in 1914, it would account for the immense and widespread exultation and relief that greeted the outbreak of war. It would also account for the apparently paradoxical juxtaposition of fear and the urgent readiness to risk decisive action or war which appears among the leaders of the European powers. In England, it was men like Sir Arthur Nicolson and Eyre Crowe, who feared for the British Empire, who urged firm action against Germany, and who wanted to convert the ententes into alliances. The social fears that underlay a book like Gustav Le Bon's *The Mob,* which in turn had such baleful influence on French strategic doctrine, unmistakably reveal themselves in Gen. Henri Bonnal's advocacy of the doctrine of the offensive, and in his warning that solidarity and *élan* were necessary to overcome the egoism of the common soldier which was as dangerous to the army as it was to social solidarity.[58] The Russian foreign minister warned the Austro-Hungarian ambassador: "When one looks around the world, one sees with horror how the enemies of the existing order, the antidynasts, everywhere gain strength."[59] In Germany, self-confident businessmen assured the government that with twenty years of peace, Germany would dominate the continent, but the fearful, fatalistic chancellor, Bethmann-Hollweg, the self-doubting chief of the general staff, Gen. Helmuth von Moltke, and the unstable emperor, who could not rid himself of his fears of socialism, the Yellow Peril, or the Slavic Flood—all felt that the time had come for a final reckoning. The German emperor's letter of condolence to Emperor Francis Joseph rang all the changes:

The horror of the crime of Sarajevo has thrown a

> harsh light upon the disastrous tumult of mad fanatics and the subversion of the state by Pan-Slav agitation . . . I regard it not only as the moral obligation of all *Kulturstaaten* but as a command of self-preservation to oppose with all the means of force the propaganda of the deed which primarily seeks out the firm structure of monarchies as an object of attack."[60]

It has been argued here that the Austro-Hungarian decision-makers were responding to real problems and real threats, but that they responded to them unrealistically. They had been subject to accumulating stress and fears from a wide range of sources long before the assassination and were seeking to reduce stress through a variety of psychological mechanisms. After the assassination, particularly given the symbolic and emotional importance of such an event, they could not tolerate the further stress entailed by uncertain negotiations over uncertain solutions. The assassination therefore acted as an immensely powerful catalyst that both raised their fears and anxieties to levels that burst the restraints that had hitherto contained them, and presented an external enemy, Serbia, upon whom such fears and their resultant aggression could be discharged. In the face of the psychological needs thus generated, war with Russia literally did not matter.

NOTES

This paper has benefitted greatly from the searching criticism imposed on earlier drafts by my colleagues, Professors Paula S. Fichtner, James P. Johnson, Christoph Kimmich and Bela K. Kiraly. I am very grateful to them.

1. Fritz Fellner (ed.), *Schicksaljahre Österreichs: Das politische Tagebuch Joseph Redlichs* (Graz, 1953), I, 194; Carl Bardolff, *Soldat im alten Oesterreich* (Jena, 1943), p. 177; G. Franckenstein, *Diplomat of Destiny* (New York, 1940), pp. 44-45; Ludwig Bittner and Hans Uebersberger (eds.), *Österreich-Ungarns Aussenpolitik von der bosnischen Krise 1908 bis zum Kriegsausbruch 1914* (hereafter *Ö.-U.A*) (Vienna, 1930); Mensdorf to Vienna, Sept. 29, 1911, *Ö.-U.A.*, VIII, 804. Austro-Hungarian envoys to Russia, including Berchtold when he was stationed there, were sure war would bring on a revolution in Russia, *Ö.-U.A.*, I, 493; V, 622, and VII, 581-82, 758.

2. Julius Szilassy, *Der Untergang der Donau-Monarchie* (Berlin, 1921), pp. 219, 234, 236; Franz Conrad von Hötzendorf, *Aus meiner Dienstzeit,*

1906-1918 (Vienna, 1921-25), III, 82-83; Hugo Hantsch, *Leopold Graf Berchtold: Grandseigneur und Staatsman* (Vienna, 1963), I, 100.

3. Most historians argue that Tisza first opposed war with Serbia and then changed his mind between July 9 and 14. Norman Stone, "Hungary and the Crisis of July 1914," in Walter Laqueur and George Mosse (eds.), *1914: The Coming of the First World War* (New York, 1966), pp. 153, 160; Oskar von Wertheimer (ed.), *Graf Stefan Tisza Briefe, 1914-1918* (Berlin, 1928), I, 28; Gustav Erenyi, *Graf Stefan Tisza* (Vienna, 1935), pp. 251-253. The question is not that clear. Tisza was always opposed to an attack without warning, but from July 7 he never wavered from the line that, if a firm note was sent and Serbia returned an unacceptable answer, war would follow. He was, however, always more aware of the risks of Russian intervention than his colleagues.

4. Historians are usually reduced to the assertion that the actions are inexplicable. Luigi Albertini concluded that "Vienna, which had no eyes save for the Austro-Serbian conflict, never faced the possibility of a European war." *The Origins of the War of 1914* (London, 1952-57), II, 286. Joachim Remak writes of the "reckless and inadequate people in Vienna" in "1914-The Third Balkan War: Origins Reconsidered," *Journal of Modern History* (hereafter cited as *JMH*), XLIII (1972), 363. Gerhard Ritter described the Austro-Hungarian response as an "elemental outburst of passion that could no longer be satisfied." *Sword and Scepter*, Vol. II: *The European Powers and the Wilhelminian Empire, 1890-1914* (Coral Gables, Fla., 1970), 233, 234, 235. P.W. Schroeder, while rightly regarding such formulations as inadequate, himself says only that the empire abandoned restraint "when it seemed too hopeless and humiliating, and violence appeared to be the only recourse." "World War I as Galloping Gertie," *JMH*, XLIV (1972), 322-342.

5. Among such studies which deal particularly with the origins of World War I are Ole R. Holsti, *Crisis, Escalation and War* (Montreal, 1972); Nazli Choucri and Robert C. North, *Nations in Conflict* (San Francisco, 1975); E.V. Nomikos and R. C. North, *International Crisis* (Montreal, 1976); R. C. North and N. Choucri, "Background Conditions to the Outbreak of the First World War," *Peace Research Society [International Papers*, IX] (1968), 125-137; Dana A. Zinnes, "The Expression and Perception of Hostility in Prewar Crisis: 1914," in J. David Singer (ed.), *Quantitative International Politics* (New York, 1968), pp. 85-119; O. R. Holsti, et al., "Perception and Action in the 1914 Crisis," in *ibid.*, pp. 123-154; R. C. North, "Perception and Action in the 1914 Crisis," *Journal of International Affairs*, XXI (1967), 103-122; Alan N. Sabrosky, "From Bosnia to Sarajevo," *Journal of Conflict Resolution*, XIX (1975), 3-24. For a critique of the methodology of content analysis, which is used in many of the above studies, see Robert Jervis, "The Costs of Quantitative Study in International Relations," in Klaus Knorr and James N. Rosenau, *Contending Approaches to International Politics* (Princeton, 1969), pp. 177-217.

6. The psychological assumptions of this paper are based upon Fred Weinstein and Gerald Platt, "The Coming Crisis in Psychohistory," *JMH*, XLVII (1975), 202-228. They reject the "ontogenetic familial orientation" of classical psychoanalysis used by most psychohistorians because they regard it as an inadequate model for historians seeking to explain adult responses to real problems. They propose, instead, a model based upon ego-psychology which postulates an ego adapting to present reality rather than merely reenacting

childhood trauma. "Social conflict arises not from drive expression but from responses to real problems in the social world which affect the capacity of people to act on internalized standards . . . Social conflict stems from different and competing orientations to action based on incompatible views of reality, a situation which arises when internalized standards become ineffective or dysfunctional because of social change." *Ibid.*, 221-22. Behavioral psychologists operate with similar assumptions. After describing changes in the behavior of a nonconforming member of a government policy group when he assumed a leadership role, Joseph H. de Rivera commented: "The behavior of an individual is seen to result from the structure of the situation rather than from his personality. The postulate asserts that *anybody* who is in the described situation will react in the prescribed way" (emphasis in the original). *The Psychological Dimension of Foreign Policy* (Columbus, 1968), p. 211.

7. On the impact of organizational structures and institutional restraints, see Samuel R. Williamson, Jr., "Theories of Organizational Process and Foreign Policy Outcomes," in Paul Lauren (ed.), *Diplomacy: New Approaches in History, Theory and Policy* (New York, 1979), pp. 127-161. On the role of immediately preceding experience, see Schroeder, "World War I as Galloping Gertie," and Williamson's essay, "Vienna and July 1914: The Origins of the Great War Once More," in this volume.

8. In this paper I shall refer to the Austro-Hungarian Monarchy as a whole as Austria-Hungary or the monarchy or the empire, to its Hungarian half as Hungary, to its non-Hungarian half as Austria. Legally, the non-Hungarian part was designated "the kingdoms and countries represented in the Reichsrat," and sometimes called Cisleithania. Cf. A. J. May, *The Hapsburg Monarchy, 1867-1914* (Cambridge, Mass., 1951), p. 43.

9. Memorandum by Szápáry, Jan. 20, 1914, *Ö.-U.A.*, VII, 55 ff.; memorandum by Tisza, Mar. 15, 1914, *ibid.*, 975 ff.; Foreign Ministry memorandum completed prior to June 24, 1914, *ibid.* VIII, 186 ff.; R.A. Kann, *Erzherzog Franz Ferdinand Studien* (Munich, 1976), p. 220.

10. *Ö.-U.A.*, VIII, 343-344.

11. *Ibid.*, 346. Krobatin also dismissed Tisza's "details," noting that the Balkan and Russo-Japanese wars had all begun without declarations of war.

12. *Ibid.*, 851 ff.

13. Conrad von Hötzendorf, *op. cit.*, IV., 149-151; Albertini, *op. cit.*, II, 665-666; Ritter, *op. cit.*, II, 245-255. On the proposal itself see Mensdorf to Vienna July 29, 30, 1914, *Ö.-U.A.*, VII, 877, 922; Berchtold and Tschirschky conversation of July 30, and July 31, Council of Ministers, *ibid.*, 909-910, 976 ff.; Grey to Goschen and Buchanan, July 29, 30, G. P. Gooch and H. Temperley (eds.), *British Documents on the Origins of the War, 1898-1914*, (London, 1926-38) (hereafter cited as *BD*), XI, 181-182, 196-197.

14. *Ö.-U.A.*, VIII, 976-979.

15. Content analysis searches diplomatic and other documents for certain categories of communication such as statements of intent, perceptions of hostility, assessments of capability, perceptions of actions or expressions of hostility by other powers, statements regarding time or the intentions of, or options open to, other powers, etc. These statements are then tabulated and arranged by power over time, or whatever is indicated by the analysis, and the results are used to test various models of international behavior. In this paper, I am using the results of such studies only to indicate the kind of perceptions Austro-

Hungarian leaders were open to. Brief descriptions of this methodology can be found in North, "Perception and Action in the 1914 Crisis." pp. 116-120; Zinnes, *op. cit.*, pp. 90-99; Jervis, *op. cit.*, pp. 179-182.

16. Holsti, *op. cit.*, pp. 146, 154; Nomikos and North, *op. cit.*, p. 55; D. A. Zinnes, *et. al.*, "Capability, Threat and the Outbreak of War," in James N. Rosenau, *International Politics and Foreign Policy* (New York, 1961), p. 471.

17. Zinnes, "Capability," p. 472. Ritter, *op. cit.*, II, 229, notes that Conrad von Hötzendorf's comparative analyses of troops strengths were usually confined to comparisons between the monarchy and Serbia and Italy.

18. Holsti, *op. cit.*, pp. 11-23.

19. Stephen V. Withey, "Reaction to Uncertain Threat," in G. W. Baker and D. W. Chapmen (eds.), *Man and Society in Disaster* (New York, 1962), pp. 117-118; Rudolf Sieghart, *Die Letzten Jahrzehnte einer Grossmacht* (Berlin, 1932), p. 169; Fellner (ed.), *op. cit.*, I, 184.

20. "Perceptions of one's own inferior capability, if anxiety, fear, or perceptions of threat or injury are intense enough, will fail to deter a nation from going to war." North, "Perception and Action," p. 117. See also Zinnes, "Capability," pp. 470-471. On perceptions of inadequate time, see de Rivera, *op. cit.*, 153-156; Holsti, *op. cit.*, p. 228; Nomikos and North, *op. cit.*, p. 1.

21. Holsti, *op. cit.*, p. 138, after noting the drop in the number of perceptions of time once war broke out, comments, "There is also evidence that after a nation has been drawn into war time pressure dropped sharply. It appears that after being faced with the problem of the prewar crisis, those of waging war actually provided some relief from time pressure." Among Austrian memoirs, see Auffenberg-Komarow, *Aus Oesterreichs Hohe- und Niedergang* (Munich, 1921), pp. 260-263 (People frequently said they felt war was like a release - "*wie eine Erlösung*"); Freiherr von Musulin, *Das Haus am Ballplatz* (Munich, 1924), p. 234 (News of serious steps against Serbia were greeted with a measure of "relief"); Ernest U. Cormons (Emanual Urbas), *Schicksale und Schatten* (Salzburg, 1953), p. 68 ("grotesque as it may appear to us today, the outbreak of war in August 1914 was greeted by youths as a relaxation of tension, yes, as a release"). Many of the Austrian intelligentsia shared these feelings. C. E. Williams, *The Broken Eagle* (New York, 1974) pp. 37, 44, 149, 188.

22. Szilassy's descriptions of the post-assassination atmosphere are enlightening. He writes that it would have taken a "steely" personality to stand up to the war party after the assassination and great moral courage to speak out against the "madness" *(Wahn)*. *Op. cit.*, pp. 224, 268. For the pressures on Tisza, see Wertheimer (ed.), *op. cit.*, pp. 26-31; Erenyi, *op. cit.*, pp. 251-253. For theoretical discussion, Nomikos and North, *op. cit.*, p. 28; de Rivera, *op. cit.*, pp. 209-211. There are useful comments in R. C. Raack, "When Plans Fail: Small Group Behavior and Decision-Making in the Conspiracy of 1808 in Germany," *Journal of Conflict Resolution*, XIV (1970), pp. 7-9, and notes 8, 9.

23. Robert Jervis, *Perception and Misperception in International Politics* (Princeton, 1976), pp. 382-406; de Rivera, *op. cit.*, p. 79.

24. *Ibid.*, pp. 150-153; Holsti, *op. cit.*, p. 17; Withey, *op. cit.*, pp. 117-118.

25. *Ö.-U.A.*, VIII, 564-566, 890.

26. Heinrich Graf von Lützow, *Im diplomatischen Dienst der k.u.k. Monarchie* (Munich, 1971), p. 221; Sieghart, *op. cit.*, p. 169; Joseph M. Baernreither, *Fragmente eines politschen Tagebuchs* (Berlin, 1928), p. 329;

Cormons (Urbas), *op. cit.*, p. 158; Giesl, *Zwei Jahrezehnte im Nahen Orient* (Berlin, 1927), p. 214; E. C. Corti and Hans Sokol, *Der Alte Kaiser* (Graz, 1956), p. 421; Conrad von Hötzendorf, *op. cit.*, IV, 127.

27. Nomikos and North, *op. cit.*, p. 1; Holsti, *op. cit.*, p. 9.

28. Dieter Senghaas, *Rüstung und Militarismus*, (Frankfurt a/M., 1972), pp. 27, 46 and *passim;* Kenneth E. Boulding, *Beyond Economics* (Ann Arbor, 1968), pp. 288-302, particularly pp. 294-297. Boulding tends to stress the structure of the international system as a source of irrational behavior while Senghaas sees a broad range of sources for the irrational decisions of elites. W. A. Scott, "Rationality and Non-rationality of International Attitudes," *The Journal of Conflict Resolution,* II (1958), 1-7, argues, however, that foreign-policy elites are less likely to be irrational than the general public.

29. A. D. Sabrosky, *op. cit.*, p. 17; Zinnes, "The Expression and Perception," p. 110; North, *op. cit.*, p. 117.

30. Senghaas, *op. cit.*, p. 51; Withey, *op. cit.*, p. 118; de Rivera, *op. cit.*, pp. 79, 153.

31. *Germany and the Approach to War in 1914* (London, 1973), pp. 62-63, 166-167, 213-214; *Rüstung and Machtpolitik* (Düsseldorf, 1973), pp. 84-92. See the somewhat similar analysis of the role of the irrational in Dieter Groh, *Negative Integration and revolutionärer Attentismus* (Frankfurt a/M., 1973), pp. 622 ff. and his fascinating argument to the effect that even the Social Democratic leadership, under the peculiar pressures of their political and ideological situation, were beginning to regard war as a way out. *Ibid.*, pp. 184-192, 195, 236, 247, 343, 491, 574, 708-710.

32. See n. 6 *supra*.

33. Michael Haas, "Societal Approaches to the Study of War," *Journal of Peace Research,* II (1965), 316; Withey, *op. cit.*, pp. 114, 117-118; Lennart Levi (ed.), *Emotional Stress: Proceedings of an International Symposium Arranged by the Swedish Delegation for Applied Medical Defense Research, Stockholm, Feb. 5-6, 1965* (New York, 1967), pp. 62, 166, 229, 246, 249.

34. Fritz K. Ringer, *Education and Society in Modern Europe* (Bloomington, Ind., 1979), pp. 18-22; T.W. Bamford, *Rise of the Public Schools* (London, 1967), pp. 16, 75; Antoine Prost, *Histoire de l'enseignement en France, 1800-1967* (Paris, 1968).

35. On artisans, see Mack Walker, *German Home Towns: Community, State and General Estate, 1648-1871* (Ithaca, N.Y., 1971); Schulamit Volkov, *The Rise of Popular Anti-modernism in Germany: The Urban Master Artisans, 1873-1896* (Princeton, 1978). On rural aristocrats in Austria, see Otto Brunner, *Adeliges Landleben und europäischer Geist* (Salzburg, 1949). On the Austrian high nobility and bourgeois society, Hans Siegert (ed.), *Adel in Oesterreich* (Vienna, 1971), p. 7. On conservative antimodernism among German intellectuals, see Fritz Stern, *The Politics of Cultural Despair* (Berkeley, Cal., 1963), particularly, p. xxix.

36. Lützow, *op. cit.*, p. 172; Alexander Hoyos, *Der deutschenglischen Gegensatz und sein Einfluss auf Balkanpolitik Oesterreich-Ungarns* (Berlin, 1922), pp. 9, 20, 66, 93; Cormons (Urbas), *op. cit.*, pp. 22-23 and *passim.;* Fritz Stern, "Bethmann-Hollweg and the War: The Limits of Responsibility" in Leonard Krieger and Fritz Stern (eds.), *The Responsibility of Power* (New York, 1968), pp. 271-307.

37. Leslie C. Tihany, "The Austro-Hungarian Compromise of 1867-1918: A Half-Century of Diagnoses, Fifty Years of Postmortem," *Central European History,* II (1969), 114, 138, 127-128; Baernreither, *op. cit.,* pp. 171, 240-247; Cormons (Urbas), *op. cit.,* pp. 154-155.

38. The quotations are a montage selected from the enormously excitable *chargé d'affaires* in Belgrade, Wilhelm Ritter von Storck, from another official in Belgrade, from Berchtold and from Szapáry, *Ö.-U.A.,* I, 206; IV, 479; VIII, 218-19, 495.

39. If the conflicting pressures are strong enough, "the organism will tend to escape from the situation, which means that the behavior will be regarded as irrational, neurotic, etc. . . ." Levi (ed.), *op. cit.,* p. 62; de Rivera, *op. cit.,* p. 79.

40. Krobatin, Bilinski, and Stürgkh all complained bitterly of the monarchy's condition and insisted upon a decisive show of strength, arguing that the loyalty of their Croatian, Slav, and Muslim subjects depended upon the appearance of overwhelming power so that irredentist aspirations would be outside the realm of practical politics. *Ö.-U.A.,* VI, 332, 334; VIII, 241, 243.

41. May, *op. cit.,* pp. 429-434; Fellner (ed.), *op. cit.,* I, 111, 141, 222.

42. John W. Boyer, "Freud, Marriage and Late Viennese Liberalism: A Commentary from 1905," *JMH,* L (1978), 78 n. 10.

43. Erenyi, *op. cit.,* p. 240.

44. Fellner (ed.), *op. cit.,* I, 90, 93, 99, 134, 153, 166, 205, 235, 239, 240, 253.

45. Hoyos, *op. cit.,* pp. 9, 12, 20-21, 66, 93-95; Fellner (ed.), *op. cit.,* I, 245-246.

46. Harald Bachmann, *Joseph Maria Baernreither (1845-1925)* (Neustadt a. d. Aisch, 1977); *Ö.-U.A.,* VII, 344-45, 347; Baernreither, *op. cit.,* pp. 179-189.

47. I thus disagree with those historians who tend to regard war as a conservative's game as, for example, Fritz Fischer, *Krieg der Illusionen* (Düsseldorf, 1969); Arno J. Mayer, "Domestic Causes of the First World War" in Krieger and Stern, *op. cit.,* pp. 318-319 and "Internal Causes and Purposes of War in Europe, 1870-1956: A Research Assignment," *JMH,* XLI (1969), 298-299. Zara S. Steiner, *Britain and the Origins of the First World War* (New York, 1977), pp. 252-253, has pointed out the difficulties of the Fischer or Mayer line of argument.

48. Hoyos wrote that because of conditions in Hungary, they could proceed only by slow, gradual form. But a gradualist approach could succeed only if irredentist movements were suppressed, so that the aspirations of their domestic nationalities could be kept in bounds. *Op. cit.,* p. 43. Cormons (Urbas) noted that reformers divided into two groups. The first continued to argue that foreign conflict must be avoided until internal stability had been achieved by reform, but a second group argued that only a victorious war would create the proper atmosphere for reform. *Op. cit.,* pp. 70-71. In neither case was war regarded as a means of preserving the status quo.

49. Minutes of May 2, 1913 Council, *Ö.-U.A.,* VI. 324-334.

50. The completed policy statement of June 24, is in *ibid.,* VIII, 186 ff. It was based upon earlier memoranda and drafts by Berchtold, Tisza, Szápary and Flotow in *ibid.,* VII, 1ff., 198, 974 ff.; VIII, 1 ff. For a detailed analysis, see H.

Bertil A. Peterson, "Das österreichischungarische Memorandum an Deutschland vom 5. Juli 1914," *Scandia* XXX (1964) 138-190. Professor Williamson in his essay in this volume (pp. 000) judges this policy statement as more aggresive than I do.

51. See Erik H. Erikson, *Childhood and Society* (2nd. rev. ed.; New York, 1963), p. 347; Edwin G. Burrows and Michael Wallace, "The American Revolution: The Ideology and Psychology of National Liberation," *Perspectives in American History,* 1972, pp. 270-274; Kenneth E. Boulding, *The Image* (Ann Arbor, 1956), p. 64; Michael Walzer, "On the Role of Symbolism in Political Thought," *Political Science Quarterly,* LXXXII (1967), 191-204, 194. I am indebted to my colleague, Professor Edwin G. Burrows, for these citations.

52. Szilassy, *op. cit.,* p. 265. "Rejoice, rejoice, enemies of Austria . . . You have destroyed the hope of our future," Danzer, one of the archduke's publicists, quoted in Vladimir Dedjier, *The Road to Sarajevo* (New York, 1966), p. 601; Cormons (Urbas), *op. cit.,* p. 158; Fellner (ed.), *op. cit.,* I, 237; Georg Franz, *Erzherzog Franz Ferdinand und die Pläne zur Reform der Habsburger Monarchie* (Brünn, 1943), p. 115. For the Austro-Germans in particular, the assassination was deeply unsettling. The dependence and loyalty of the subject nationalities was an essential part of their self-image as guardians of the smaller nations of Central Europe. Williams, *op. cit.,* pp. 34-35, 42, 64-65, 238.239.

53. Quoted in Hantsch, *op. cit.,* II, 374, 471. On nightmares and sleeplessness, see *ibid.,* pp. 374, 455, 475 n. 14, 500, 520 citing Berchtold's diaries.

54. Memoranda of August 6, 1913 and March 15, 1914, *Ö.-U.A.,* VI, 112; VIII, 975, 976.

55. *Ö.-U.A.,* VIII, 250-252 ff. There is a detailed comparison of the June 24 statement and the July 5 memorandum in Peterson, *op. cit.,* pp. 159-176. The Austrian editors and most historians assumed that both memoranda were completed before the assassination and that the latter memorandum was hastily adapted to take the assassination into account. Almost everyone, and I at one point, assumed that both documents were substantially similar and incorporated a generally peaceful diplomatic program. See Stone, *op. cit.,* p. 155. This view was consistent with the portrait of a weak, vacillating Berchtold sending the Germans an essentially peaceful memorandum and asking for a blank check, which in turn led to disputes over what it was the Germans thought they were being asked to do. Peterson makes clear that the aims of the two memoranda are quite different. There are further details on their history in Cormons (Urbas), *op. cit.,* pp. 161-162. The Austrian editors' comments on the memoranda are at *Ö.-U.A.,* VIII, 195, 252, 261.

56. Bilinski, in a series of wartime interviews with the journalist Heinrich Kanner, described Berchtold as "unshakably strong" after the assassination and adds that "the ultimatum was his work." R. A. Kann, *Kaiser Franz Joseph und der Ausbruch des Weltkrieges* (Vienna, 1971), p. 11. The usual portrait of a weak, vacillating, relatively unwarlike Berchtold is curiously at odds with his post-assassination behavior. The discrepancy is usually explained by saying that after the death of the archduke, Berchtold was no longer strong enough to stand up to the war party. Kann, *Erzherzog Franz Ferdinand,* pp. 239-240; S.R. Williamson, "Influence, Power and the Policy Process: The Case of Franz

Ferdinand, 1906-1914,'' *Historical Journal,* XVII (1974), 417, 430. But see Williamson's essay in this volume for a different view. Albertini, for example, first leaves open the question whether Berchtold agreed to war from his own convictions or because of the pressure of stronger men, and then concludes by describing him ''as a man entirely lacking strength of will and power of decision.'' But in between he describes a Berchtold doggedly avoiding every effort to deter him from war with Serbia. *Op. cit.*, II, 125, 669. So does S.B. Fay, *The Origins of the World War,* (New York, 1930), II, 198. Ritter, *op. cit.*, II, 237, describes a hitherto ''unsure and fainthearted'' Berchtold ''suddenly turned into a strong man'' after he was certain of German support. But it is clear that Berchtold was bent upon war from at least June 30 onwards.

57. See the stimulating comments by Franco Fornari, *The Psychoanalysis of War* (New York, 1974), pp. vii-xxxi. Fornari works with a psychoanalytic model in which ''conflicts connected with specific historical situations reactivate the more serious conflicts which each of us had experienced in infancy . . . The confusion between the real historical events and the unconscious vicissitudes lies at the basis of the transference of the problems of our internal world into the external world.'' He goes on to say that ''in time of peace society requires the individual to adopt realistic defenses for controlling his unconscious anxieties, in time of war it proposes as a defense the institutionalization of the expulsion of the Internal Terrifier onto the enemy.'' This Internal Terrifier he calls ''an internal, absolute enemy similar to a nightmare.'' To relieve themselves of the intense fear and anxiety induced by the Internal Terrifier, people find a concrete, external enemy that can be dealt with. *Ibid.*, pp. xvi, xxvi-xxviii. Although Fornari roots these internal fears and anxieties in childhood experiences in accord with psychoanalytic theory, the behavior he describes is consistent with the behavioral model used in this essay. See n. 6 *supra*.

58. The influence of Le Bon's work on the French military is set out in Robert A. Nye, *The Origins of Crowd Psychology: Gustav Le Bon and the Crisis of Mass Democracy in the Third Republic* (London, 1975). Bonnal's warning is at p. 136.

59. Czernin to Vienna, March 28, 1914, *Ö.-U.A.*, VII, 1013.

60. *Ö.-U.A.*, VII, 442-443. On German businessmen's belief in the advantages of peace, see Groh, *op. cit.*, pp. 413-414 n. 199.

SCHORSKE'S GARDEN TRANSFORMED AGAIN: WAR PROPAGANDA, AESTHETICS, AND THE CONSERVATIVE REVOLUTION

Paula Sutter Fichtner

Among the many ideological by-products of World War I, few have been more lastingly volatile than the so-called Conservative Revolution. The term was first used in Germany, but the program it embodied appeared in many guises throughout Europe. Hostile both to liberal representative government and the Marxist rhetoric of class warfare, its supporters called for the regeneration of individual states along national lines by new "elites" closely attuned to the "spirit" of all their countrymen. Emphasizing action at the expense of procedure, and personal rather than institutional ties between leadership and people, the movement had close affinities to Fascism and Nazism.[1] For this reason, the term "conservative" can still be one of reprobation in liberal and leftist circles.

The discontent of many with their contemporary environment gave rise to the Conservative Revolution even before World War I. Among the most articulate in their disaffection were large number of artists, intellectuals, and scholars. The tasteless opulence and smug materialism of their bourgeois surroundings repelled them. The proclivity of new, nationally based constitutional regimes to fall into sterile interparty squabbles prompted them to reject the political status quo. The subjective focus of their intellectual and aesthetic preoccupations troubled them; as a way of transcending this self-alienation, some proposed to use their art and writing in the service of national renewal. In France the novelist Maurice Barrès, Italy and Germany the poets Gabriele d'Annunzio and Stefan George saw themselves in this role.

It was Germany's great misfortune, however, to lose both a war and a government, and none felt this more keenly than the country's antiliberal, anti-Marxist intellectuals. There was wide agreement among them that the left-liberal Weimar Republic was even more unacceptable than its predecessor, and the alternatives they offered were what collectively came to be classified as the Conservative Revolution. At the University of Heidelberg the literary historian Friedrich Gundolf called for a "new Caesar," and Oswald Spengler dreamed of a revival of Prussian self-discipline.[2]

Yet it was not a German national, but an Austrian, the poet, playwright, and essayist Hugo von Hofmannsthal, whose gloss of the term Conservative Revolution seems to have found the deepest resonance among Germans of his day. In a widely applauded adddress entitled "Das Schrifttum als geistiger Raum der Nation," delivered before a gathering of prominent artists and politicians at the University of Munich on January 10, 1927, Hofmannsthal described the movement as a kind of moral awakening. According to him, German intellectuals had characteristically been highly individualistic—he cited the titanic self-destructiveness of the *Sturm und Drang* school and the self-indulgence of Romantic *Schwärmerei* as examples. Now he saw among this selfsame group of people a willingness to accept communal bonds and responsibilities, where once they had rejected them. The institutional arrangements of politics played little role in this process; indeed, it issued forth unforced from individuals themselves. It was, in Hofmannsthal's words, "a political construction of the spiritual and a spiritual construction of the political," something in which all could participate.[3]

Why should an Austrian have been so eloquent a spokesman for this development? True, the experiences of Austrian and German intellectuals had much in common. The truncated, German-speaking state carved out of the old Habsburg Empire after World War I suffered financial and political dislocations which dwarfed those of its neighbor to the north. From the point of view of middle-class excess, prewar Vienna matched everything that Berlin or Munich had to offer. The Ringstrasse alone indicates that the bourgeoisie of the Habsburg capital was second to none in its taste for self-congratulatory extravagance. Most important of all, Hofmannsthal's career duplicated those of many artists and intellectuals throughout Europe who were caught up in the syndrome of malcontent that spawned the Conservative Revolution. As Carl Schorske, the closest student of the relationship between art and politics in turn-of-the-century Vienna, has shown, the poet had for some time been trying to move beyond the limits of the egocentric aestheticism which had characterised his early work and to fashion a new synthesis of art and life.[4]

But Hofmannsthal's pre-1918 Austria-Hungary differed in one important respect from d'Annunzio's Italy, Barrès's France, and George's Germany. The recently created kingdom of Italy and the Wilhelmine *Reich* were affirmations of a nationalism that had aroused much idealistic fervor in the nineteenth century. Germans and Italians had been promised that greater destinies awaited them once national unification was achieved. France's Third Republic depended for survival in part on its ability to maintain its identification with the national mission of regaining Alsace-Lorraine, lost to Germany after 1871. But none of the institutions established to carry out these awesome trusts were able to do so. Industrialization and urbanization further fragmented Italy and Germany; the Third Republic was too weak internally to challenge Prussia, and corruption was everywhere. This was the view of prewar radical conservatives, and it was for this reason that they felt that spiritual renewal was necessary for their countrymen.[5]

In the Habsburg Empire, on the other hand, nationalist expectations, while everywhere aroused, were nowhere triumphant. Therefore they could not be said to have been disappointed in the same way as in Italy, Germany, and France. One important precondition for the development of the Conservative Revolution would thus seem to be missing in the Dual Monarchy. Yet Hofmannsthal's ability to project the sense of the movement to those who heard him in 1927 suggests that he and others like him must have experienced the same kind of alienation from existing institutions as led him to celebrate the spiritualization of politics in his Munich lecture. It may therefore be of value to look more closely at the relationship between artists, scholars, and political institutions in Vienna before 1918 in order to understand why Austria-Hungary was also a fertile breeding ground for the Conservative Revolution.

* * * *

It was World War I that provided Hofmannsthal and many other Viennese intellectuals with the long-sought opportunity to put their art and scholarship at the service of a wider public. Leading Austrian intellectuals jumped almost frenetically into propaganda work and semiofficial political journalism. In Hofmannsthal's case, such purposive employment allowed him to overcome his long-term spiritual crisis and did much to elevate cultural-political concerns to a central place in his thought. Feeling that a population engaged in war required spiritual sustenance, Hofmannsthal believed that he was uniquely qualified to provide it.[6]

Though they may have done less in the area of cultural propaganda than the Germans, various branches of Austro-Hungarian officialdom were aware that they might win friends both at home and abroad with such activities.[7] Count Leopold Berchtold, the foreign minister at the outbreak of the conflict, apparently watched for such items in local papers.[8] The War Archives became a center for a number of literary luminaries such as Stefan Zweig, Alfred Polgar, Felix Salten, and, for a short time, Rainer Maria Rilke. They, along with others, turned out a flood of material on the activities of the Imperial and Royal Army. Indeed, General Maximilian von Hoen, who became director of the archives during the war, fretted that their sheer productivity would lower his institution's reputation for scholarly meticulousness. The foreign ministry had a *Literarisches Bureau,* founded as early as 1868 with the design of influencing the foreign press in favor of the empire. During the war it expanded its concerns to include sponsorship of such things as tours of the Vienna Philharmonic orchestra and *Burgtheater* to neutral territories such as Switzerland, and even experimented with propaganda films abroad. [9]

Hofmannsthal's activities were of two kinds – that of an occasional lecturer in such places as Poland and Scandinavia as a quasi-official representative of the Foreign Office, and in a purely private capacity, that of editor and author of various publications calculated to explain the Austrian cause and win supporters to it. Toward the latter end, the poet did the bulk of the editing and production work for a series called the "Österreichische Bibliothek" which appeared between 1915 and 1917. Its importance in this context is not its wide circulation. Despite its low price – sixty pfennigs in Germany, eighty hellers in the Habsburg lands – and special field editions, it sold poorly. The Insel Verlag of Leipzig, which published it, discontinued it after twenty-six of the little volumes had appeared.[10] Rather, because many authors contributed to its openly political purposes, it is a highly suggestive starting point for any investigation of the intellectual environment out of which the Conservative Revolution emerged.

Hofmannsthal's idea to bring out such a series, which he hoped would make the Austrian cultural, historical and intellectual heritage more accessible to all, came to him in discussion with other like-minded individuals late in 1914. He initially planned to call it "Bücher aus Österreich" and to publish it under the fifteenth-century motto of Emperor Frederick III: AEIOU *(Austria erit in orbe ultima).* His prospectus for the project bespoke his long-term concern with the role art was to play in the reintegration of society. Though he never reached the point where he was able to include medieval municipal chronicles, family histories, and old trade and industry reports in the endeavor, Hofmannsthal thought that they belonged there, along with more conventional subjects.

The strong historical orientation of the "Bibliothek" was neither psychologically nor ideologically surprising. The empire that Hofmannsthal and his cohorts sought to defend was one whose political integrity was very much in question at home and whose survival was very much doubted abroad. In such situations, common experiences, even past ones, are useful rallying points. Their historical character is even something of an advantage in a world where the daily reality of politics is ceaseless and unpleasant change.[11]

But although intended as propaganda, the "Österreichische Bibliothek" had a remarkably idiosyncratic flavor. Two themes appear consistently in the introduction to individual volumes. One was the significance of leadership in the Austrian tradition. This in itself is a familiar simplification of most war propaganda. What is striking, however, is the almost complete absence of any mention of the institutional framework which supported that leadership, or of the structures through which the decisions of that leadership were communicated to the body politic as a whole. Thus Hofmannsthal, in his contribution entitled *Grillparzers politisches Vermächtnis,* argued that the two most important constellations in Austrian politics were ruler and people. In *Deutsches Leben in Ungarn,* Adam Müller-Guttenbrunn attributed the prosperity of Swabian settlements in Baranya and Tolna counties in Hungary after the Turks left the area solely to German hard work and the protection of the emperor. The nineteenth-century Austrian military adventurer, Friedrich zu Schwarzenberg, is praised simply for the strength of his personality, which enabled him and those like him to shape their destinies rather than allowing others to do it for them. Ernst Molden's presentation of Field Marshall Joseph Radetzky belittles concrete historical detail in developing an Austrian version of the Cincinnatus myth. Radetzky's memory, according to the author, has endured not because of any documentable accomplishments, but simply through the force of the great general's personality. The Austrian state, Molden claimed, differed from other polities in the way that great crises and great figures had shaped it. Not based on any single people, the Habsburg Empire needed major trials and tests to renew its vigor, and heroic men to give it new life and direction in the settlement that followed any crisis. Such people were Eugene of Savoy, Maria Theresa, Joseph II, Radetzky, and "perhaps" Prince Klemens von Metternich.[12]

The second theme was equally unusual, though not entirely unrelated to the first – the superiority of art to politics, the value of subjective perception in understanding the past as opposed to historical fact, the stuff of "experimental politics" as the conservative polemicist Joseph de Maistre once said.[13] If there were great epochs in Austrian history, they occurred only when the barriers between art and politics were lowered, and the former could shape the latter. Thus, referring to the opera at the court of Leopold I, Richard von Kralik extolled the Baroque as a period when art was used to explain political, social, and moral ideas to the broad public.[14] Hofmannsthal himself described the "Bibliothek" as something "created out of his own head," which was the way he preferred to work but which political considerations sometimes made very difficult.[15]

What he regarded as spiritual boundaries were far more significant than the conventional ones of politics.[16] Where he tried to explain his notions of politics, he did so in terms of an artist's vision. Politics, he argued, were simply a higher form of anthropology, and commanding political figures were those who best understood the human psyche, particularly its irrational side. It was the role of the artist to point out more precisely the nature of men. For this reason, according to Hofmannsthal, the Austrian dramatist Franz Grillparzer had a superior "political head." Grillparzer's observation that "Metternich was a good diplomat but a poor politician" was, according to the poet, a model of political insight because it described Metternich the man so accurately. Hofmannsthal argued that the playwright could have contributed much to practical politics if he had been old enough to do so during the Napoleonic wars. By 1848, he was "too mature" to mix himself up in the political "chaff," as Hofmannsthal put it.[17]

And just as politics could be approached through the avenue of human feeling, so could an understanding of the past. In his little anthology in the "Österreichische Bibliothek" on the *Deutschmeister,* the regiment to which Vienna's elite belonged, Max Mell scorned rooting around "in the dust of history" as a way of coming to know something about the organization. What was meaningful to him was the use of historical material to dissolve the barriers of time and history so that the *Deutschmeister* would seem to his audience part of an eternal present, at least emotionally.[18]

Of course none of this by itself should be taken as a statement of personal belief. When dealing with war propaganda, one draws with utmost caution the line between what is genuinely meant and what is said to suit official purposes. When one finds, however, that letters, diaries, and other writings of the people who worked with Hofmannsthal on the "Österreichische Bibilothek" dwell on exactly the same themes, although in greater detail, as found in the little series, then it is clear that the "Bibliothek" has some genuine source value. Indeed, it is a measure of how deeply these questions disturbed the authors who appeared in the "Bibliothek" that they would rehearse them in works intended for the widest possible readership. Let us turn then to these other materials to establish more fully the reasons for this contempt for the daily realities of politics and history, and for this deinstitutionalization of political relationships, which marked the "Österreichische Bibliothek" and resurfaced in the Conservative Revolution.

The editorial consultants and authors whom Hofmannsthal chose for the "Bibliothek" were a most unusual group of publicists and war propagandists. Among them were leading artists, writers, scholars, journalists, and in a few cases, military and political figures such as Joseph Redlich, Leopold von Andrian, the diplomat, and Maxmilian von Hoen, already mentioned in connection with the War Archives.[19] Most of them were as concerned about the integrity of their positions as artists and scholars as they were about political matters. Regardless of the genre in which they wrote, it was judged as art. Hofmannsthal, who preferred to think of his propaganda activities as *"kulturpolitisch"* rather than literary, spoke to Redlich, a political scientist, about the "art form" of a didactic treatise which the latter was to contribute to the "Bibliothek". Maxmilian von Hoen's historical writing was later compared to that of an artist – work shaped not only by the discipline, learning, and critical acumen of the trained scholar, but also by the gift of the artist to make the past live again through sheer intuitive insight.[20]

Along with the concern, which the people around the "Österreichische Bibliothek" felt for the aesthetic and scholarly value of even their war propaganda, went a sharply critical posture toward the day-to-day conduct of the empire. The rigid facade of the last years of Franz Joseph's reign masked a ferment of activity among many in Vienna who were deeply concerned with reform of the monarchy in order to preserve it. The editors and many of the authors of the "Österreichische Bibliothek" had contacts with many in these circles and were frequently central to them. Perhaps the most important of these groups, in terms of its relationship to the "Bibliothek" was the so-called *Dienstagverein* which, under the chairmanship of Hans Schlitter, director of the Haus-, Hof- und Staatsarchiv, met in his office there during the first years of the war. Editors and authors in the series, such as historians Heinrich Friedjung and August Fournier, Leopold von Andrian, and occasionally Hofmannsthal himself, joined Schlitter and others in discussions of the monarchy's future. Most of them had connections in high places. Schlitter was a confidant of many in the foreign office. Count Alexander Hoyos was a close advisor of Berchtold. Leopold Chlumecky was editor of the influential *Österreichische Rundschau* and repeatedly entrusted with sensitive diplomatic missions. Almost all had been partisans of the assassinated heir to the throne, Archduke Franz Ferdinand; their chief purpose, once the war began, was to develop a program of organizational change for the empire which the new crown prince, Archduke Charles, could carry out.[21] In general, they rather naively believed that centralization around the German element in the monarchy could solve many of its problems. As a result, they were consistently unfriendly toward the Magyars. However, they were not programmatically intolerant of other nationalities, and were quick to sympathize with all who had suffered under what they saw to be bureaucratic incompetence in Vienna.[22]

Their alienation from the current political system varied in intensity among the group and those with whom they communicated, and stemmed from several sources. In the case of Richard von Kralik, one can hardly speak of any conscious disenchantment at all, since he believed that the imperial ministry deserved unconditional trust and confidence. But this may have been due to his belief that individuals and institutional forms mattered very little in any case. For Kralik ideas and ideas alone were the forces behind events. Thus, for all the constitutional innovations it had experienced in the nineteenth century, the Habsburg monarchy had not changed fundamentally. The emperor remained representative of what Kralik called "the Austrian idea," a kind of suprainstitutional concept which depended very little upon the individual characteristics of parliamentary bodies, ministers, committees, and the like.[23]

For others it was the war and the events that surrounded it which provoked an acute sense of dissociation between themselves and their political and social system. The novelist Robert Michel, one of the few in the circle of the "Österreichische Bibliothek" who saw extended military service, believed that soldiers who had died in combat should not be sent home for burial. Rather, in Michel's view, they should be interred in the ground which their blood had sanctified. Their experience had been such that the graves of the civilian world were no longer suitable for them. In answering their call to duty, they had been forever severed from normal life. These collective dead would have an impact, however, on future politics which Michel described in critical and angry terms. He asked his readers to envision all these corpses as one giant who, when he stamped his foot, would shake the entire world.[24]

The incompetent management of the war drove the poet Anton Wildgans to increasingly pessimistic views about the day-to-day conduct of political and military life. Habsburg diplomacy was irresolute, its leadership like the fish "which begins to stink at the head." By the end of the war, Wildgans had elaborated an Austrian variant of the more famous German "stab in the back" theory in which it was imperial Austria that was undermined on the home front. He accused Emperor Charles of taking weapons out of the hands of the army at a decisive moment in the war through his imperial manifesto of October 1918, which in effect federalized the Austrian half of the monarchy.[25]

Others such as Schlitter and Joseph Redlich, for whom high political office seemed a possibility for a time, saw the Habsburg regime from the inside and were especially embittered as a result. Politically speaking, Redlich found little to praise in the empire. In his view, it had not enjoyed competent statecraft since the time of Maria Theresa. A convinced liberal, a persuasion unusual among the men who frequented the *Dienstagverein* and participated in the "Österreichische Bibliothek," Redlich was deeply distressed by military domination of the Habsburg war government. He put part of the responsibility for this state of affairs at the feet of Count Stürgkh, the Austrian minister president, and contended that if the minister had not given up on the idea of a truly civilian administration at the outset of the war, military dictatorship would have been impossible. Redlich also implicated the emperor, who in his view had a misplaced faith in the capacities of the army to save the regime.[26]

Schlitter's contempt for the weakness of the leading personnel in the monarch's government, especially in the Ballhausplatz, was near obsessive. No one there, he claimed, had reported that Russia had been "arming and mobilizing" for war since 1912. Nor, beyond Germany, had Austria's diplomacy won the empire any friends.[27] He took a kind of dark satisfaction in recounting jokes, such as the following, about the incompetence of Franz Josef's ministers:

> The emperor to Count Berchtold: "But my dear Count Berchtold, you do stupid things *every* single day."
> Berchtold to the emperor:
> "Yes, your Majesty, I can't do them *all* in a *single* day."[28]

Hofmannsthal, too, while less involved in the mechanics of politics, shared the distaste of his acquaintances for the way government was conducted in the empire. Both politicians and the press, the latter closely censored during the war, were—in the poet's view—corrupting influences on the population as a whole.[29]

Some positive forces persisted in this otherwise deteriorating society. One was the army which Schlitter and Wildgans believed could have been far more effective had the civilian regime not neglected it. Schlitter thought in 1914 that, if peace were concluded in Austria's favor in Galicia, a military rather than a civilian regime should temporarily be installed there. In his judgment, the army was energetic, a quality notably missing from the civilian bureaucracy.[30]

The people as a whole also had much good in them; Hofmannsthal and others found in them an admirable, blind heroism. With deep respect, Schlitter related the story of a wounded reservist from Josefstadt in the neighborhood of Lemberg (now L'vov). The man's injuries were not his real worry, but rather the damage that the Russians had done to his house and fields. When promised by an imperial spokesman that the state would compensate him, the man replied that he could not ask for that since the state had far more important things to do with its money.[31] By 1916 Wildgans thought that if anyone should choose diplomats it should be the Austrian parliament, remodeled to consist of genuine representatives of the people.[32]

What this people and army needed above all was effective leadership. Hofmannsthal tried to deal with this problem on an aesthetic level in essays on Prince Eugene of Savoy and Maria Theresa, an activity he viewed as a way of giving people "heroes," at least vicariously. Both the military man and the empress were, in Hofmannsthal's eyes, visionaries and builders, distinguished by their ability to rise above the constraints of the bureaucracy that surrounded them. Others criticized Habsburg leadership more directly. For Wildgans, it was the duty of the state to foster talent and then to position it correctly for effective service, something the contemporary regime had obviously not done. Schlitter bemoaned the lack of brave men who could stand before the emperor and tell him that he had been lied to and betrayed. Only an "iron regime," not precisely defined by Schlitter, could bring needed change.[33]

As one would expect in any monarchical state, Schlitter's concern was with both ruler and the quality of his advisors. Significantly, however, he stressed the importance of the single leader over and above any advisory intermediaries to the point where it was only leadership that mattered. He was not alone in this attitude. Even Redlich, the liberal, based his admiration for eighteenth-century Austrian statecraft on the achievements of a lone figure, Maria Theresa.[34]

To a certain extent, some were led to this conclusion by the internal logic of their own political positions. Richard von Kralik, for example, seemed to believe that there was a preordained harmony between emperor and people which made intermediate institutions superfluous.[35] Anton Wildgans described the basic problem of the Austro-Hungarian state as one of reconciling its multinational character with the need for German direction. This was, of course, a virtually unrealizable demand which made his conclusion that only a Bismarckian figure could meet it all but inescapable.[36]

But a good deal of this longing for decisive leadership stemmed from the frustration of many around the "Österreichische Bibliothek" which the murder of Archduke Franz Ferdinand had provoked. To almost all he had embodied the larger-than-life quality needed to turn the monarchy toward constructive reform. Like Friedrich zu Schwarzenberg in the "Bibliothek," he was admired for having shaped his world largely through his own force of will. Maxmilian von Hoen said that it was his personality that had turned both army and navy into functioning defense units.[37] Hoen argued that Franz Ferdinand's murder was more than a crime against the heir apparent to the Austro-Hungarian thrones, it was the murder of a powerful personality.

In Schlitter's eyes, Franz Ferdinand's death was not "merely" *(blos)* the death of an archduke, but the end of his reform program as well. Indeed, for Schlitter, the dynasty had not only lost much of its content with the death of the archduke, but his connection with it had downright malevolent consequences. The archivist took the emperor and his advisors to task for not forbidding the archduke to appear publicly in Bosnia when they knew very well the dangers that awaited him there. Schlitter was also furious that the remaining Habsburg archdukes and archduchesses remained aloof from Franz Ferdinand's bereaved family because of the protocol surrounding his morganatic marriage. Wilhelm II of Germany, he pointed out, was quick to send a message of condolence to the heir apparent's children.[38]

But the preoccupation with the crisis of leadership in the Habsburg Empire was not the only reason for the disdain which the circle of the "Österreichische Bibliothek" accorded the institutional aspects of daily politics. A second source for this attitude was the belief of almost all of them that an unbridgeable gulf lay between the demands of art and scholarship on the one hand and war and politics on the other. In part this feeling resulted from the ambivalent way in which the Habsburg war regime treated the activities of Hofmannsthal and his acquaintances. On some levels, Austrian authorities were both receptive and helpful. Thanks to the intervention of Stürgkh, Hofmannsthal was spared all forms of military service from 1915 on, thus enabling him to devote himself completely to the editing of the "Österreichische Bibliothek," as well as other endeavors. Stürgkh went so far as to call the poet "irreplaceable" for such tasks.[39]

But such sentiments were rare in the Vienna bureaucracy. Professional administrators and politicians simply did not take artists and scholars seriously, or, perhaps more accurately put, regarded them as tangential to the main theaters of diplomatic, political, and military action. Literary men were continually frustrated by the slowness and clumsiness of Austrian censorship and by a lack of recognition for their efforts. The ministry of education dragged its feet for what Hofmannsthal felt was much too long before recommending the publisher of the "Österreichische Bibliothek," Dr. Anton Kippenberg, for a citation.[40]

After writing an article on Emperor Charles's coronation in Buda in 1917, Richard von Kralik was asked by the minister of the interior to do something similar for the same event in Vienna. The essay, presented to the imperial couple, Charles and Zita, led the empress to summon the author to her for closer consultation. The unusual invitation stirred up much discussion in the Austrian capital; Kralik reported that many were excited to hear that the empress was "for the first time" speaking "with a literary man" *(mit einem Literaten)* of his caliber. After this, however, he heard nothing more from the emperor or his wife or from the minister. Kralik called this rebuff a neglect of what he described as the "positive forces of preservation" in the monarchy.

But even greater insults were in store for him and other artists and scholars. When in 1917 Charles decided to call back to life the Austrian parliament, which had not met since the beginning of the war, Kralik's name was suggested to him for appointments to the *Herrenhaus* or upper chamber. The Habsburg ruler turned him down, however, along with Peter Rosegger, the Styrian novelist, and Heinrich Friedjung. He did see fit to appoint such celebrities as Field Marshal Fritz Conrad von Hötzendorf and seven other generals, Constantin Dumba, the ex-ambassador to Washington, Moritz Benedikt, the pliant editor of the *Neue Freie Presse* and Karel Škoda, the armaments magnate.[41] Despite all of Leopold von Andrian's efforts, Count István Burián, Berchtold's sucessor as foreign minister, denied Hofmannsthal an official citation of thanks for the latter's cultural propaganda work in Poland with the laconic comment that he had no desire "to react" to Andrian's request.[42]

But the artists and intellectuals were not the one-sided victims of the scorn of politicians; they in turn rejected politicians for reasons grounded in their artistic and scholarly standards. For all their desire to be supportive of the Habsburg war effort, Hofmannsthal and his acquaintances seem to have come away from their experiences with the conclusion that their interests and those of government and its institutions were all but mutually exclusive. There were those, Hofmannsthal included, who hoped that the war would serve to revivify old art forms and to create new ones, but this did not mean that they thought that artistic activities were intrinsically related to the realities of war and politics.[43] Indeed, for all their desire to overcome their aesthetic and academic isolation, the circle around the "Österreichische Bibliothek" seems to have decided during the war that the sacrifice of integrity and independence would be too great. Anton Wildgans found it necessary while the conflict was on to pay close attention to what he called his "spiritual personality" in a world where artistic values, at least temporarily, had low priority. Max Mell, too, felt there was an insuperable split between artistic sensibilities and the conditions of war. He described roommates invalided with him during the hostilities, including a hollow-eyed Czech who had the unsettling habit of interrupting conversations with hoarse imitations of cannon and machine-gun fire, as unable to understand what he, a writer, saw in a volume of Rosegger which he had been given. In a story written in 1917, "In der Bukowina," Mell depicted a young career officer who was merely enduring his present service until he could give it up and become an artist. The figure who represents Mell in the tale and the officer have much in common.[44]

For Robert Michel as well, the demands of military life and the artistic imagination virtually excluded each other. In his thinly fictionalized *Briefe eines Landsturmleutnants an*

Frauen, he tells of a young war painter whose nerves grow increasingly frayed when he is forced by the pace of events to work at the same tempo as journalists and photographers. The artist and a woman he meets in the course of the war are accidentally thrown into a kind of idyllic Robinson Crusoe existence with one another when he loses contact with his unit. When the couple finally decide to rejoin the world, the painter discovers that an experience in which he has had to care only for essentials has so changed him that he can no longer draw scenes of war, only of peace.[45] When the historian Wilhelm Bauer decided in 1917 to found a new periodical, *Österreich,* to help Austrians become acquainted with their past, he argued that it should not be too blatantly patriotic since "the less we dress ourselves up with official connections, the more likely we are to have the desired effects."[46]

Hofmannsthal, too, for all his initial enthusiasm about engaging in useful activity, nevertheless remained keenly aware of the distance between himself as an artist and the political and military realm. True artistic creation came from within, he observed in 1916, and a certain amount of solitude was necessary for it. When politics were mixed up in the process, this isolation was difficult to maintain. Furthermore, when he finished a piece of political writing, he did not have an audience on whom he could count for approval as he did for his artistic endeavors. Even Stürgkh, whom Hofmannsthal conceded had shown him a great amount of goodwill, had couched this in a "formal" manner which the poet found less than satisfying. He looked forward to a cultural propaganda tour he was to make in Scandinavia in 1916 in part because it was his name that would draw audiences there, not names like Stürgkh, Tisza, and Count Gyula Andrássy. The latter carried prestige and power in Austria, but abroad, he was happy to say, they had no meaning. By 1917, having given up his political enterprises and turned once again to artistic creation, Hofmannsthal described himself as engaged in "productive" work, implicitly stamping his political activities as less than that.[47]

Thus in 1927, when Hofmannsthal pointed to the new spiritualization of politics, he did so having had first-hand experience of the institutional inadequacies of the Habsburg

Empire, and having come to the conclusion that art and politics marched to the tunes of different drummers. There were two choices open to him and to those like him – to retreat from political life altogether, or to formulate politics in a way that was compatible with aesthetic values. Hofmannsthal chose the latter course, much as d'Annunzio or George had once done. It was a quite unremarkable decision, for even in his propaganda work, which had a specific political purpose, he and his circle in Vienna could not sacrifice the values of art and scholarship for those of quotidian politics. While part of Hofmannsthal's political perceptions in the twenties undoubtedly stemmed from the total collapse of the Habsburg Empire in 1918, their roots extended somewhat further into the past. The war years left the poet and the circle around the "Österreichische Bibliothek" with the same conviction that was harbored by radical conservatives throughout Europe – that political leadership spoke less and less to the needs of anyone, especially to the needs of aesthetes and intellectuals, and that this ought to change.

NOTES

1. Salvatore Saladino, "Italy," in Hans Rogger and Eugen Weber (eds.), *The European Right: A Historical Profile* (Berkeley, Cal., 1966), pp. 208-260; George L. Mosse, *The Crisis of German Ideology: The Intellectual Origins of the Third Reich* (New York, 1964), pp. 1-66. On the appearance of the term Conservative Revolution in Germany see Klemens von Klemperer, *Germany's New Conservatism* (Princeton, 1968), p. 10.

2. Friedrich Gundolf, *The Mantle of Caesar,* (New York, 1928); Oswald Spengler, *Preussentum und Sozialismus* (Munich, 1920).

3. Hugo von Hofmannsthal, *Gesammelte Werke,* (Frankfurt a/M, 1946-59), VI, 390-413. For contemporary reactions to Hofmannsthal's address, both positive and negative, see *Bayerische Staatszeitung und Bayerischer Staatsanzeiger,* Jan. 11, 1927, p. 3; *Bayerischer Kurier und Münchner Fremdenblatt,* Jan. 13, 1927, pp. 3-4; *Münchner Post,* Jan. 12, 1927, p. 3. Cf. *Münchner Neueste Nachrichten,* Jan. 12, 1927, p. 1; *Neue Freie Presse* (Vienna), Jan. 11, 1927, p. 8.

4. Carl E. Schorske, "The Transformation of the Garden in Austrian Literature," in *Fin-de-Siècle Vienna: Culture and Politics* (New York, 1980), p. 315. Cf. Egon Schwarz, "Hofmannsthal as a Critic," in Arthur R. Evans (ed.), *On Four Modern Humanists: Hofmannsthal, Gundolf, Curtius, Kantorowicz* (Princeton, 1970), p. 16; Herman Rudolph, *Kulturkritik und konservative Revolution: Zum kulturellpolitischen Denken Hofmannsthals und seinem problemgeschichtlichen Kontext* (Tübingen, 1971), pp. 41-80.

5. Saladino, *op. cit.*, pp. 211-212; Mosse, *op. cit.*, pp. 5-6; Eugen Weber. "France," in Rogger and Weber (eds.), *op. cit.*, p. 83.

6. Rudolph, *op. cit.*, pp. 93, 107; Heinz Lunzer, "Hofmannsthals politische Tätigkeit in den Jahren 1914 bis 1917" (Ph.D. diss., Vienna, 1978), p. 89. I am deeply grateful to Dr. Lunzer for the loan of his dissertation and for his generosity in placing the library at the *Dokumentationsstelle für neuere österreichische Literatur* at my disposal in the summer of 1979.

7. Emil Charlet to Captain Krauss, Dec. 29, 1916 in Kriegsarchiv (hereafter referred to as KA), Nachlass Hoen, Konv. 1*a*, no folio no., Vienna. Charlet was a former member of the division in the German Foreign Office for cultural propaganda.

8. Hans Schlitter, unpublished "Tagebuch" in Haus-, Hof-, und Staatsarchiv, Nachlass Schlitter, Karton 6, fo. 209, Vienna.

9. Kurt Peball, "Literarische Publikationen des Kriegsarchivs im Weltkreig 1914 bis 1918," *Mitteilungen des österreichischen Staatsarchivs,* XIV (1961), 247, 253, 259; Franz Rottensteiner, "Das literarische Bureau; Pressepolitik, Organisation und Wirksamkeit 1877-1918" (Ph.D. diss., Vienna, 1967), pp. 6, 182-189, 206-207.

10. Lunzer, *op. cit.*, p. 92; Felix Braun, *Zeitgefahrten* (Munich, 1963), p. 27. Individual titles were as follows:

1. Hugo von Hofmannsthal (ed.), *Grillparzers politisches Vermächtnis*
2. Max Mell (ed.), *Heldentaten der Deutschmeister 1697-1914.*
3. Heinrich Friedjung, *Custozza und Lissa.*
4. Franz Zweybruck (ed.), *B̂ismarck und Österreich.*
5. Felix Braun (ed.), *Audienzen bei Kaiser Joseph.*
6. Otto Zoff (ed.), 1809: *Dokumente aus Österreichs Krieg gegen Napoleon.*
7. Helene Bettelheim-Gabillon *Österreich Fürst Friedrich zu Schwarzenberg,* der *"Landsknect": Bilder aus Alt-Österreich.*
8. Richard von Kralik (ed.), *Abraham a Sancta Clara.*
9. Felix Braun (ed.), *Beethoven im Gespräch.*
10. Ernst Molden (ed.), *Radetzky: Sein Leben und Wirken.*
11. Robert Michel, *Auf der Sudostbastion unseres Reiches.*
12. Anton Wildgans, *Österreichische Gedichte.*
13. Friedrich Eckstein (ed.), *Comenius und die böhmischen Brüder.*
14. Max Mell (ed.), *Die österreichischen Lande im Gedicht.*
15. Franz Grillparzer, *Ein Bruderzwist in Habsburg.*
16. Stefan Zweig (ed.), *Nickolaus Lenau an Sophie Löwenthal.*
17. Irma Hift (ed.), *Prinz Eugen: Aus seinen Briefen und Gesprächen.*
18. Adam Müller-Guttenbrunn, *Deutsches Leben in Ungarn.*
19. Karl Burdach (ed.), *Walter von der Vogelweide: Gedichte und Sprüche in Auswahl.*
20. Wilhelm Bauer (ed.), *Briefe aus Wien.*
21. Paul Eisner (ed.), *Tschechische Anthologie: Vrchlický, Sova, Brezina.*
22. Richard Smekal (ed.), *Adalbert Stifters Briefe.*
23. Ernst Molden (ed.), *Ein österreichischer Kanzler: Der Fürst von Metternich.*
24. Max Pirker (ed.), *Alpensagen.*
25. Josef Kallbrunner (ed.), *Maria Theresia als Herrscherin: Aus den deutschen Denkschriften, Briefen und Resolutionen (1740-1756).*

26. Felix Braun (ed.), *Schubert im Freundeskreis.*

11. Hugo von Hofmannsthal and Anton Wildgans, "Briefwechsel," (ed.), Norbert Altenhofer, *Hofmannsthal Blätter,* VII (1971), 3; Hofmannsthal, *Werke,* VI, 285, 287, 289; Eckart Koester, *Literatur und Weltkriegs-ideologie: Positionin und Begrundungszusammenhänge des publizistischen Engagements deutscher Schriftsteller im ersten Weltkrieg* (Kronberg/Ts, 1977), p. 178; Hannelore Schlaffer and Heinz Schlaffer, *Studien zum ästhetischen Historismus* Frankfurt a/M, 1975), p. 19.

12. *Politisches Vermächtnis,* p. 5; *Deutsches Leben,* p. 80; Bettelheim-Gabillon, *Schwarzenberg,* p. 3; *Radetzky,* p. 3-4.

13. "Study on Sovereignty," in Jack Lively (ed.), *The Works of Joseph de Maistre* (New York, 1971), p. 114.

14. *Abraham a Sancta Clara,* p. 6.

15. Hugo von Hofmannsthal to Leopold von Andrian, Nov. 17, 1915, Walter Perl (ed.), *Briefwechsel* (Frankfurt a/M, 1968), p. 221.

16. Hofmannsthal, *Werke,* VI, 322.

17. *Grillparzers politisches Vermächtnis,* pp. 4-7.

18. *Heldentaten,* pp. 54-55.

19. Hoen's participation was minimal since his work in the War Archives consumed the entirety of his attention. Werner Volke, " 'Auf der Sudostbastion unseres Reiches': Zum 100. Geburtstag von Robert Michel und als Beitrag zur Geschichte von Hofmannsthals *Osterreichische Bibliothek,*" *Hofmannsthal Blätter,* XIV (1976), 132; Peball, *op. cit.,* pp. 240-260, *passim.* On the attitudes of Austrian historians toward the war, especially those associated with the *Österreichische Bibliothek,*" see Gunther Ramhardter, *Geschichtswissenschaft und Patriotismus: Österreichische Historiker im Weltkreig 1914-1918* (Vienna, 1973), pp. 17, 27-28, 62, 182.

20. Hugo von Hofmannsthal to Count Stürgkh, Sept. 4, 1915, in Hugo von Hofmannsthal and Joseph Redlich, *Briefwechsel,* ed. Helga Fussgänger (Frankfurt a/M, 1971), p. 135; Hugo von Hofmannsthal to Joseph Redlich, Aug. 23, 1915, *ibid.,* p. 18; Edmund von Glaise-Horstenau, "Feldmarschall-leutnant Hoen," Nachlass Hoen, Konv. 7, no folio no. The memoir is undated but internal evidence clearly alludes to its composition in 1926.

21. Lunzer, *op. cit.,* pp. 49, 54, 58-59, 67, 70, 90.

22. *Ibid.,* p. 69; Schlitter, "Tagebuch," fos. 194-195.

23. Richard von Kralik, *Vom Weltkrieg zum Weltbund: Abhandlungen, Aufsätze, Gedanken, und Stimmungen* (Innsbruck, 1916), pp. 261, 174, 283, 286.

24. Robert Michel, *Briefe eines Hauptmanns an seinen Sohn* (Berlin, 1916), pp. 182, 185.

25. Anton Wildgans, *Sämtliche Werke* (Vienna, n.d.), VII, 114, 143, 153.

26. Josef Redlich to Hugo von Hofmannsthal, Oct. 23, 1915, *Briefwechsel,* p. 22; Josef Redlich, *Österreichische Regierung und Verwaltung im Weltkriege* (Vienna, 1925), p. 137.

27. Schlitter, "Tagebuch," fo. 193.

28. *Ibid.,* fo. 254. Emphasis Schlitter's.

29. Lunzer, *op. cit.,* pp. 45, 90.

30. Schlitter, "Tagebuch," fos. 265, 212; Wildgans, *Werke,* VII, 148-149.

31. Lunzer, *op. cit.,* pp. 45, 90; Schlitter, "Tagebuch," fo. 200. Cf. Brian D. Coghlan, *Hofmannsthal's Festival Dramas* (London, 1964), pp. 127-128.

32. Wildgans, *Werke,* VII, 124.

33. Koester, *op. cit.,* p. 179; Coghlan, *op. cit.,* pp. 96, 101; Wildgans, *Werke,* VII, 123; Schlitter, "Tagebuch," fo. 265.

34. Schlitter, "Tagebuch," fos. 429-430; Josef Redlich to Hugo von Hofmannsthal, Oct, 23, 1915, *Briefwechsel,* p. 22, It is interesting to note that between 1860 and 1930, a veritable flood of publications about Maria Theresa appeared. Pia Maria Plechl, "Maria Theresia regiert wieder in Schönbrunn," *Die Presse,* July 17, 1979, p. 5.

35. Kralik, *Weltkrieg,* p. 130.

36. Anton Wildgans to Hugo von Hofmannsthal, Dec. 7, 1914, "Briefwechsel," pp. 9-10.

37. Maximilian von Hoen, "Österreichische-ungarische Kriegskorrespondenz," June 27, 1917, Nachlass Hoen, Konv. 2, no folio No. The "Kriegskorrespondenz" was prepared as a press release.

38. Schlitter, "Tagebuch," fos. 153-154.

39. Lunzer, *op. cit.,* p. 133; Georg Freiherr von Franckenstein to Albert Count Nemes, Sept. 1, 1915, Hofmannsthal-Redlich, *Briefwechsel,* p. 134. Franckenstein was the imperial commissar to the *Legationsrat* in Brussels.

40. Rottenstein, *op. cit.,* p. 6; Lunzer, *op. cit.,* pp. 66-67; Leopold von Andrian to Hugo von Hofmannsthal, Oct. 24, 1916, Hugo von Hofmannsthal to Leopold von Andrian, Nov. 1, 1916 and Feb. 15, 1917, *Briefwechsel,* pp. 243-244, 248.

41. Richard von Kralik, *Tage und Werke: Lebenserinnerungen* (Vienna, 1922), pp. 190-191.

42. Lunzer, *op. cit.,* pp. 54, 36I n. 16; Hofmannsthal-Redlich, *Briefwechsel,* p. 185.

43. Josef Redlich to Hugo von Hofmannsthal, Oct. 23, 1915, *Briefwechsel,* p. 22; Koester, *op. cit.,* p. 185; Wildgans, *Werke,* VII, 118-119.

44. Wildgans, *Werke,* VII, 118; Max Mell, *Prosa-Dramen-Verse* (Munich, 1962), IV, 45, 47-48, 247.

45. (Berlin, 1917), pp. 85-100. The problems about the pace of work are pp. 90-91.

46. Wilhelm Bauer to Maximilian von Hoen, 1 June, 1917 Nachlass Hoen, Konv. 1*a,* no folio No. *"Je weniger wir mit offiziellen Beziehungen prunken, desto eindringlicher scheint uns die erwünschte Wirkung zu sein."*

47. Hugo von Hofmannsthal to Leopold von Andrian, July 31, 1916 and Hugo von Hofmannsthal to Leopold von Andrian, Sept. 27, 1917, *Briefwechsel,* pp. 234, 236, 252.

II. CASE STUDIES ON EAST CENTRAL EUROPEAN PRISONERS OF WAR IN WORLD WAR I

Peter Pastor, Editor

SIGNIFICANT PRISONER OF WAR CAMPS

IN THE RUSSIAN EMPIRE (1914 – 1917)

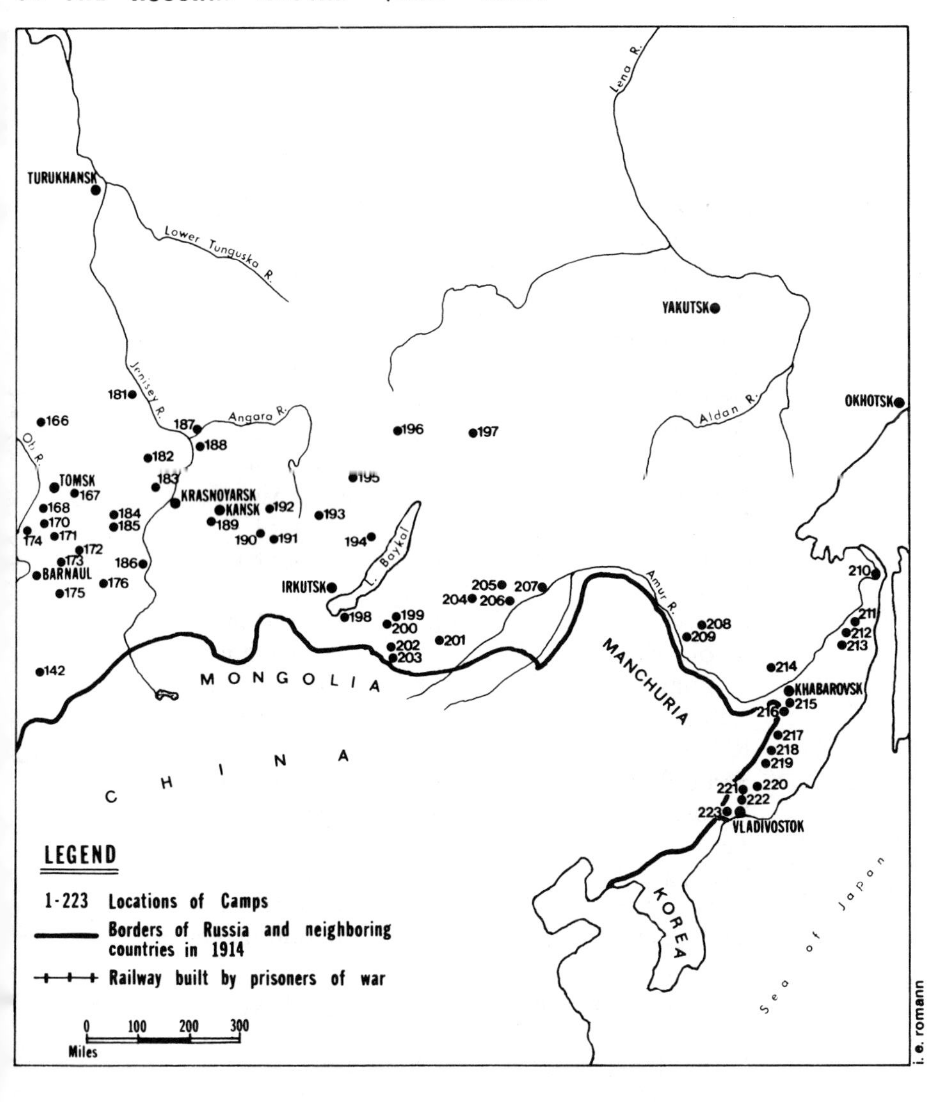

TURUKHANSK
Lower Tunguska R.
Lena R.
YAKUTSK
Jenisey R.
Angara R.
Aldan R.
OKHOTSK
Ob R.
181
166
187
188
182
183
TOMSK
167
KRASNOYARSK
KANSK
168
170
171
174
172
173
BARNAUL
175
176
184
185
186
189
190
191
192
193
194
195
196
197
L. Baykal
IRKUTSK
198
199
200
202
203
201
204
205
206
207
Amur R.
208
209
210
211
212
213
214
KHABAROVSK
215
216
217
218
219
220
221
222
223
VLADIVOSTOK
142
MONGOLIA
MANCHURIA
CHINA
KOREA
Sea of Japan
LEGEND
1-223 Locations of Camps
Borders of Russia and neighboring countries in 1914
Railway built by prisoners of war
0
100
200
300
Miles
i.e. romann

LEGEND

Locations below are in addition to camps identified by name on the map.

1. Narva
2. Yuryev (Tartu)
3. Pskov
4. Ostrov
5. Borovichi
6. Novgorod
7. Vologda
8. Olonets
9. Vytegra
10. Petrozavodsk
11. Kondopoga
12. Povenets
13. Kem
14. Kandalaksha
15. Kola
16. Onega
17. Dvinsk
18. Baranovichi
19. Mogilev
20. Bryansk
21. Orel
22. Kromi
23. Roslavl
24. Smolensk
25. Vyazma
26. Kaluga
27. Rzhev
28. Serpukhov
29. Borovsk
30. Tver
31. Yaroslavl
32. Rybinsk
33. Sologalich
34. Lyubim
35. Ivanovo-Voznesensk
36. Kovrov
37. Nizhni-Novgorod
38. Vladimir
39. Gus-Khrustalny
40. Ryazan
41. Serpukhov
42. Tula
43. Saransk
44. Spassk
45. Kerensk
46. Tambov
47. Yelets
48. Gomel
49. Chernigov
50. Rovno
51. Lemberg (Lvov)
52. Zhitomir
53. Darnitsa
54. Kursk
55. Zadonsk
56. Sumy
57. Belgorod
58. Voronezh
59. Volchansk
60. Biryuchiy
61. Ternopol
62. Chernovtsy
63. Uman
64. Krivoy-Rog
65. Kremenchug
66. Poltava
67. Kadiyevka
68. Boguchar
69. Yekaterinoslav
70. Lugansk
71. Bakhmut
72. Makeyevka
73. Novocherkassk
74. Novonikolayevka
75. Azov
76. Taganrog
77. Simferopol
78. Yeysk
79. Novorossiysk
80. Maykop
81. Stavropol
82. Kuberle

83. Krasniy Yar
84. Tsaritsyn
85. Dubovka
86. Nikolayevsk
87. Volsk
88. Kuznetsk
89. Penza
90. Simbirsk
91. Syzran
92. Vetluga
93. Yarensk
94. Nikolsk
95. Mezen
96. Vozhgora
97. Slobodskoy
98. Vyatka
99. Kotelnich
100. Izhevsk
101. Muzhi
102. Raztov
103. Nadezhdinksi Zavod (Serov)
104. Filkino
105. Perm
106. Nizhniy Tagil
107. Irbit
108. Kungur
109. Birsk
110. Kushva
111. Zlatoust
112. Minyarski Zavod (Minyarsk)
113. Chelyabinsk
114. Troitsk
115. Magnitogorsk
116. Troitsk
117. Buzuluk
118. Totskoye
119. Ivanovskoye
120. Uralsk
121. Krasnovodsk
122. Kizyl Arvat
123. Ashkabad
124. Tadzhent
125. Merv (Mary)
126. Katta-Kurgan
127. Chardzou
128. Kokand
129. Hodzhent
130. Zolotaya-Orda
131. Gorchakovo Stantsiya
132. Namangan
133. Andizhan
134. Chimkent
135. Turkestan
136. Pispek
137. Verny (Alma Ata)
138. Petrovsk
139. Kazalinsk
140. Karaganda
141. Akmolinsk
142. Ust Kamenogorsk
143. Semipalatinsk
144. Ekibastuz
145. Pavlodar
146. Petropavlovsk
147. Kurgan
148. Ishim
149. Ust Ishim
151. Tyumen
150. Tara
152. Nevyansk
153. Alapayevsk
154. Verkhoturye
155. Staro-Lyayinsk
156. Aleksandra
157. Melovka
158. Padun
159. Romanovsk
160. Borovskaya
161. Shurgutka
162. Tobolsk

163. Yushkova
164. Sychovo
165. Byezek
166. Turnutavskoye
167. Mariinsk
168. Anzhero Sudzhensk
169. Kainsk
170. Kemerovo
171. Danikova
172. Kuznetsk
173. Rostovsk
174. Novonikolayevsk
175. Biysk
176. Subinsk
177. Turgay
178. Kamislopsk
179. Bsipulsk
180. Sukharovsk
181. Sym
182. Bogotol
183. Achinsk
184. Shushlova
185. Znamenka
186. Minusinsk
187. Yeniseysk
188. Ust-Yansk
189. Rybinskoye
190. Nizhneudinsk
191. Tulun
192. Chistyakovo
193. Ust-Uda
194. Verkholensk
195. Ust-Kut
196. Kirensk
197. Bodaibo
198. Mysovsk
199. Berezovka
200. Verkhneudinsk (Ulan Ude)
201. Dauria
202. Troitskosavsk (Kyakhta)
203. Kyakhta
204. Chita
205. Antipikha
206. Nerchinsk
207. Sretensk
208. Aleksandrovsk
209. Blagoveshchensk
210. Nikolayevsk
211. Yevgentyevska
212. Malmyzh
213. Valki
214. Okhansk
215. Krasnaya Rechka
216. Pervaya-Rechka
217. Bikin
218. Iman
219. Spassk (Spassk-Dalni)
220. Razdolnoye
221. Nikolsk-Ussuriysk
222. Shkotovo
223. Almazovka

INTRODUCTION

Peter Pastor

When Europe went to war in August 1914, few contemplated the cataclysmic consequences of the conflict. Neither governments nor peoples were prepared to fight a long and bloody war. They expected quick victory, peace, and the swift return of captives.

These assumptions, including those about the prisoners of war, soon proved to be wrong. Those soldiers who had been captured by the enemy experienced deprivation and long months or, in most cases, years of captivity. They were separated from their families and forced to endure physical and mental pain. A great many died of exhaustion and illness. Their death was even more lamentable than that of their comrades on the battlefield.

Most of the more than two million East Europeans captured had been fighting in the Habsburg army on the Russian and Italian fronts. A reexamination of the history of their activities in captivity was the responsibility of a panel of experts at a recently held conference on war and society. Their scholarly contributions presented herein complement each other. The reader is offered a tableau bound together by similar themes and by conclusions that are remarkably alike.

The essays focus on the fate of the prisoners of war in Russia. They indicate that the tsarist state, which was the least prepared to fight the long war, was also unprepared to care for the large number of captured soldiers. Most of these men were captured *en masse* in the wake of the Russian offensives, though some crossed to the Russian side and surrendered. The Russians were signatories of the 1907 Hague Convention on the fair treatment of captured enemy soldiers. Yet the Russian military leadership's callous handling of its own troops also extended to the prisoners of war. "When the forest is cut down, splinters fly" states a popular Russian proverb. In this case, the prisoners of war, the "splinters," became victims of the Russian government's attitude, best expressed by this adage.

Like the GULags of Stalin's time, the prisoner-of-war camps in Russia formed a veritable archipelago across the Russian empire. In fact, these camps, which held millions of inmates, could be considered prototypes of those set up later by the communists. The prisoner-of-war camps included a "first circle" reserved for Slav captives expected to be won over to the Russian cause. These camps were found in European Russia. The "lower depths" – the worst camps – were found near the Arctic Circle, in Siberia and in Central Asia. They were inhabited mostly, though not exclusively, by captured Germans, Austrians and Hungarians. Regardless of the qualitative differences between the camps, they were all dismal and often inhumane communities.

The prisoners of war were often used for labor on large-scale building projects in a hostile environment. Their situation had a great deal in common with that of the *zeks* of Stalin's camps. Like the victims of the thirties, hundreds of thousands of prisoners of war died on similar projects and in comparable camps as a result of accident, malnutrition and disease. One of the survivors of a Siberian camp, the Hungarian publicist Jenő Lévai, whose work is cited by two contributors, recalled that at Krasnoyarsk the officers had a sense of *déjà vu* in their situation, similar to what Fedor Dostoevsky described in *The House of the Dead.* From the descriptions in these essays, however, it appears that for the majority of the captive enlisted men in any number of camps, Dostoevsky's Siberia would have seemed like a rest and recuperation station.

The historian of the GULags, Aleksandr Solzhenitsyn, emphasized the inaccuracy of parallels between prison camps of the nineteenth century and those of the twentieth. Contrary to Solzhenitsyn's claim, however, the new type seems to have come into being, not under the communists, but under the tsarists. Their first victims were the prisoners of war. It can only be wondered if Stalin's view of labor camps was influenced by his sight of the Krasnoyarsk camp, which housed 15,000 prisoners of war when he was in that town late in 1916.

Although the style of warfare when World War I opened was like that of the previous century, methods of mass psychological warfare soon came to be applied. These were intended to preserve the morale of peoples called on to bear immense sacrifices and systematically to subvert the enemy citizenry's loyalty through propaganda, as Professor Krammer indicates.

The East Central European prisoners of war were subject to these tactics as well. The Czecho-Slovaks and the South Slavs were particular targets of all successive Russian governments. The Austro-Germans and Hungarians attracted only the attention of the Bolshevik government. The liberal government of Italy also tried to reach the Czecho-Slovak prisoners of war. The hopes were that Russia and Italy could expand their spheres of influence after the war if their brand of ideology were carried into enemy territory, as Professor Kalvoda suggests.

Varieties of nationalism to recruit volunteers from among the South Slav and Czecho-Slovak prisoners of war were used by the tsarist and Kerenskiy governments. Attempts to enlist the majority of prisoners of war fell short of expectations, however. Professor Banac explains that perceptions of the future of the Balkan states divided the South Slavs, such as the Serbs and the Croats. Professor Kalvoda points out that differences of opinion about the future of Bohemia and Slovakia also existed among the Czech and Slovak prisoners of war. These differences of opinions between fraternal ethnic groups were in part responsible for the low number of volunteers.

A more important reason for the reluctance of the prisoner of war to volunteer was his demoralized, and thus apolitical, position. He was preoccupied with survival under adverse conditions. Russian propaganda and the deferential treatment of selected groups of prisoners of war exacerbated ethnic animosities between Austro-Germans and Hungarians on the one side and South Slavs and Czecho-Slovaks on the other. The contributors demonstrate, however, that these tensions did not inspire most of the ethnic Slavs to join the volunteers and fight in the name of a new type of nation state such as a Greater Serbia, or multinational entities like Yugoslavia or Czechoslovakia. Many of those who did join made their decision solely in the hope that life in the volunteer barracks would be superior to that in the prisoner-of-war camps. Significantly, Professor Williams's essay shows that under the more civilized conditions that obtained in Italy, the Czechs and Slovaks joined the volunteers in greater numbers.

Ideology was used as a weapon by the Bolshevik government of Russia. Lenin considered the prisoners of war as carriers of the "bacilli of bolshevism" into Europe. He also expected those prisoners of war who were of the worker and peasant class majority to fight for the Bolshevik cause in Russia. The number of volunteer Internationalists from the various nationalities treated in these essays fell short of Bolshevik expectations. Again, most of those who joined were motivated by personal rather than by ideological considerations. It was either hunger or the need for self-defense that pressed so many to join the Red Guards and the Internationalists.

The question of whether or not the Internationalists saved the Soviet system in Russia is open to debate. Yet it is evident that the participation of prisoners of war in the civil war lengthened its duration and increased the death toll as well as the human suffering. Participation on one side or another was often along ethnic lines. Most of the Czecho-Slovaks were anti-Bolshevik, the Hungarians were pro. This ethnic formulation of the sides indicates that within the Russian civil war there was also a civil war of the East Central Europeans.

It is significant to note Professor Kalvoda's argument that in the civil war the Czech Legion took the side of the Whites in order to leave Russia quickly. Most of the Hungarians, as the present author's essay indicates, joined the Reds for the same reason – to get out of Russia. These pragmatic considerations motivated many of the South Slavs as well.

Professor Banac describes how some of these men switched loyalties from one side to another in order to achieve the selfsame goals.

Professors Banac, Davis, Krammer and the present author indicate that Lenin's hope that the repatriated prisoners of war would revolutionize East Central Europe also proved to be incorrect. Although many of the leaders of the East Central European communist movement gained their first experience in Russia, they were unable to attract the masses at home. Neither were they able to count on the support of most of the returned prisoners of war.

Although the treatment and manipulation of the prisoners of war did not bring about the expected results, these policies had an impact on contemporary history in other ways. The Czecho-Slovak legions did not influence the outcome of the war on the Eastern and Western fronts, but their activities in Italy and, more importantly, their war against the Bolsheviks contributed substantially to the fact that the concessions to the Czecho-Slovak leaders' territorial demands at the Paris Peace Conference were not only what they wanted but also surpassed their highest expectations.

A less tangible consequence of the inhumane treatment of the prisoners of war was the acclimatization of the European mind to the existence of concentration camps. The *voennoplenniy arkhipelag* (prisoner-of-war archipelago) was followed by the GULags of Russia and by the extermination camps of Hitler's Europe. The "barbed-wire disease" mentioned by Professor Davis may have left scars on the psyche of the repatriated prisoner of war. The impact of the camp experience on the peacetime behavior of the former inmate had to be considerable. Historical inquiry in this direction may be valuable. It is also hoped that the present collection of essays will not only contribute to a better understanding of the history of the East Central European prisoners of war during the era of the Great War, but will be followed by new monographs on the subject as well.

SOUTH SLAV PRISONERS OF WAR IN REVOLUTIONARY RUSSIA

Ivo Banac

In Russ·land sind vie·le Sol · da·ten

Gebeš Mirko, a pockmarked Home Guard private with pale tubercular cheeks, was wounded several times before he fell into Russian captivity during a mad Austrian charge on the Dniester. He roamed the Siberian POW camps and finally returned to our barracks as one of the first heralds of the Russian tempest. . . . To everyone in our *Marodezimmer* Gebeš described Lenin as an ordinary Russian muzhik who spoke to the peasant soldiers about rural revolt, about their barracks, about the War, and how it was shameful to carry a gun and bleed and shoot for the bosses, and not *at* the bosses! . . .

"You don't say?! Revolt?! Street war against the bosses?! That's all Jewish nonsense! Shut up?"

That was Sergeant Benčina, an old front-liner. On two occasions he barely escaped death. He took great pride in displaying his trophy: a coat cribbled with seven machine-gun bullets. . . .

Benčina felt that Gebeš had overstepped the limits of order and discipline, and so he pulled rank to inform the private that it would be best if Gebeš would simply shut his trap and stop barking this brainless nonsense.

Miroslav Krleža (1924)[1]

Private Gebeš and Sergeant Benčina parted ways not only on the question of loyalty to Austria-Hungary but also on attitude toward the Russian revolution. Among more than 200,000 soldiers of Serb, Croat, Slovene, and other South Slav nationality who surrendered to the Russians or were captured on the Eastern front during the course of the war, there were many who relinquished all loyalty to Vienna and Pest, but were not quite ready to follow the red banner.[2] These largely peasant recruits (some 80 percent were from the countryside) became the prize in the contest between the two rival modern ideologies; small-nation *Staatenbildung* and Leninist socialism. Various emissaries from the Entente countries sought to involve their POW compatriots in movements for national independence. In the South Slav case, representatives of the London-based *Jugoslavenski odbor* (South Slav Committee or JO) and the Serbian exile government recruited volunteer detachments among the captives, in a program that was supported by Tsar Nicholas II, and—after February 1917—by the Provisional Government. The Bolsheviks after the victory of the October revolution (and to a considerable extent even before that) tried to win adherents among the POWs, or at least to persuade them not to join the interventionist or White units.

The volunteers recruited among the prisoners of war in Russia were not a decisive factor on the battlefield. The emergence of the East European successor states was largely unrelated to the military stature of the Polish, Czech, or Serbian volunteer corps. Similarly, the Boshevik victory in the civil war was not determined by the POWs who joined the Red Army, however helpful their actual contributions may have been. The value of the volunteer movement, which in fact attracted only a relatively small minority of the POWs in Russia (only some 10 percent of the South Slavs), was on the whole symbolic, and it is probably because of this that the importance of the movement has been somewhat exaggerated.[3]

In her postwar account of the dissident forces among the South Slav volunteers who withdrew from the Serbian Volunteer Corps in Odessa soon after the February revolution, MIlada Paulova noted that their battalion "roamed across Russia for a long time and encountered various problems, but lacked any political weight. In similar fashion other dissidents were also lost in the Russian Revolution."[4] Paulova presumed that the loyalist volunteers who went on to the Salonika front exerted far more influence on the course of events, and this interpretation was fostered in the semiofficial literature of interwar Yugoslavia:

> Volunteer units, whose disciplined and heroic display surprised all the leading and military circles in Europe, quite apart from their deep psychological significance, were meaningful in an important military-political way. Not only did the volunteers weaken Austrian military might, but they also strengthened Serbian divisions. . . . The volunteers elevated the prestige of Serbia and with their own blood testified to doubting Europe that the Yugoslavs from the Austro-Hungarian Monarchy demanded unification with Serbia.[5]

Soviet historians have always been equally generous in their praise of the former POWs in Red units, though the accolades reserved for the foreign Internationalists are always carefully phrased in order not to diminish the leading role of the revolution's domestic, specifically Russian, participants. Moreover, Soviet historians rightfully feel that it would be inaccurate to overplay the military contributions of the pro-Bolshevik POWs. Thus they tend to view the foreign Red Army men as veterans of an agitational front which demoralized the interventionists and mitigated anti-Bolshevik sentiment in their home countries.[6]

The Soviet desire to stress the continuity and reciprocity of revolutionary traditions in the USSR and the eastern-bloc countries is also reflected in contemporary East European research on the pro-Bolshevik volunteers. In Yugoslavia, however, such scruples have not obtained since 1948. On the contrary, when any Yugoslav historians venture to display a bit of party-mindedness on this matter, they are likely to inflate the role of the South Slav Internationalists, not for the purpose of promoting solidarity with Russia, but rather to underscore Yugoslavia's individual contributions to the international communist movement. Their unanimity on this is similar to the official Yugoslav interpretation of partisan experience in 1941-1945, which generally emphasizes the contributions of Tito's partisans to the common Allied cause, and minimizes the aid given to them by the Allies, including the USSR.

On the other hand, contemporary historiography in Yugoslavia does not hide South Slav participation in interventionist units. For example, Ivan Očak, the foremost authority on the South Slav POWs in Russia, decided to publish some of his findings on this sensitive subject only after his recent repatriation from the Soviet Union to Yugoslavia.[7] Yet all students of the South Slav volunteer movement in Russia must be very critical in their evaluation of the literature on this subject, of whatever provenance.

From the beginning of the war in 1914, Austria-Hungary was afflicted by the problem of desertion. The South Slav soldiers in the Austro-Hungarian army, especially the Serbs, refused to believe that the war against Serbia, Montenegro and Russia was in their interests. During Serbia's counter-offensive in December 1914, the Užice division together with Montenegrin units advanced deep into eastern Bosnia as far as the outskirts of Sarajevo.[8] Some 50,000 Bosnians, most of them Serbs, crossed into Serbia during this period.[9] Since the Serbian army did not keep records of the participation of the early volunteers in its units, it is not known how many of these deserters and refugees joined Serbia's cause.[10] These deserters, mainly South Slavs and Czechs, increasingly sought to persuade the Russian authorities that they wanted to be used in combat against Austria-Hungary, most often as soldiers in Serbian units.[11] Similar requests flowed into Serbian diplomatic missions from the POW camps in Russia[12] and from the South Slav colonies overseas, especially in the Americas.

The Serbian government welcomed these manifestations of support, and whenever possible aided the volunteers in their efforts to secure Allied cooperation. It did what it could to lessen the expensive and delicate problems of transporting them from neutral countries, but it made no attempt to give the volunteers a separate status or to employ them in the propaganda war against Austria-Hungary. The exiled South Slav politicians thought the volunteers should not be taken so much for granted. After weeks of discussion, an assembly of Croat, Serb, and Slovene émigrés meeting in Rome decided on January 11, 1915, to form a volunteer unit, to be called the Adriatic Legion, which would demonstrate to the world the determination of the Habsburg Monarchy's South Slavs to free themselves from Austro-Hungarian tutelage and join with Serbia to form a new Yugoslav state.[13]

The aim of the émigrés—from the spring of 1915 officially the *Jugoslavenski odbor (JO)*—was to enlist the support of the Entente governments and international opinion, as well as of South Slav emigrants in overseas countries, for the cause of South Slav unification, which, in their view, could be accomplished only by a formal agreement between the JO and the Serbian government. The South Slav state, as envisioned by the JO, would be a new entity created by the free will of the Serb, Croat, and Slovene "tribes" of the single Yugoslav people. The integralist Yugoslavism of the JO rejected a separate Serb, Croat, or Slovene statehood, and also implicitly opposed the Greater Serbian solutions of the South Slav question that were deeply entrenched in the governing institutions of royal Serbia.

The challenge to the Serbian prime minister, Nikola Pašić, and the ruling Radical party was to transform the idea of integralist Yugoslavism in such a way as to ensure Serbian domination. They found it inconceivable that "one" people should enter into a pact with itself. The moving force for unification could only be Serbia, which had "earned" a leadership position by its sacrifices, its national independence and statehood, and its loyalty to the cause of its allies, primarily tsarist Russia. The unification of the South Slavs would therefore, according to Pašić, be accomplished by Piedmontization. These differences in conceptions of South Slav unification were too deep ever to be reconciled, and the JO and the Serbian government were bound to cross swords on many issues. Pašić was not interested in forming an Adriatic Legion or any volunteer units that were not under control of the Serbian army. He did not want the JO to have an independent combatant force on the side of the Entente, because the Serbian government maintained the notion that "Serbia alone was the 'liberating' factor [among the South Slavs], and . . . jealously guarded the Serbian character of its army and of the entire [unification] action."[14]

Under pressure from the JO, backed by thousands of POW and emigrant demands for volunteer units, the Serbian government decided to anticipate any independent action by the JO, and in the summer of 1915 it announced a volunteer program of its own. Implementing it was not easy. The Russian government, generally ignorant of Balkan affairs, resisted the conscription of POWs as contrary to international law.[15] In Petrograd, particularly among A. A. Bashmakov's Orthodox Neo-Slavophiles, there was strong opposition to all movements toward South Slav unification.[16] And despite Bulgaria's overtures to the Central Powers, Russian opinion still favored Sofia over Belgrade on the question of Macedonia.[17] Nevertheless, Serbian diplomats made some headway with the sluggish Russian bureaucracy. Marko Cemović, Serbia's consul general in Odessa, succeeded in persuading the Russians to allow the formation of a small unit, which ostensibly protected Serbian food depots in Black Sea harbors, but large-scale mobilization of the POWs did not become a reality before Field Marshal August von Mackensen's offensive against Serbia in the fall and winter of 1915.[18]

Bulgaria's participation in the crippling campaign against Serbia and Montenegro closed the Danube route to the Serbian battlefields, and with it the only way of transporting the volunteers that Russia had hitherto tolerated. At this decisive moment the method of mobilizing the POWs had to be revised. Petrograd had to be persuaded to allow the formation of large volunteer detachments on Russian territory. Undaunted, Cemović turned to the tsar himself to change Russian policy. As a result of the consul's audience with Nicholas II in October 1915, Russia not only permitted the immediate establishment of the Serbian Volunteer Corps in Odessa, but also facilitated this action with generous financial grants and tactical support.[19] In truth, the slow dying of Serbia's flames and the Albanian calvary of the retreating Serbian army changed Petrograd's attitude in favor of full support for Serbian war aims.

With the imperial permission to assemble the South Slav volunteers, Russian camp authorities started delivering large contingents of POWs to Odessa. Some of these men were forcibly gathered; others, including many Czechs, Poles,

Ukrainians, and even Italians, came along, lured by promises of better living conditions.[20] Initial anarchy was stemmed by Serbian diplomatic personnel loyally assisted by Ante Mandić, the representative of the JO in Russia, but among the Croat and Slovene POWs the units acquired a taint of Serbian exclusiveness. Only a narrow layer of intelligentsia among these men supported the ideal of South Slav unification. The Croat and Slovene rank and file remained skeptical. Partly for this reason only some 85 Croat and Slovene soldiers had joined a total of 5,365 volunteers by mid-March 1916. However, Croats and Slovenes predominated among an additional 181 officers gathered in Odessa.[21] This imbalance was less pronounced by the end of the war, but the Serbs continued greatly to outnumber the other South Slavs in the volunteer corps, which totaled some 42,000 men at its peak in early 1917.

Although for many Croats and Slovenes mistrust of the Serbs was initially perhaps the most powerful deterrent to joining the volunteer corps, threats of reprisals by the Austro-Hungarians were also effective, and there were numerous other drawbacks.[22] Yet life in the Russian POW camps was far from being an attractive alternative. Only a fraction of the POWs benefited from the 1915 Russian decision to permit the employment of captives in factories and public works.[23] The lot of the POWs was harsh indeed. They were poorly fed and clothed, they were much abused by the authorities, and they were forced to perform difficult labor in most unfavorable conditions.[24] For all this, most Croats and Slovenes never attempted to enlist in the volunteer corps (which in any case could not have accommodated them all). Along with the anti-Serb sentiment, there was a certain lingering sense of loyalty to the Habsburg Monarchy. Some volunteers, for example, recalled that their decision to enlist in the corps frequently elicited catcalls and scornful spitting from other POWs, not only from the Austrian Germans and Hungarians, but also from their fellow South Slavs.[25] An as time went on, those who were not aroused by the hopes of South Slav unification became even less inclined to volunteer as reports of the hardships of the corps units filtered back to the POWs.

Their bad reputation was not due simply to the fact that the command of the volunteer units was entrusted to Serbian officers. Conditions in Odessa were terrible. A Slovene miller recalled that he was greatly disappointed with what he found there: "They assigned me to a rope factory, which was cold and filthy. We were full of lice, without straw mattresses or blankets, and in clothes that were no match for the frost of 1916. Disagreements among the volunteers hurt most of all."[26] The attitude of the Serbian officers, dispatched to Odessa from Corfu, the seat of the Serbian government-in-exile, made matters worse. Colonel Stevan Hadžić, who arrived to Odessa in April 1916, together with a staff of twelve other Serbians, shared the opinion of his superiors that the volunteers were merely another branch of the Serbian army. The Pašić government made it clear that Hadžić's task was to fashion "firm, disciplined units, inspired with Serbian ideas."[27] Any discussion about the name of the corps (most volunteers demanded that the units be called "South Slav" rather than "Serbian"), as well as any political activity or participation in decision-making by the volunteers, was forbidden as unacceptable. The POWs concluded that their volunteer status was at stake, as was the larger question of South Slav unification on the basis of equality among the constituent nationalities.

The situation was not helped by the Serbian officers' bad judgment in punishing dissident volunteers. According to Franko Potočnjak, a JO emissary who was summoned to Odessa to reassure the volunteers, "matters had gone so far there that [the officers] threatened those who espoused 'Yugoslavism' with the death penalty."[28] Some volunteers withdrew in protest. Rumors about the intolerable conditions in the corps were fueled by a number of Croat and Slovene politicians in Petrograd who were close to the Neo-Slavophile circles, and who argued for separate Croat and Slovene volunteer units.[29]

Morale in the corps sank even lower after its first taste of combat on the Dobrudja front against the Bulgarians in August and September 1916, in which it suffered heavy losses–1,978 dead and over 8,000 wounded.[30] Potočnjak remembered that "the wounded returned to Odessa filthy and completely neglected, without clothes, without greatcoats, without spare underwear, without a penny in their pockets. Both officers and men waited in blood-stained shirts at the gate of the English quarantine–and wept."[31] The survivors viewed the Dobrudja campaign as a senseless and misdirected venture. When the Russians started forcible recruitment of a new division of South Slav POWs to make up for the Dobrudja losses, resentment boiled over. Thirteen of the impressed troops *(silovoljci)* were killed in disturbances that erupted in the corps's garrison on October 23, 1916. After the rebellion, 44 percent of the volunteers either deserted or withdrew.[32] Some men of Capt. Milorad Majstorović's auxiliary battalion in Odessa were killed outright and their bodies were thrown into the Black Sea.[33]

These events that blackened the corps's reputation still further came at an unfortunate time. During its last months, the tsarist regime seemed determined to loosen its ties with the Serbian government and the JO. Of several ministries of that period, the cabinet of B.V. Stürmer was openly commited to curtailing the Czechoslovak and South Slav volunteer movements, which were regarded as obstacles to Russia's possible separate peace with the Central Powers. Stürmer's purpose was well served by the dismal state of the Serbian Volunteer Corps, whose reputation did not improve despite the growing support for the unification of the South Slavs on the part of the center and left groups in the Russian Duma.

Obstacles placed in the path of volunteer recruitment were removed by the February revolution. Still, the collapse of autocracy in Russia did not usher in a period of unimpeded opportunity for the promoters of the volunteer corps. To be sure, they profited from Foreign Minister P.N. Miliukov's unambiguous statement that the war goals of the revolutionary government included the liberation of the oppressed peoples of Austria-Hungary and the establishment of a "solidly organized Yugoslavia."[34] (Indeed, Prince L'vov's foreign minister was the first Allied statesman to come out in favor of a unified South Slav state.) Nevertheless, democratization of the Russian army and its steady involvement in political controversies could not bypass the foreign soldiers in Russia. The curtailment of the unrestrained power of the Corfu martinets in Odessa encouraged the dissidents in the corps, and the authority of the Serbian high command was further undermined by the decision of the Russians to permit on-demand transfer of the volunteers into the Russian army. Before the revolution, the dissatisfied officers or men could only go back to the deplorable POW camps. The revolutionary authorities allowed a far better alternative. Thus, according to Capt. Adam Gašparović, a volunteer officer, the revolution "shook the foundations of the corps, because the moral-disciplinary means of 'fear of fetters' was lost."[35]

Soon after the February revolution the corps experienced a new wave of desertions, which the command attributed to rumors stemming from the local soviets that all foreign units would be disbanded and their men sent back home. Entire detachments refused to obey orders, disrupted assemblies, or fled.[36] Astute observers, however, refused to credit these events to the revolution alone: "It would take too long, Mr. Chairman," wrote Cemović to Pašić in August 1917, "to demonstrate that the revolution did not obstruct the continuation of our work, and that the dissolution of the [volunteer] units occurred as a result of an *entire series of our errors.*"[37]

The erosion of discipline that followed the February events also manifested itself in numerous demands advanced especially by dissatisfied officers. Remedies against brutalized conditions in the corps and calls for the end of inequality in status and pay between the volunteer officers and their Serbian counterparts from Corfu figured prominently among the malcontents' claims. Nevertheless, most officer petitions addressed the functional purpose of the corps. The dissidents wanted the corps freed of narrow Serbian interests and manipulation by Pašić's cabinet. They wanted a "Yugoslav Corps," which would not be strictly military but would also be used to promote ideas of Yugoslav unity and communality. As a political corps, it should not be made to engage in combat on the Russian battlefields, but should serve only on the volunteers' native soil. There is evidence that the dissidents believed that their demands had the backing of the JO.[38]

All this had the clear ring of integralist nationalism. The Croat and Slovene officers who withdrew from the corps in May 1917 denounced the goals of fighting for a "Great Serbia," a "Great Croatia," or a "Great Slovenia" as "criminal utopias" that must be replaced by the alternative of a "federative Yugoslavia," an edifice of tolerance that would become an "element of reconciliation in the Balkans, that unfortunate carbuncle of Europe full of megalomaniacs and predatory chauvinism, where no people knows what belongs to it and what to others."[39] Pašić patched over the differences between the volunteers and the Corfu staffers by extending Serbian citizenship to all volunteers. Second Lieutenant Gustav Barabaš, a Croat from the Zagreb area, noted that this was an unsatisfactory substitution for genuine Yugoslavism, among other reasons, because of what was likely to follow. Barabaš foresaw "something horrible for us all, but not to be excluded, namely, that the time might come when our [Croat] people may rise up against the hegemony of the Serb people, and I, as a Serbian officer, reservist, and subject, would be obliged to lift my hand against my own people."[40]

Although hostility to Serbian supremacy in the corps motivated the officer dissidents, the disaffected troops were more interested in immediate improvements in their amenities, the end of harsh conditions, and participation in policy decisions. The soldiers' councils of the Russian army presented themselves as a ready model, and also as a democratic innovation that the Provisional Government was not prepared to oppose, despite the fact that the councils were the handiwork of the Petrograd Soviet. As of April 12, 1917, the prerogatives of the councils were defined, and their activities were fostered by the Russian supreme staff within all military units on Russian territory. Greater interest in the councils on the part of ordinary volunteers, who were mainly Serbs, stands in contrast to the aspirations of the dissident officers, mainly Croats and Slovenes. Differences in nationality structures between officers and men played as great a role here as class distinctions. According to a Serb working-class dissident:

> Soldier dissidents from the First [Volunteer] Division were ethnic Serbs (95 percent), while the rest were Croats, Slovenes, Czechs, and Muslims. In 98 percent of cases, officer dissidents were Croats and Slovenes, and the rest—Serbs and others. Soldier volunteers waged a collective and organized struggle and gave socialist earmarks to their movement, while the officers, although mutually connected, fought individually and gave a purely national character to their

> movement. Workers and peasants—veterans of the workers' movement—were at the head of the soldiers' struggle. Among the officers, the leaders were exclusively intellectuals who belonged to the [Yugoslav] nationalist movement.[41]

The April 12 decision on councils by the Russian supreme staff was greeted by a demand for councils by the volunteer corps rank and file. There were protest assemblies, illegal elections of soldiers' deputies. Some officers even took up the call. General Mihailo Živković, the head of the corps since July 1916, was obliged to submit to these calls, largely under Russian pressure. On April 18 he issued an order authorizing the establishment of soldiers' councils and specifying their structure and functions.[42] As it turned out, despite the resistance of some officers, the councils did not create chaos in the corps. Rather, in most cases they became a reliable conveyor belt whereby the command exercised firmer control over the troops than before. In any case, except in those units where the dissidents already had a firm foothold, the councils acted as beneficial safety valves for rebellious spirits.[43] A few days before the introduction of the councils in the corps, the Pašić government authorized the renaming of the volunteer units as the Volunteer Corps of the Serbs, Croats, and Slovenes (rejecting the Yugoslav nomenclature).[44]

These modest concessions by the Pašić cabinet improved the situation in the corps and persuaded the command to crack down on the active dissidents. The dissidents had already established contact with the Odessa Soviet, actually the local supplementary executive committee, in which the Bolsheviks had considerable influence, and the command rightly suspected that they were being swayed by Russian left-wingers who feared the potential misuse of the corps against the Russian revolution. As a result, a fortnight after the authorization of the councils within the corps, Gen. Živković ordered that all officers and men who disagreed with the aim of the units were to be expelled. Special commissions were established to supervise and verify this task of separation.[45] As Mandić later remarked, "Nothing else remained but to localize the fire and to separate the 'faithful' from the 'dissidents.' "[46] At this point 149 officers and 12,741 soldiers left the corps. According to nationality, the numbers broke down as follows:

	Serbs	Croats	Slovenes	Others	Total
Officers	4	96	42	7	149
Soldiers	7,352	3,787	1,241	360	12,740
Total	7,356	3,883	1,283	367	12,889

This represented some two-fifths of all volunteers registered at the beginning of 1917. In percentages, the numbers of those who withdrew in the various categories were significant:

	Serbs	Croats	Slovenes	Others	Total
Officers	1.20%	60.76%	56.76%	2.72%	18.13%
Soldiers	33.10%	77.43%	82.84%	43.27%	42.13%
Total	32.63%	76.91%	71.24%	21.95%	41.49%

These figures are a fairly accurate representation of how the corps was accepted by different nationalities and ranks.[47] The majority of the Croats and Slovenes—soldiers even more than officers—opted out. Two-thirds of the Serb soldiers and practically all the Serb officers chose to stay, which certainly meant that they did not find life in the corps unbearable. The losses suffered by the corps after the withdrawal of the dissidents were offset slightly by an influx of new volunteers—2,008 soldiers and 112 officers who enlisted in the late spring and summer of 1917. But the decline in the overall number of volunteers was more than compensated for by a marked improvement in discipline that followed the split and was noted in all reports.[48]

The deteriorating situation in Russia in the summer of 1917 created new problems for the corps. Under pressure from the workers' soviets, which were demanding the disbandment of the volunteers, the Provisional Government insisted that the corps, whose operational costs were covered by the Russians, was to be deployed on the Rumanian front. After a great deal of wrangling some units were sent there, though against the advice of Gen. Živković, who believed that the Serbs (especially those from the Banat) could not fight effectively for a country that sought to annex their native regions. For one thing, he and others feared that the epidemic of "fraternalization" on the fronts might affect the loyalty of the volunteers. The Serbian government and the JO were painfully aware that the Russian maximalists encouraged revolutionary defeatism and had no scruples about offering to return the volunteers to "their own men" in the Austro-Hungarian army. This in fact almost happened to a Czech unit on the Austrian front.[49] And the corps command feared that under growing political pressures the volunteers would become as demoralized as the Russian soldiers. Živković, writing in July 1917, commented: "I believe that this is the last moment to save the corps, because Russian committees, both military and civilian ones, which today decide on everything in Russia and which know the disciplines and order of our volunteers in the corps, are publicly agitating for and working for the disbandment of the corps, because they say that we hinder their liberty and republican principles."[50]

In August, after reversals on the Rumanian front, the Serbian government succeeded in getting the Russians to allow the volunteer corps to be withdrawn and reassigned to the Salonika front. The bulk of the troops, including the staff, the Second Division, and the First Brigade of the First Division, reached Arkhangel'sk before the October revolution and were transported by Allied ships to Britain, and thence to France. They were dispatched through France and Italy to Taranto and finally to Salonika, which they reached by January 1918. The new Bolshevik authorities prevented the Second Brigade of the First Division from reaching the White Sea. The brigade was ordered instead to gather at Iaroslavl, and then in January 1918, with Leon Trotsky's express permission, it set out eastward through European Russia, Siberia and Manchuria to Dairen in China. From there British ships transported it by way of Singapore and Suez to Salonika, where all of its members arrived by May 1918. During the transport to Salonika 2,514 officers and men deserted or withdrew. A large group of 150 men (with one officer) joined the Baikal and Amur area cossack units of Gen. G.M.

Semenov, and fought on against the Bolsheviks until the end of the civil war in the Far East.[51]

The *semenovtsy* were not the only anti-Bolshevik formation to attract the South Slavs. In Siberia especially, where according to some accounts there were as many as 20,000-30,000 South Slavs at the beginning of 1919,[52] they could be found in small groups in practically every counter-revolutionary unit. Most were attached to the Czechoslovak Legion and were stationed from the Volga to Vladivostok, and along the way in Tiumen, Omsk, Novonikolaevsk (now Novosibirsk), and Krasnoiarsk. They were also in the retinues of various hetmans. Fifty served in the personal guard of Gen. Khorvat in Khabarovsk. There were 400 in A.V. Kolchak's camp, including Gen. Batić, Kolchak's aide-de-camp.[53]

These groups were of no consequence, however. Far more significant were the larger remnants of the volunteer corps which were attached to the interventionist and White units. Of these, the supplementary battalion of the volunteer corps, some 2,000 officers and men, was the most important. The British and French retained the battalion in Karelia during the withdrawal of the other volunteers. The battalion was to defend the Petrograd-Murmansk railroad from the Bolsheviks and the German-backed Finns, and in general to help the Allies in protecting the harbors of Murmansk and Arkhangel'sk from the Germans, with whom the Bolsheviks concluded a separate peace treaty on March 3, 1918, at Brest-Litovsk.

The enthusiasm of the volunteers for this venture was certainly not greater than that of Radoslav S. Jovanović, the ranking Serbian diplomat in Bolshevik-held territory and Pašić's confidant, who regarded any shedding of "fraternal Russian blood by our arms . . . as a terrible crime against our future and a direct assassination of our national honor and conscience."[54] Throughout their struggles in northern Russia, where they operated as part of the British 257th Brigade largely between Kandalaksha and Lake Onega, the volunteers encountered evidence of POW presence. A Slovene military physician noted that in this area "during the war the POWs built a 1,000-kilometer railroad line from Zvanka near Petrograd to Murmansk":

> [The line] was constructed at the cost of great losses, because the POWs were ravaged by various infectious diseases and by scurvy due to a lack of fresh food. Many cemeteries along the line speak of these victims. I read the inscriptions on the humble crosses and, though some had German and Hungarian names, I found the majority to be Slavic names. No wonder so many POWs did not and never will return from Russia.[55]

Despite its relative successes against the Bolsheviks, the battalion was demoralized, felled by Spanish influenza, and increasingly restless and rebellious. It was evacuated in October 1919 on orders of the government in Belgrade, bringing to an end the official involvement of Serbia (and of the new Yugoslav state) in Russian military affairs.[56]

Nearly all the remaining South Slav troops in Russia—whether White or Red—were related in one way or another to the dissident movement. Of the 13,000 volunteers who left the corps in early May 1918, the officers were turned over to the Russian district commands in Odessa and Ekaterinoslav (now Dnepropetrovsk), and the soldiers sent to the POW camps in Darnitsa (near Kiev) and Ekaterinoslav. The entire leadership of the dissident soldiers' committee was in Darnitsa, including Nikola Grulović (1883-1959) and Nikola Kovačević (b. 1890), the president and secretary, respectively, both veteran Social Democrats. By the end of May, the Darnitsa group had obtained the status of Russian soldiers, though this recognition exposed them to new pressures, because Serbian diplomats in Kiev and elsewhere in Russia had a stake in reversing the Russian decision on their status. As long as withdrawal from the corps did not occasion dire consequences, other volunteers could choose to follow the dissidents, but the dissidents were spreading very damaging stories about the corps, and these were bound to have an effect on Serbian efforts to attract new volunteers, especially in Darnitsa, one of the principal recruiting points. "Wherever they go," wrote one Serbian officer, "the dissidents spread all sorts of things about the corps, except a good word. And they disrupt further work. An offended Slav takes revenge to the end."[57]

The status of the dissidents in Darnitsa and elsewhere underwent several reversals until June 1917, when the officers and men agreed on the establishment of a dissident military unit that would enter the Russian army. This proposal won the backing of A.F. Kerenskii, who wished to buttress the position of the Provisional Government with the aid of the ex-POW units. According to Grulović, who had no reason to be partial to Kerenskii, the Socialist Revolutionaries (Kerenskii's party) were the only Russian faction interested in the dissident movement.[58] This perhaps explains the steady influence of the Socialist Revolutionaries in Darnitsa, especially among the officers.

With Kerenskii's approval, a Serbian shock battalion of some 600 men and twenty-four officers was formed in early summer of 1917. In keeping with the steady radicalization of the troops, and the dissidents' stand on the question of South Slav unity, its name was soon changed to the South Slav Revolutionary Shock Battalion. Those men who remained outside the unit were assigned to various workers' groups in Kiev and elsewhere in the Ukraine. Simultaneously, the dissidents created a political organization, the South Slav Revolutionary Alliance, which enlisted some 20,000 POWs in the summer of 1917, mainly in the western Ukraine. The alliance was directed by its central committee, headed by Maksim Čanak (1888-1918) and Nikola Kovačević. Ninety to 95 percent of the members were of peasant origin, and there was a sprinkling of workers. Officers were discouraged from joining, except in the cases of well-known radicals.[59] The aim of the organization was "to fight for the liberation of [the South Slavs] from foreign rule, for equality, and for social and political justice."[60]

The alliance and the shock battalion wished to remain neutral in Russian political disputes, but this was not easy since most of the leaders of the alliance were left-wing Social Democrats who approved of the policies of various Russian revolutionary groups—though it is clear that the Bolsheviks did not have any significant following. Grulović, who later became a communist, wrote that, at the time of the Kornilov affair in September 1917, "most of the [soldiers] came out for the Socialist Revolutionaries and Kerenskii, while a smaller number was for the Social Democrats, for the

Mensheviks. Nobody spoke badly of the Bolsheviks, nor did any of the soldiers back Kornilov. Half of the officers spoke for Kornilov, while a significant number was neutral."[61] Most officers backed the Russian moderates. This was especially the case of a handful of Serbian officers from Corfu, who joined the dissidents in the wake of the Dimitrijević-Apis affair.[62] Foremost among them, Col. Vojislav Gojković, who commanded the shock battalion, openly sided with Kornilov. Gojković also advocated an exclusively Serbian name for the battalion, a viewpoint already rejected by the dissidents.[63]

The Bolshevik seizure of power in November 1917 further polarized the South Slav Revolutionary Alliance. Though the Bolsheviks favored full equality for foreign nationals (including the POWs), they were suspicious of organized foreign groups, which were viewed as potential allies of the counterrevolution. Moreover, since the Bolsheviks were trying to conclude a separate peace with the Central Powers, they had to restrict the activities of the POWs. This in turn strengthened the apprehensions in the exile community that the Bolsheviks might agree to repatriation of captured enemy soldiers, including those—such as the members of various anti-Habsburg units—who might be charged with treason in their home countries. The decidedly anti-Habsburg South Slavs were also concerned about the ambiguous demand for "immediate peace without annexations," which Lenin included in his famous decree on peace issued immediately after the October revolution. The South Slavs felt that this decree at the very least showed an indifference to their aim of constituting a Yugoslav state on the rubble of Austria-Hungary.

The alliance congress that convened in Kiev in January 1918 was unable to resolve the differences between the factions. Participants have claimed that most soldier delegates were by then on the whole pro-Bolshevik.[64] Still, the congress reached a compromise platform: "The congress hailed the October revolution in order to satisfy the [allegedly pro-Bolshevik] majority. And so that the minority would not feel dissatisfied and offended, the resolution included a claim that the South Slav Revolutionary Alliance would wage a pacifist revolutionary struggle for the realization of its socialist ideals."[65] In fact, the alliance was already disintegrating. With the beginning of the civil war and Bolshevik attempts to create ex-POW units under the firm control of the revolutionary regime, the time for neutrality had passed.

There was much wavering, however. For example, the shock battalion of Aleksandar Srb, one of the Corfu officers who joined the dissidents, first fought against the Ukrainian nationalists on the Boshevik side. Srb was killed in Taganrog in April 1918 on orders of the Serbian mission in Petrograd.[66] Under the command of Maj. Matija Blagotić, his battalion then joined the Red units in the defense of Kazan' in August 1918. It switched sides in the thick of the battle, and helped the Whites and their Czechoslovak allies capture Kazan'. Its men then participated in the murder of thirty wounded Serb and Croat communists.[67] Several upheavals later, after the men had killed Blagotić, the battalion became part of the South Slav regiment within the Czechoslovak Legion in Cheliabinsk. It fought against the Red Army on several occasions, but in September 1919 the remaining members rebelled, killed their new commander, and joined the Red Army. The unit later fought in eastern Siberia.[68]

The First South Slav Regiment, also a part of the Czechoslovak Legion, had an equally checkered history. This regiment, not connected with the dissident movement, was formed in Siberia out of the remnants of the volunteer corps joined by the POWs from Petropavlovsk. It was dominated by a group of left-wing officers led by Robert Valdgoni (1892-1938) and Pavle Gregorić (b. 1892), both Croats. They organized a successful underground officers' organization and renamed the regiment "Matija Gubec," after the leader of the 1573 Croat peasant uprising. The group wanted to preserve the regiment from internal Russian struggles and to effect its safe return home. The officers also fostered integralist Yugoslav nationalism, but along radical, antimonarchist lines. Above all, they wanted to prevent the regiment from fighting against the Bolsheviks. To this end, they entered into secret contacts with the Siberian Red partisans. In January 1920, two of the regiment's three battalions passed to the side of the Red Army in Nizhneudinsk.[69]

These cases demonstrate that units that were at the outset counterrevolutionary joined the Red Army as a result of concerted Bolshevik agitation. Much the same can be said of the armed groups that sided with the Soviets without major upheavals. Similarly, Bolshevik organizational skills helped fashion Red units out of the passive majority of the ex-POWs, who demonstrated no apparent loyalties after their capture at the fronts. South Slav Red Guard units mushroomed soon after the October revolution. The first such unit was created in Odessa in December 1917 with the aid of men sent by the Kiev leadership of the South Slav Revolutionary Alliance, which increasingly took the Bolshevik side.

From the Bolshevik point of view, the alliance was not an acceptable vehicle for the further growth of Red units among the South Slavs. Active Communist groups alone could perform this political-organizational task. By the end of 1917 the Bolsheviks were already encouraging the Petrograd POW organization, which was solidly pro-Soviet, to popularize revolutionary ideas among the exiles. Dr. Mijo Radošević (1884-1942), who represented Croat socialists at the Stockholm conference and later served in the Serbian mission in Petrograd, stood for the leftist South Slav POWs in this organization. Since he preferred to stress the need to continue struggling against the Central Powers, he sided with the liberal intellectuals, the founders of the new South Slav Revolutionary Federation in Russia, which was backed by the Serbian mission.

After the All-Russian Congress of Prisoners of War, which was held in Moscow in April 1918, the liberal and moderate forces were on the defensive. With Bolshevik encouragement, the congress favored full engagement of the POWs on the Red side in the civil war, and the promotion of trained political leaders among the POWs, who would be schooled to direct revolutionary struggle in their homelands. The revolutionary alliance, which had been increasingly abandoned by its leftist leadership, had ceased functioning altogether in March. The nascent liberal federation soon became the target of concerted attacks by the radicals, who flocked to Moscow hoping that the Bolshevik leaders would entrust them with the task of creating communist South Slav groups. One liberal leader recalled that the Bolsheviks tolerated the activities of the federation, viewing its members as victims of German imperialism. There were no obstacles to its further work,

> until at the last moment Nikola Kovačević appeared in Moscow and, in company with the famous psychopath Dr. Vukašin Marković,[70] convinced the Bolshevik Olympus that all of us in the South Slav Revolutionary Federation were counterrevolutionaries, that we had no influence over our POW masses, and that these must be joined within an exclusively Communist organization. The Russian Bolsheviks accepted this, and subsequently the South Slav Communist soviet was founded in Moscow. The South Slav Revolutionary Federation was scattered, the printing of its organ *Sloboda* [Freedom] was stopped, and the press "nationalized" and turned over to the South Slav soviet, which was at first directed precisely by the above mentioned Dr. Marković and Kovačević.[71]

The pro Bolshevik South Slavs, including Bulgar communists, first established in April 1918 the so-called South Slav Group of International Social Democracy, with its organ, *Revolucija.* A month later, after the Bolsheviks created the Federation of Foreign Communist Sections attached to the Central Committee of the Russian Communist Party (Bolshevik) [RKP(b)], the group's plenary meeting petitioned to become a section of the RKP(b). The proposal was accepted. The section's official name ultimately became the South Slav Group of the RKP(b). The Bulgars left in October 1918 to establish their own national communist section. Meanwhile, on July 3, 1918, the South Slav group elected its leadership, headed by Vukašin Marković, who also edited the new weekly *Vsemirnaia revoliutsiia* (World Revolution), published in editions of 10,000-18,000 copies, with texts in Slovene, Croat, Serbian, and Bulgarian. Vladimir Ćopić (1891-1938?), a Croat lawyer from Senj, served as secretary. When the People's Commissariat for the Nationalities (Narkomnats) established its South Slav section in August 1918, Marković and Ćopić held the identical offices in this agency of the Soviet state.

The South Slav Communist group was subject to the Central Committee of the RKP(b). Its initial mission was to school cadres to spread the message of Bolshevism to their exiled countrymen and ultimately in Yugoslavia. Hundreds of trained agitators were then sent to the Red Army units that included substantial numbers of South Slav recruits. Many were also infiltrated into White South Slav units in order to break them up. The South Slav section of the Narkomnats included special subsections devoted to the organization of South Slav units of the Red Army, employment of idle POWs, cultural and educational activities among the POWs, and, of course, political agitation.[72] In addition to its headquarters in Moscow, the South Slav communist group established organizations in Petrograd and elsewhere in Russia, the Ukraine, Siberia, and Turkestan. In 1920 there were 450 members and 50 candidate members of the group in the Russian Federation; 49 members, 133 candidates, and 2,419 non-party sympathizers were in Siberia and Kazakhstan.

In the wake of the Treaty of Brest-Litovsk, as part of Bolshevik measures to discredit the military missions of still-warring Austria-Hungary, Germany and Serbia, the Soviet authorities decided to organize these countries' nationals within the system of soviets for the purpose of paralyzing the missions' anti-Bolshevik activities. South Slav sections were organized within the Austro-Hungarian soviet, and in March 1919 a South Slav Soviet of Workers' and Peasants' Deputies was established in Moscow. Its president was Ilija Milkić (1884-1970), a veteran Serbian Social Democrat who came to Russia from exile in Switzerland at the beginning of 1919. In addition to its attempts to supplant the work of the former Serbian military mission, the soviet aided all the activities of the South Slav communists in Russia. It was especially active in repatriation work. From 1921 on, it had authority over the transport of the remaining POWs to Yugoslavia, and it denied clearance to all "former officers, capitalists, landowners, and other counterrevolutionary elements."[73]

The most important accomplishment of the South Slav communist leadership in Russia was the recruitment of some 30,000 ex-POWs into the Red Army. This is not to say that each of these Red Army men fought for the Bolsheviks at the instance of his communist countrymen. Many enlisted without any intermediaries. Since the national units of the

Red Army were fairly few and far between, South Slav recruits were scattered all over the vast Russian land, in the Ukraine, Siberia, and Turkestan. Their exploits, a story in themselves, are a part of the extremely complicated history of Russia's civil war.

The role of several celebrated South Slav Red Army commanders may be mentioned briefly. Danilo Srdic (Serdich) (1896-1937), a Serb from the Lika region of Croatia, studied in Belgrade before the war, and in 1912 went to Russia to pursue military studies. He fought in the Russian army during the war, then joined the Serbian Volunteer Corps in Odessa and defected after the February revolution. Srdić was one of the very few South Slavs who participated in the storming of the Winter Palace in the October revolution. He later commanded the First Serbian Soviet unit in Ekaterinoslav. In the late summer and the fall of 1919 he commanded the newly formed First South Slav Communist Regiment, which was under the direct supervision of the South Slav Group of the RKP(b). The regiment distinguished itself on the Tsaritsyn (now Volgograd) front. Srdić later commanded various Soviet Cavalry units.

Another legendary Red cavalryman was Tomo Dundić (1897-1920), known in Russia as Oleko Dundich, or simply Red Dundich. Dundić was a Croat from the environs of Imotski in Dalmatia, who joined the Serbian volunteer corps in Russia after his territorial *(domobran)* unit was captured.[74] After the October revolution he organized a Red partisan unit in the Ukraine, and then joined the Soviet troops at Tsaritsyn. He rose to become S.M. Budennyi's deputy in the Red Cavalry, commanded the Model Cavalry Division attached to the staff of the First Red Army, and was killed near Rovno on July 7, 1920, during the Polish-Soviet war. Dundić's superhuman heroism is the stuff of Soviet Red Cavalry legend, maintained through the years in dozens of plays, novels, and biographies.

Incongruous stories of South Slav experiences in revolutionary Russia demonstrate that some lives certainly *habent sua fata.* From Janez Košir, a Slovene Bolshevik who became a deputy to the president of the Kirghiz Soviet Republic in 1921, to his countryman Viktor Engelsberger, a dissident volunteer, who spent the Christmas of 1917 in

Tabriz drinking his *arak* with the last tsarist soldiers in Iran,[75] they all underwent a memorable travail. It should be stressed that little is known of the "good portion of the [South Slav] element [in Russia] which does not even want to hear [of loyally serving the cause of the new Yugoslav state], but instead continues to bow to the old [Austrian] idols."[76] But if one leaves out this group—in fact the vast majority of the POWs who minded their own affairs in Russia—can the reasons for Bolshevik successes among the POWs, which were greater than those of the Yugoslav nationalist recruiters, be attributed to any specific causes?

Bolshevik ideology was not more attractive to the peasant POWs because of any innate appeal. Enthusiasm for national independence, encouraged by the Entente, had considerable influence, especially among the Serbs, whereas the Croat and Slovene intellectuals preferred an integral, or, in some cases, federated, Yugoslavia. Nevertheless, the Bolsheviks invested by far the greater imagination and organizational skill in propagating their ideas among the POWs. The political role of the South Slav Group of the RKP(b) and its highly effective and varied press had no equivalent among the adherents of the Serbian government or the JO. Nor did the royalists and Whites know how to train dedicated agitators or how to infiltrate them into the enemy camp through clever subterfuge. Moreover, the Red Army established its own élan and camaraderie, which Budennyi rightly felt was unique to revolutionary armies. This was a reflection of the revolution's utopian dream, which, while it lasted, could not be matched by its enemies. Precisely the opposite was true of the practices of the Murman interventionist units. There, according to *Vsemirnaia revoliutsiia* (World Revolution) "the English treat the Serb soldiers with unconcealed contempt. While [the English] live in warm cars the Serbs inhabit cold freight wagons."[77] Finally, if nothing else worked, the Bolsheviks relied on terror. Some of the South Slav interventionists, captured near Arkhangel'sk in 1918, experienced all the terrors of the Cheka's arbitrary methods in Butyrki prison near Moscow, as they were alternately condemned to death and then spared.[78]

After the breakup of Austria-Hungary in November 1918, the South Slav Communist Group became increasingly anxious to organize the return of their pro-Bolshevik countrymen to the homeland. The new leadership of the group, headed by Lazar Vukićević (1887-1942), a veteran Social Democrat from Bosnia, as well as Ćopić and Kovačević, decided to initiate communist activities in nascent Yugoslavia, where organized communist groups had not yet been formed.

The decision of the South Slav communist leadership to return home influenced the process of differentiation in Social Democratic ranks that had already commenced within Yugoslavia. According to one source, "a total of 114 emissaries, that is, only a fifth (20.86 percent) of all party-organized South Slav cadres in Soviet Russia," had returned to Yugoslavia by December 20, 1918.[79] In fact, activist returnees made up at most one percent of all repatriates from Russian captivity. Among them were members of the South Slav communist leadership in Russia, such as Vladimir Ćopić, Nikola Kovačević, and Nikola Grulović. After their return to Zagreb in early December 1919, Ćopić and Kovačević became instrumental in creating an underground communist network in Croatia-Slavonia and Bosnia.[80] Vukićević and Grulović, who like most organized returnees decided to make the Vojvodina their base, initiated the so-called Pelagić Alliance of Communists in early March 1919, soon after they arrived in Novi Sad. All the activist returnees propagated unconditional adherence to Bolshevik positions, a break with Social Democracy, and the building of illegal communist organizations.

Little is known about the fate of the rank-and-file Red Army men after their return to Yugoslavia. Their presence was surely felt in an outburst of rural violence that engulfed Croatia-Slavonia in the fall of 1918. There quasi-Bolshevik republics proclaimed in Banova Jaruga and Novo Mesto testify to their continued insurrectionary engagement. Most would remain anonymous, or at least for a while. Josip Broz Tito, whose woolen cap bore the traces of the red star badge when he returned to Croatia in the summer of 1920, was destined to lead the Communist Party of Yugoslavia (CPY) to power two decades after the end of Russia's civil war.[81] Pavle Gregorić and Nikola Grulović were among the chief organizers of partisan struggle in Croatia and Vojvodina, respectively, and later served as high state and party officials. Ilija Milkić stayed in Moscow and represented the CPY at the first three Comintern congresses, but later returned home and quit the party.

The fate of the other prominent South Slav veterans of the revolution was less fortunate. Lazar Vukićević was executed by the Nazis in 1942. Vladimir Ćopić, Robert Valdgoni, and Danilo Srdić fell victim to Stalin's purges. So did Vukašin Marković. In 1920 he first attempted to start a revolution in Montenegro and then fled to Russia. An eccentric to the end (he would go to bed fully clothed "because the enemy never sleeps"), he was arrested by the NKVD and died in a Soviet camp during World War II. Nikola Kovačević, like Ćopić a Loyalist commander in the Spanish Civil War, remained a Stalinist, and was arrested in Tito's purge of the Cominformists in 1948.

Incidentally, Krleža tells us that his fictional antagonists in the great debate among the South Slav POWs also succumbed. Private Gebeš was sentenced to death by an Austro-Hungarian court martial and was executed a few months before the Monarchy's collapse. Sergeant Benčina was killed by nationalist sailors in the pay of the National Council of the Slovenes, Croats, and Serbs during the fall of 1918. The heritage of the revolution is not evident.

NOTES

1. Miroslav Krleža, "Domobrani Gebeš i Benčina govore o Lenjinu," in *Hrvatski bog Mars* (Zagreb, 1962), pp. 462, 464.

2. The number 200,000 is a standard estimate for all the South Slav POWs, including a small group of Bulgarian captives. Altogether there some 2,000,000 Austro-Hungarian, German, Turkish, and Bulgarian POWs in Russia during the war. See A. Manusevič, "Učešće internacionalista u borbi za sovjetsku vlast u Rusiji 1917-1920," *Prilozi za istoriju socijalizma* (Belgrade), V (1968), 320-321.

3. Bibliographical guides to the literature on the South Slav POWs in Russia are selective. See the appropriate sections in Žarko D. Protić *et al, Socijalistički i radnički pokret i KPJ (1867-1941); Bibliografija (1945-1969)* (Belgrade, 1972); E.M. Kan (ed), *Oktiabr' i revoliutsionnoie dvizhenie v stranakh Tsentral'noi i Iugo-Vostochnoi Evropy (1917-1923 gg.): Ukazatel' literatury (1945-1965)* (Moscow, 1968); Ferdo Čulinović, "Učešce Jugoslovena u Oktobarskoj revoluciji, *Naučni skup "Oktobarska revolucija i narodi Jugoslavije,"* III (Belgrade and Kotor, 1967), 20-23.

4. Milada Paulová, *Jugoslavenski odbor: Povijest jugoslavenske emigracije za svjetskog rata od 1914-1918*. (Zagreb, 1925), p. 321.

5. Ernest Turk, "Zgodovinski oris pokreta jugoslovanskih vojnih dobrovoljcev v svetovni vojni," in Ernest Turk *et al.* (eds.), *Dobrovoljci kladivarji Jugoslavije,* (Ljubljana, 1936), p. 104.

6. Manusevič, *op. cit.*, p. 333.

7. This is not to suggest that Očak's recent publications are in any way a departure from his earlier writings published in the USSR. They are only thematically different. See Ivan Očak, "O Jugoslavenima u bjelogardejskim jedinicama u Rusiji za vrijeme gradjanskog rata (1918-1920)," *Časopis za suvremenu povijest* (Zagreb), I (1974), 39-56.

8. Josip Horvat, *Privi svjetski rat: Panorama zbivanja, 1914-1918* (Zagreb, 1967), p. 189.

9. Paulová, *op. cit.*, p. 156.

10. Ante Mandić, *Fragmenti za historiju ujedinjenja* (Zagreb, 1956), p. 40.

11. Paulová, *op. cit.*, p. 157.

12. Samples of these requests can be found in Nikola Popović (ed.), *Jugoslovenski dobrovoljci u Rusiji, 1914-1918; Zbornik dokumenata* (Belgrade, 1977), pp. 1-5.

13. Franko Potočnjak, *Iz emigracije,* IV: *U Rusiji* (Zagreb, 1926), pp. 87-89.

14. Mandić, *op. cit.*, p. 40.

15. Paulová, *op cit.*, p. 157.

16. *Ibid.*, pp. 164-167.

17. *Ibid.*, pp. 162-163.

18. Mandić, p. 43.

19. *Ibid.*, pp. 43-45 Cf. Paulová, op. cit., pp. 172-174.

20. *Ibid.*, 191-192.

21. *Ibid.*, p. 192. For a detailed account of the SerbianVolunteer Corps in Russia see Ilija Jovanović *et al.*, *Jugoslovenski dobrovoljački korpus u Rusiji: Prilog istoriji dobrovoljaćkog pokreta (1914-1918)* (Belgrade, 1954). Figures on the numerical standing of different nationalities in the corps are given on pp. 135 and 184 of this volume.

22. For a dramatic autobiographical account of Austro-Hungarian retribution, see a memoir of a Slovene volunteer captured by the Bulgarians in Dobrudja and later sentenced to death by an Austro-Hungarian court-martial: Tone Habe, "Skozi tri fronte in štiri ujetništva," in Turk *et al.* (eds.), *op. cit.*, pp. 348-351. In this case the sentence was commuted. It is not apparent that the Austrians generally showed such consideration to the captured volunteers, or — as it were — deserters.

23. Paulová, *op. cit.*, p. [169].

24. For a vivid account of the conditions in one camp in the Vitebsk *guberniia,* see Potočnjak, *op. cit.*, pp. 245-247.

25. Franjo Lah, "Iz robstva v slobodo," in Turk *et al.* (eds.), *op. cit.*, p. 627.

26. Anton Kovačić, "Pota dobrovoljca — kmeta," *ibid.*, p. 575.

27. Javanović *et al.*, *op cit.*, pp. 19-20.

28. Potočnjak, *op. cit.*, p. 7.

29. Krunoslav Heruc (Geruts), the founder of the Croat Križanić Society in Petrograd, and Josip Tuma, Heruc's Slovene associate, were the most important of these figures. After the February Revolution some Great Serbian elements in

the corps plotted to kill these politicians. Another slated victim was V. I. Lenin. See Vladimir Košćak, "Prilog za historiju 1917, godine," *Historijski zbornik* (Zagreb), X (1957), No. 3-4, 131-136. For more on Heruc and Tuma consult Mandić, Paulová, and Potočnjak, *passim*.

30. Paulová, *op. cit.*, p. 250.

31. Potočnjak, *op. cit.*, p. 42.

32. Paulová, *op. cit.*, *254*.

33. Nikola Grulović, *Jugosloveni u ratu i Oktobarskoj-revoluciji* (Belgrade, 1962), p. 84.

34. Paulová, *op. cit.*, pp. 289-290, 313-317.

35. Popović, *op. cit.*, p. 316.

36. *Ibid.*, p. 205.

37. *Ibid.*, p. 297.

38. *Ibid.*, pp. 272-273.

39. *Ibid.*, p. 260.

40. Pero Damjanović *et al.* (eds.), *Uchastie iugoslavskikh trudiashchikhsia v Oktiabr'skoi revoliutsii i grazhdanskoi voine v SSSR: Sbornik dokumentov i materialov* (Moscow, 1976), p. 32.

41. Grulović, *op. cit.*, p. 142.

42. Popović, *op. cit.*, pp. 196-200.

43. For details on the soldiers' councils in the volunteer corps, see especially Bogumil Hrabak, "Komiteti u jugoslovenskoj dobrovoljačkoj vojsci u Rusiji 1917, godine," *Istorija XX veka: Zbornik radova,* III (Belgrade, 1962), 277-343.

44. Popović, *op. cit.*, pp. 195-196.

45. *Ibid.*, pp. 217-218.

46. *Ibid.*, p. 380.

47. The figures in both tables are based on information from the memorandum of Captain Gašparović, *ibid.*, pp. 311-312, 315-316. I have corrected a calculation error in the original.

48. *Ibid.*, p. 381.

49. *Ibid.*, p. 257.

50. *Ibid.*, p. 286.

51. Jovanović *et al.*, *op. cit.*, pp. 184-191.

52. Očak, *op. cit.*, p. 45.

53. *Ibid.*, p. 48.

54. *Ibid.*, p. 40.

55. Valentin Meršol, "V težkih urah," in Turk *et al.* (eds.), *op. cit.*, pp. 541-542.

56. For additional personal accounts of the Murman and Karelia episode in the volunteer chronicle, see Alojzij Trstenjak, "Naši dobrovoljci v Koreliji," *ibid.*, pp. 514-529; Ernst Gorišek, "Boji ob jezeru Onega in zavzetje Dianove gore," *ibid.*, pp. 530-533.

57. Popović, *op. cit.*, p. 317.

58. Grulović, *op. cit.*, p. 133.

59. Ivan D. Očak, *Jugosloveni u Oktobru* (Belgrade, 1967), p. 133.

60. Grulović, *op. cit.*, p. 153.

61. *Ibid.*

62. Colonel Dragutin Dimitrijević-Apis (1877-1917), the reputed mastermind of the assassination of Archduke Franz Ferdinand in 1914 and head of the

Black Hand, a secret society of Great Serbian nationalist officers, was executed in Salonika in June 1917. The Serbian government charged him with conspiracy to assassinate Regent Aleksandar. In fact, Apis was a victim of an artfully contrived plan which could have assured a separate peace between Serbia and Austria-Hungary. No negotiations with the Austrians were possible, however, as long as Apis and his closest associates remained at large. Moreover, Pašić and Regent Aleksandar both feared Apis's power in the army and his links with the South Slav nationalist circles outside Serbia. Therefore they had Apis arrested, arranged a rigged trial conducted by a Serbian military court in Salonika, and — after the defendant's condemnation — authorized the quick exectuion of Apis and some of his aides. Even earlier, after Apis's arrest in December 1916, Pašić's government set out to weed the officer corps of Apis's followers, members of the Black Hand. At least six of them were in Odessa in the command of the volunteer corps. They refused to cooperate with their superiors or to return to Corfu, withdrew from the Serbian army and the volunteer corps, and joined the Russian army. Among them were Lt. Col. Božin Simić, Vojislav Gojković, Aleksandar Srb, and Sima Cenić. CF. Jovanović *et al.*, *op. cit.*, p. 176-179.

63. Očak, *Jugosloveni u Oktobru*, p. 75.

64. Grulović, *op. cit.*, p. 172. The surviving text of the resolution issued by the convention does not mention any pacifist approach, and in fact does not include terror as a means of struggle for national liberation. It does, however, advocate neutrality in internal Russian affairs. Damjanović *et al.*, (eds.), *op. cit.*, pp. 66-69.

65. Grulović, *op. cit.*, p. 173.

66. *Ibid.*, pp. 246-247.

67. Očak, "O Jugoslavenima," *op. cit.*, p. 47.

68. *Ibid.*

69. *Ibid.*, pp. 50-54. In their proclamation made on the eve of defection to the Bolsheviks, the officers declared that their ideal, the unification of all Serbs, Croats, and Slovenes into a single and independent Yugoslav state, founded on the principles of democracy and national equality, had been betrayed by the Yugoslav bourgeoisie which was establishing a reactionary regime based on Serbian hegemony. They therefore chose to fight on the side of the Soviet army against the enemies of their own people and of all humanity. For the full text, see Damjanovic *et al.* (eds.), *op. cit.*, pp. 66-69.

70. Dr. Vukašin Marković (1874-1943), a Montenegrin from the Piperi clan of the Zeta valley, had lived in Russia since 1892, where he attended first a seminary and later medical and veterinary schools. A tempestuous personality and an eternal iconoclast, he joined the Bolsheviks in 1903. For more on his life see Dimitrije-Dimo Vujović, "Učešće dr Vukašina Markovića u oktobarskoj revoluciji i njeni odjeci u Crnoj Gori," *Prilozi za istoriju socijalizma* (Belgrade), V (1968), pp. 489-514

71. Arhiv Instituta za historiju radničkog pokreta Hrvatske (Zagreb), Sig. IX, k. 1, 1921, Grupa IX: Repartirci, Kr. redarstveno redateljstvo u Zagrebu (Broj: 1515 res. 1921, 12, XII. 1921).

72. Očak, *Jugosloveni u Oktobru*, pp. 111-117.

73. *Ibid.*, p. 195. For a detailed study of the South Slav soviets see Bogumil Hrabak, "Jugoslovenski sovjeti u Rusiji i Ukrajini, 1919-1921, godine," *Tokovi revolucije: Zbornik istorijskih radova* (Belgrade), II (1967), 3-55.

74. Dundić's origin and place of birth have been contested for years. The information given here, which seems reliable, is from an article in the *Voronezhskaia kommuna* of November 18, 1919. See Damjanovic *et al.*, (eds,), *op. cit.*, p. 347.

75. Viktor Engelsberger, "Kavkaška odisejada," in Turk *et al.*, (eds,), *op. cit.*, p. 474.

76. "Povratak u domovinu," *Naš list* (Tomsk), Aug. 7, 1919, p. 3.

77. Očak, "O Jugoslavenima," p. 42.

78. Fedor Šlajmer, "Ječa smrti," in Turk *et al.* (eds.) *op. cit*, pp. 455-460.

79. Bogumil Hrabak, "Komunistička partija (boljševika) Srba, Hrvata i Slovenaca," *Jugoslovenski istorijiski časopis* (Belgrade), 1969, Nos. 1-2, 7-27.

80. *Ibid.*, pp. 21-22. The extensive organizational undertakings of the activist returnees in Crotia-Slavonia and Bosnia have been carefully detailed by Ivan Očak. In an excellent recent study he reconstructed the exploits of Ćopić, Kovačević, and others from December 1918 to early spring 1919. This group created tens of illegal communist organizations in cooperation with the local leftists (an underground communist group functioned in Zagreb as early as December 1918) and financed the network with funds obtained in Council Hungary. It also established a liaison system and even a number of insurgent units (frequently referred to as "Red Guards"). The returnees' bold initiatives did not, however, culminate in a planned uprising. See Ivan Očak, "Povratnici iz Sovjetske Rusije u borbi za stvaranje komunističkih organizacija uoči prvog kongresa SRPJ(k)," *Historijski zbornik* (Zagreb), XXVII-XXVIII (1974-75), 1-26, esp. pp. 2-8. This article forms a chapter in Očak's *U borbi za ideje Oktobra: Jugoslavenski povratnici iz Sovjetske Rusije 1918-1921* (Zagreb, 1976), pp. 203-236. For an appraisal of the returnees' activities during and after the Unification Congress of the Communist Party of Yugoslavia, see *ibid.*, pp. 236-250, 287-372.

81. Tito's role in Russia was — in his own words — "extremely modest." He joined the South Slav Group of the RKP(b) in Omsk. Tito claims that this was in the winter of 1917-1918. As we have seen, the party group was founded only in the spring of 1918. During the same spring he claims that he fought against the Czechoslovak Whites: "The struggle lasted for four days, forces were unequal and they [the Czechoslovaks] completely defeated us. I fled to a nearby village. But a punitive Cossack unit came there looking for the former Red Guard fighters. I fled once again to a Kirghiz village sixty versts from Omsk. I started working there as a mechanic at a mill. I had already returned to Omsk in the winter of 1919-1920 when the Bolsheviks came there, and in August 1920 I returned to Yugoslavia. Well, that was my entire participation in the civil war." Josip Broz Tito, *Govori i članci*, XI (Zagreb, 1959), 449.

HUNGARIAN POWs IN RUSSIA DURING THE REVOLUTION AND CIVIL WAR

Peter Pastor

Although justifiable attention has been paid to the history of the Russian revolution and civil war by American Slavists, the examination of the considerable role played by POWs during that time has yet to be undertaken. Sole exception to this is the research done on the Czechoslovak Legion. Made up mainly of former Czech and Slovak soldiers of the Austro-Hungarian army, this force sided with the enemies of the Bolshevik Revolution. There is less known, however, about the Magyar POWs, many of whom sided with the Bolsheviks and contributed to their triumph.

Soviet literature describes the activities of the POWs on behalf of the communist revolution as having been motivated by the class solidarity of the worker-peasant soldiers liberated from concentration camps.[1] Hungarian historiography of the last thirty years does not deviate from this thesis, although a careful reading of the texts may lead to a different conclusion.[2] This reading supports the thesis of pre-World-War-II historians who stressed that most POWs were apolitical. They emphasized that camp conditions were a major cause for the support that the Bolsheviks received from the POWs.[3] Western historians still share this view.[4]

It has been estimated that during the war approximately 2,110,000 troops of the Austro-Hungarian army fell into Russian hands. Of these, 54,146 were officers. One quarter, or about 500,000 to 600,000 of the captured men, were

Magyars. This was a somewhat higher proportion than the number of Magyars who served in the Austro-Hungarian army (23%).[5]

The Russian government tried to divide the captives into camps according to their nationalities. Camps made up mostly of Slav, Italian or Rumanian POWs seemed to be better equipped than those that housed Austrian and Magyar POWs. While the Slavs were placed in camps in European Russia, Magyar, Austrian and German POWs were sent to the Urals, Siberia and Turkistan.[6] Most of the 300,000 who died came from these camps. Some observers have noted that the conditions to which the Magyars were subjected were among the worst of that time.[7]

The conscious effort of the tsarist government to differentiate among the nationalities, coupled with traditional national dislikes brought from their homelands, made nationalism the primary ideology of the camps.[8] These generally housed 2,000-10,000 inmates, although some camps had as many as 30,000 prisoners.[9]

The government began to use POW labor for non-military public work as early as September 1914. The increasing labor shortage soon forced the authorities to utilize cheap captive labor in most industries, including railway construction and mining. By 1916-1917 the POWs constituted 20-25 percent of the work force. Beginning in March 1915, POW labor was also used in agriculture.[10] Although many POWs looked upon labor as an escape from death, labor conditions in Siberia, Turkistan and on the Murmansk railway construction project were not much better than camp conditions. Until 1916 wages were calculated to match treasury costs for keeping a POW incarcerated. That year a government *ukaz* called for a fairer salary, with rights for the POWs to save that part of their earnings not paid to the treasury. This policy aimed at increasing productivity and reducing work stoppages.[11]

The February revolution overthrowing tsarism was welcomed by the POWs. Interwar historians claimed that most prisoners were not aware of the ideological aspects of the revolution. Instead, they hoped that the revolution would bring about a separate peace and a speedy return home.[12] Marxist historians, however, claim that the laboring POWs, numbering about a million and a half in February 1917, saw their own salvation in the Russian workers' struggle.[13]

During the first weeks of the revolution the situation in the camps was a reflection of the world outside. Discipline in the camps broke down and POWs were given freedom of movement. The consolidation of authority in the hands of the Provisional Government, however, led to a worsening of conditions for the POWs. The Provisional Government hoped that the revolution would lead to Russian victories at the front, and had no intentions of pursuing peace negotiations without Allied acquiescence. On August 12 (July 30) Premier Aleksandr Kerenskiy ordered punitive treatment for prisoners. Camps were to be supervised by Russian escapees from Austro-Hungarian camps. It was expected that their thirst for revenge would make them ruthless wardens. To break POW morale, officers were not allowed contact with enlisted men.[14] While these harsh measures were being applied to the Austro Germans and Magyars, Slav POWs were being allowed to move out of the camps and be housed among civilians.[15]

The organization of Czech and South Slav troops for use at the French front was approved by the government, but no attempt was made to raise troops among the Austrian or Magyar POWs with pro-Entente feelings.[16] This policy clearly furthered national animosities among the POWs as it indicated that the policies of the Provisional Government differed little from those of its predecessor. Another *ukaz*, reducing Austro-Magyar pay to treasury costs, made this even more apparent.[17]

Among the political parties, only the Bolsheviks appear to have heeded the plight of the POWs. Since their program called for immediate peace, they believed that better treatment of the Austro-Hungarian captives could increase the chances of a separate peace agreement. This conciliatory policy, coupled with Marxism – a familiar theme among socialist POWs – induced some of them, such as Béla Kun, to pay attention to Lenin and his followers. Others sympathised with the Bolsheviks because, like most Russians, they believed the Provisional Government's charge that Lenin and his entourage were German agents. These POWs hoped therefore, that Bolshevik victory would lead to a speedy separate peace between Russia and the Central Powers, and their prompt return home.[18]

With continuing defeats at the front, chaotic conditions returned to Russia. Camp inmates often found their camps guardless. This helped some prisoners strike out and try to make it home on their own. For most, however, camp guards meant protection from the hostile native population. For the sake of security POWs joined the Red Guards and were assigned to guard the camps.[19] Attitudes among POWs were thus clearly split along national lines. Because of their support of the war effort and of the Provisional Government, Czech, Slovak and South Slav POWs seemed assured of an exit from Russia. Austrian and Magyar POWs could only wish for another revolution – one that would bring to power a government seeking immediate peace with the Central Powers. The October revolution of the Bolsheviks seemed to assure the Austrians and Magyars of a speedy repatriation.

It is with this in mind that some Magyar POWs participated in the overthrow of the Provisional Government. Their motive was reported in the Hungarian dailies which faithfully covered the Russian events.[20] Among the first orders of the Bolshevik government was the cessation of hostilities and a call for peace. Despite the claim of official historians that this provided an opportunity for a world revolution, most Magyars saw in the Bolshevik victory merely a new chance to return home. The nonideological nature of pro-Bolshevik sentiment among the Magyars is borne out by the fact that by November 1918 only about 300 Magyars had joined the Bolshevik party.[21] Official party historians, making an argument for the ideological awareness of the POWs, however, speak of "thousands of communists." They claim that the Magyar POWs considered Russian conditions as similar to those in Hungary, and realized that only through a communist takeover could the situation improve.[22] Whatever the interpretations, they appear to have one underlying theme – the Magyars welcomed the Bolshevik victory.

Lenin and the Bolsheviks seem to have relied on the fact that both these ambitions existed among the POWs. They hoped that the prisoners' families could pressure that Austro-Hungarian and German governments to negotiate and conclude a speedy peace with the Russians. The Russian communists also hoped that the pro-Bolshevik prisoners would spread propaganda among their compatriots on the other side of the armistice lines.[23] They were expected to support revolution in their respective countries and to act as shock troops for the cause.[24]

With these aims in mind, the Bureau of Military Affairs of the All-Russian Executive Committee established the All-Russian Prisoner of War Bureau in January 1918. Its head was Ivan Ivanovich Ulyanov, who was also a member of the All-Russian Executive Committee.[25] The bureau's role was not merely to oversee camp administration, but also to finance communist publications for the camp inmates. The bureau also sent Bolshevik agitators to the camps.

In February the bureau began recruitment among the POWs for service in the newly formed Red Army. The army's first task was to stop further German advances into Russia following Leon Trotskiy's unilateral suspension of the Brest-Litovsk peace negotiations. The few hundred POW volunteers in the Red Army came to be known as "Internationalists."[26] Yet the first significant contributions of the Internationalists to the Bolshevik cause can be associated with internal, rather than external, defense. In July 1918, the Left-Social Revolutionaries, the coalition partners of the Bolsheviks, rose in armed rebellion in Moscow and in some other localities. The Internationalist units were instrumental in crushing the uprisings. In Moscow the battle plans against the Left-Social Revolutionaries were worked out by the Hungarian Tibor Szamuely who, along with Ferenc Jancsik, took part in the recapture of the buildings held by the Left-Social Revolutionaries. Summary executions of the vanquished were done on Szamuely's orders.[27]

With the signing of the Brest-Litovsk treaty on March 3, 1918, the Soviet government expected to use the POWs to spread revolution abroad. To this end, on March 24, 1918, the Hungarian Section of the Bolshevik Party was formed out of the Internationalists. Other sections were also formed during the same period. The umbrella organization, the Federation of Foreign Sections of the Russian Communist (Bolshevik) Party, came under the leadership of Béla Kun.[28]

The Hungarian Section initially had only four members – Béla Kun, Ernö Por, Endre Rudnyánszky and Tibor

Szamuely. Once organized, the section swung into feverish activity among the POWs. Under the editorial guidance of Rudnyánszky, a semiweekly, the *Szociális Forradalom,* was printed in 15,000 to 20,000 copies, and distributed in the camps. Agit-prop schools were set up and in 1918 several hundred POWs took the courses.[29] All these activities were conducted in direct contravention of the Brest-Litovsk treaty which prohibited Bolshevik activities among the POWs.[30]

The Soviet government was also behind the organization of the All-Russian Congress of Prisoners of War which met in Moscow between April 14 and 18. The major item on the congress agenda was the organization of propaganda work among the returnees. The conferees set up the International Socialist Revolutionary Organization of Foreign Workers and Peasants. On its executive committee were two Magyars: Ferenc Jancsik and Károly Vantus.

The Moscow congress was preceded by regional conferences, including ones in Siberia, where most of the Magyars were. On March 10 a meeting in Kansk seemed to indicate a split in the POW objective. There were delegates present who demanded that the POW organizations remain apolitical. These organizations were perceived as responsible for protecting the welfare of the POWs before repatriation. Others called for active involvement in Soviet affairs and for military assistance to the Bolshevik side if the need were to arise.[31] Marxist sources claim that those favoring active support were in an overwhelming majority.[32] Since the temper in most POW camps favored nonintervention in Russian affairs, it is possible to assume that this claim is erroneous or that the delegates were not representing the will of the captives.[33] Even Marxist sources indicate that only a few thousand POWs joined the Internationalists before June 1918.[34] This attests clearly to the fact that relatively few POWs favored active participation.

The lack of mass support for the activists may be the reason why some self-styled pro-Bolshevik "delegates" of the POWs chose Tomsk for the temporary headquarters of the executive committee for all the POW organizations in northern Siberia. Tomsk was the center of communist POW activities, which were led by Béla Kun, Ernö Seidler and Ferenc Münnich. The town soviet had POW members as well.[35] The executive committee clearly aimed to put forward the Bolshevik view in the name of all POWs.

The ideological commitment of even these few thousand may be questioned, however. A report by Maj. Albert Ritter, a staff officer, that was sent to the Austro-Hungarian ministry of war and the Hungarian minister president's office, indicates that the majority of the POWs joined the Internationalists out of opportunism.[36] Ritter left the Krasnoyarsk officer's camp in mid-February. In his memorandum he claimed that the morale of the enlisted men and officers was extremely low as a result of camp conditions. He claimed that prisoners who refused to join the Internationalists were often left without food. He cited conditions in Yekaterinburg, where POWs were forced to beg on the streets. As a result, he claimed the POWs were joining the Red Guards for the sake of survival, but with the intention of deserting at the first opportune moment. The promise that service would last only six months was further inducement to join the guards. Favored treatment of Internationalists, including the right to reside outside the camps, was also reported in *Szociális Forradalom.*[37]

The charge that material incentives rather than ideological fervor motivated the POWs to join the Internationalists has been rejected by Marxist historians. One exception to this was a recently published and withdrawn biography of Béla Kun. In this work, party historian György Borsányi claimed that enlistment into the Internationalist ranks was indeed for the sake of food and clothing. The dean of Hungarian party historians, Politburo member Dezsö Nemes, criticized Borsányi's work in a long essay in which he refuted Borsányi's view of recruitment.[38]

The outbreak of full-scale civil war and intervention by the Czechoslovak Legion in Siberia necessitated the organization of Red Army units in that part of Russia. Small international units were formed within the army, and many Magyar communists, including Kun, took an active part in leading Magyar volunteers. The Czechoslovak Legion's attack on apolitical Magyar POWs helped to increase the number of volunteers in the Bolshevik forces.[39] At Omsk, the Magyar communist leaders used an ethnic rather than an ideological approach to recruit volunteers. In an appeal published in

Szociális Forradalom, they described "blood baths by Czechoslovak *druzinas*" of Magyar and German prisoners. Defense of the Bolshevik revolution was therefore equated with the survival of Magyar captives.[40] In camps which subsequently came under the control of Adm. Aleksandr Kolchak's government, the POWs looked forward to the return of the Bolsheviks as liberators.[41] The White government, which considered itself an ally of the western powers, voided the Treaty of Brest-Litovsk and returned to treating the POWs as enemies and halting their repatriation.[42]

To the POWs the Bolsheviks still seemed to offer the best guarantee for their return home. This belief is supported by statistics. By the time of the November armistice about 300,000 prisoners had returned home, leaving some 150,000 to 200,000 in Russia.[43]

After the armistice repatriation slowed down, partly because of the civil war and partly because the Allied military leaders were against the exchange of Magyar and Russian POWs. They wanted to prevent the Bolshevik government from drafting repatriates into the Red Army.[44] Official exchange was thus replaced by stragglers who made it home on their own. These POWs became a part of the mass migration that took place in Russia, a still neglected aspect of the revolution.[45] Between November 1918 and July 1919, about 44,000 Magyar captives made their way home through Galicia.[46] It is possible that most were deserters from Red Army units, but some came home with the blessing of the Bolshevik government.

A November 1918 transport of prisoners included 200 communists, among them Béla Kun, Ferenc Münnich, József Rabinovits and Mátyás Rákosi. While still in Moscow, these men, leaders of the Hungarian section of the Russian Communist Party, had formed the Hungarian Communist Party on November 4. Their task was to recruit new adherents to overthrow the revolutionary government of Mihály Károlyi, who was seen by Lenin as the Hungarian Kerenskiy.[47]

Although party historians claim that Kun and the others built a Hungarian party of 30,000 to 40,000 members, western historians estimate that 4,000 to 7,000 was closer to the truth.[48] The greatest failure of the recruitment drive was the party's inability to enlist returned POWs. Although both party papers, *Vörös Újság* in Hungary and *Szociális Forradalom* in Russia, called on returning Red Army and Red Guard veterans to report to party headquarters,[49] few of them did so.

On March 21, 1919, the Hungarian communists, led by Kun, came to power in Hungary. This renewed the hopes of the POWs still in Russia. The Magyar communists in Russia, however, pleaded with the Magyar Internationalists not to desert the Red Army but to fight on in its ranks. It was argued that this would also help the Magyar cause.[50]

On May 12, Béla Kun, in the name of his government, ordered all Magyar workers and peasants in Russia and the Ukraine between the ages of 18 and 45 to join Hungary's ally, the Red Army.[51] This order meant that POWs could now be drafted into the Red Army. Between April and June an international brigade of 5,000 was organized in the Ukraine to come to the aid of the Hungarian Red Army, than at war with the Rumanians. A large part of the brigade was made up of Magyar volunteers,[52] who seem to have been recruited by appealing to their nationalist rather than working-class instincts. It was the Rumanians in general they were to fight rather than simply the "army of the Rumanian boyars."[53] They never had a chance to fight against the Magyar nation's enemy, however, for they were transported farther and farther away from the Hungarian frontier and used to fight against White armies in southern Russia.[54]

The military success of the Hungarian Soviet Republic over its Czechoslovak neighbor had an impact on the remaining Austro-Hungarian POWs in Siberia, who still numbered around 200,000.[55] The Czechoslovak legionaries, whose national animosity toward the Hungarians was reinforced by the high proportion of Magyars among the Internationalists, were aware of the humiliating defeats at home. The news gave the legionaries additional excuses for mistreating the Magyar POWs. The summary execution of sixteen prisoners in Krasnoyarsk on August 1, 1919, gained a special notoriety.

Although the Czechoslovaks claimed that those executed were Bolsheviks, only three of them in fact were. Five others were camp leaders of a Magyar nationalist organization that championed the defense of Hungary's integrity. Another of the victims was a Czech-German who had refused to join the legion earlier.[56] The background of the victims indicated whom the Czechoslovaks considered to be their enemies.

On August 2, 1919, while the civil war was still raging in Russia, the first Hungarian experiment with communism came to an inglorious end. The rise of White terror in Hungary and the need for troops in Russia meant that the POWs again could not return home. On August 6, the Revolutionary Committee of Hungary, made up of communist prisoners, was formed in Moscow. By calling themselves a goverment in exile,[57] they could claim jurisdiction over the POWs still in Russia.

In December 1919 Hungarian kangaroo courts brought in their first series of judgments against the former leaders of the Soviet Republic in Hungary. The Moscow government replied by making hostages of 1,000 POW officers – this group had generally been handled as a class enemy during the civil war – and threatening to shoot them if harm were to come to the condemned in Hungary. The Russian action saved the lives of dozens of revolutionaries in Hungary. It also led to a revival of negotiations between the Hungarian and Soviet governments. A bilateral agreement on POW exchange was signed on May 20, 1920, in Copenhagen. The exchange of hostages was the subject of a separate treaty, signed in Riga on July 28, 1921.[58] These agreements finally resolved the fate of the Magyar POWs still in Russia.

With the civil war coming to its end, it was hoped that the returning prisoners could work toward the overthrow of Adm. Miklós Horthy's regime. The exiled Magyar communist group in Russia, which by August 1920 included Béla Kun, had done its utmost to enroll new members into the Hungarian section of the Bolshevik Party. It was reported that 3,000 new comrades joined the movement.[59] Contrary to expectations, however, these men did not proceed to build a party once they returned. Like other former POWs, they concentrated on rebuilding their lives, shattered by their captivity in Russia.

During their captivity, the POWs had concentrated on survival, fueled only by the hope to return home. Most preferred to remain aloof from involvement in the Russian revolution. The motive of most of those who did take the Bolshevik side was self-preservation rather than revolutionary zeal. It is nevertheless impressive that an estimated 85,000 to 100,000 prisoners took arms on the Bolshevik side.[60] Reports indicate that the length of service of these reluctant revolutionaries was limited to days or weeks, and ended with desertion and attempts to return home. It is also estimated that about 30,000 never succeeded in reaching home, dying in combat or on the road to Hungary. Their attempts at self-preservation were costly, the risks great, implying that the alternative was felt to be even worse.

The participation of Magyar Internationalists in the Russian revolution and civil war has been judged by party historians not to have provided decisive support for the Bolshevik cause.[61] Yet by being unable and unwilling to side with the Whites, Magyar POWs may have tipped the balance in favor of the Bolsheviks, and so have contributed to their final victory.

NOTES

1. M.A. Birman (ed.), *Internatsionalisty v boyakh za vlast' Sovetov* (Moscow, 1965), p. 12; V.A. Danilov, *Internatsionalisty na Urale i v Sibiri* (Sverdlovsk, 1972), pp. 5-6; V.S. Getman and O.I. Kurochinka (eds.), *Foreign Comrades in the October Revolution* (Moscow, 1967), p. 10. See also articles by Soviet historians in the special edition of *Hadtörténelmi Közlemények*, XXVI, No. 3 (1977), 451, 478, 496, and in Zsigmond Pál Pach and A.P. Okladnikov, *Magyar Internacionalisták Szibériában és a Távol-Keleten* [Hungarian Internationalists in Siberia and in the Far East] (Budapest, 1978), pp. 11, 43, 108, 143.

2. A.A. Zhilak, "Velikiy Oktyabr i revolutsionnogo dvizheniye voyennoplennikh vengrov v Rossii (1917-1918 gg.)," in Birman (ed.), *op. cit.*, p. 120; György Milei, "A magyar hadifoglyok forradalmi szervezkedése Szoviet-Oroszország területén (1917 november - 1918 március)" [The Revolutionary Organization of the Hungarian Prisoners of War in Soviet Russia], in Zsuzsa L. Nagy and András Zsilák (eds.), *Ötven év, A Nagy Október és a magyarországi forradalmak* [Fifty Years, The Great October and the Revolutions in Hungary] (Budapest, 1967), p. 217.

3. B. Baja and I. Lukinich (eds.), *Hadifogoly Magyarok Története* [History of the Hungarian Prisoners of War] (Budapest, 1930), II, 244; Jenö Lévai, *Fehér cártól — vörös Leninig: Magyar hadifoglyok szerepe a nagy orosz átalakulásban* [From White Tsar - to Red Lenin: The Role of the Hungarian Prisoners of War in the Great Metamorphosis] (Budapest, 193?), 7. füzet, p. 18.

4. Iván Völgyes, "Hungarian Prisoners of War in Russia, 1916-1919," *Cahiers du monde russe et soviétique*, No. 1-2 (1973), p. 59; Rudolf L. Tökés, *Béla Kun and the Hungarian Soviet Republic: The Origins and Role of the Communist Party of Hungary in the Revolutions of 1918-1919* (New York,

1967), p. 50.

5. Antal Józsa, *Háboru, hadifogság, forradalom: Magyar internacionalista hadifoglyok az 1917-es oroszországi forradalmakban* [War, Captivity, Revolution: Hungarian Internationalist Prisoners of War in the Russian Revolutions of 1917] (Budapest, 1970), p. 101.

6. Az MSzMP Kozponti Bizottságának Párttörténeti Intézete, *Tanuságtevök* [Witnesses] (Budapest, 1977), p. 10.

7. Elsa Brändström, *Among Prisoners of War in Russia and Siberia* (London, 1929), p. 225.

8. Józsa, *op. cit.*, p. 108.

9. Brändstöm, *op. cit.*, p. 68.

10. A Klevanskiy, "Voyennoplennye tsentral'nykh derzhav v tsarskoyi i revolyutsionnoyi Rossii," in Birman (ed.), *op. cit.*, p. 24; Thomas Fallows, "Politics and the War Effort in Russia: The Union of Zemstvos and the Organization of Food Supply, 1914-1916," *Slavic Review,* XXXVII, No. 1 (1978), 79; György Milei, "A magyar internacionalisták Szovjet-Oroszországért" [Hungarian Internationalists for Soviet Russia], in János Jemnitz *et al.*, *El a kezeket Szovjet-Oroszországtól!* [Hands off Soviet Russia!] (Budapest, 1979), p. 168.

11. Józsa, *op. cit.*, p. 270.

12. Baja and Lukinich (eds.), *op. cit.*, II, 244.

13. Józsa, *op. cit.*, p. 191.

14. *Ibid.*, p. 258.

15. *Ibid.*, p. 260.

16. Victor M. Fic, *Revolutionary War for Independence and the Russian Question* (New Delhi, 1977), pp. 72-77.

17. Józsa, *op. cit.*, p. 277.

18. Iván Völgyes, "Communism Comes to Hungary: An Examination of Some Causes Leading to the Establishment of the Hungarian Soviet Republic" (Ph.D. thesis, American University, 1968), p. 138; G.D. Obichkin and H. Vass *et al.* (eds.), *A magyar internacionalisták a Nagy Októberi Forradalomban és a polgárháboruban: Dokumentumgyüjtemény* [Hungarian Internationalists in the Great Socialist Revolution of October and the Civil War: Documentary Collection] (Budapest, 1967), p. 69; Lévai, *op. cit.*, 4. füzet, p. 16.

19. Józsa, *op. cit.*, p. 300.

20. László Remete (ed.), *Igy látták a kortársak* [How It Was Seen by Contemporaries] (Budapest, 1977), p. 135.

21. Obichkin and Vass, *op. cit.*, p. 48; Völgyes, "Hungarian Prisoners of War . . .," pp. 67, 73.

22. György Milei, *A Komunisták Magyarországi Pártjának megalakításáról* [About the Founding of the Communist Party of Hungary] (Budapest, 1962), pp. 6-15.

23. Milei, "A magyar hadifoglyok . . .," p. 247.

24. György Szamuely, "A Kommunisták Magyarországi Pártjának elökészítése" [Preparations for a Hungarian Communist Party], *Sarló és Kalapács* (Moscow), X, No. 4 (1932), 50; László Réti, *Lenin és a magyar munkásmozgalom* (Lenin and the Hungarian Labor Movement] (Budapest, 1970), pp. 61-62.

25. Birman, *op. cit.*, p. 11; Józsa, *op. cit.*, p. 105.

26. MSzMP, *op. cit.*, p. 17.

27. Miklós Zalka, *Szamuely* (Budapest, 1979), p. 41.

28. Branko Lazitch and Milorad Drachkovitch, *Lenin and the Comintern* (Stanford, Calif., 1974), I, 44; Birman, *op. cit.*, p. 14.

29. Obichkin and Vass, *op. cit.*, p. 22.

30. John W. Wheeler-Bennett, *Brest-Litovsk the Forgotten Peace* (New York, 1971), p. 405.

31. MSzMP, *op. cit.*, p. 178.

32. M. Csugnov, "Magyar internacionalisták a szovjetek hatalmáért a tomszki kormányzóságban" [Hungarian Internationalists for Soviet Power in Tomsk Gubernium], *Hadtörténelmi Közlemények*, XXIII, No. 3, (1977), 497, 504; Danilov, *op. cit.*, p. 45; MSzMP, *op. cit.*, p. 169.

33. Lévai, *op. cit.*, 5. füzet p. 7.

34. Milei, "A magyar internacionalisták," p. 178.

35. Getman and Kurochkina, *op. cit.*, p. 134.

36. : K.u.K. Kriegsministerium Abt. 10/Kgf No. 54439 von 1918 Wien, am 16 August 1918, in Magyar Országos Levéltár [Hungarian National Archives], M.E. 916/Kl 8140 res.

37. *Szociális Forradalom,* April 7 (March 25) 1918.

38. György Borsányi, *Kun Béla* (Budapest, 1979), p. 62; Dezsö Nemes, "Észrevételek Borsányi György: *Kun Béla politikai életrajza* cimü munkájához" [Observations on György Borsányi's *The Political Biography of Béla Kun*], *Párttörténeti Közlemények*, No. 3, 1979, p. 38.

39. Brändström, *op. cit.*, p. 256.

40. Hadtörténelmi Intézet (ed.), *Ligeti Károly válogatott irásai* [The Selected Writings of Károly Ligeti] (Budapest, 1957), pp. 142-144.

41. Brändström, *op. cit.*, p. 249.

42. *Ibid.*, p. 272; Lévai, *op. cit.*, 4, fužet, p. 16.

43. MSzMP, *op. cit.*, p. 22, p. 52.

44. Peter Pastor, *Hungary between Wilson and Lenin: The Hungarian Revolution of 1918-1919 and the Big Three* (Boulder, Colo., 1976), p. 116.

45. John L.H. Keep, *The Russian Revolution* (New York, 1976), p. 261.

46. Baja and Lukinich, *op. cit.*, II, 555.

47. Szamuely, *op. cit.*, p. 52; László Réti (ed.) *Lenin Magyarországról* [Lenin on Hungary] (Budapest, 1974), pp. 82-83.

48. Milei, *A KMP megalakulásáról...*, p. 76; Tökés, *Béla Kun...*, p. 109.

49. *Vörös Újság,* Dec. 21, 1918; *Szociális Forradalom,* Jan. 15, 1919; Tökes, *Bela Kun..., p. 105.*

50. *Szocialis Forradalom,* March 28, 1919.

51. Obichkin and Vass (eds.), *Vengerskiye internatsionalisty v oktyabr'-skoyi revolyutssi i grazhdanskoy voyne v SSSR: Sbornik dokumentov* (Moscow, 1968) II, 60.

52. MSzMP, *op. cit.*, p. 34; Antal Józsa and György Milei, *A rendithetetlen százezer* [The Tenacious Hundred Thousand] (Budapest, 1968), pp. 171-168.

53. Author's interview with a POW veteran, Budapest, June 1978.

54. V.I. Ananyev, "Lukács József magyar internacionalista" [József Lukács, Hungarian Internationalist], *Hadtörténelmi Közlemények,* XXIII, No. 3 (1970), 489.

55. Baja and Lukinich, *op. cit.*, II, 408; it is estimated that in March 1920

there were still 118, 646 Magyar POWs in Siberia and in the Far East. See, T.M. Islamov and Antal Józsa. ''A magyar internacionalisták történetének forráskutatása és historiográfiájának néhány kérdése'' [Some Questions about the Sources and Historiography of the History of the Hungarian Internationalists], in Pach and Okladnikov, *op. cit.*, p. 323.

56. Lévai, *op. cit.*, 6. füzet, pp. 10-11; Jenö Györkei, *Magyarok az Amur partján* [Hungarians along the Amur] (Budapest, 1967), p. 65.

57. Obichkin and Vass, *op. cit.*, pp. 315-316.

58. Baja and Lukinich, *op. cit.*, II, 564.

59. *Vörös Újság* (Moscow), Oct. 17, 1920.

60. Obichkin and Vass, *op. cit.*, pp. 48-49.

61. MSzMP, *op. cit.*, p. 49.

THE LIFE OF PRISONERS OF WAR IN RUSSIA, 1914-1921

Gerald H. Davis

Of all the peoples uprooted and flung into hostile lands by war, few have endured greater frustration, confusion, or agony than the German and Austro-Hungarian soldiers and civilians who became prisoners of the Russians during World War I. There were over two million of them, of which 80 to 85 percent were Austro-Hungarian soldiers of various nationality groups. Eight percent or less were Reich-German and two to three percent Turkish and Bulgarian soldiers. The rest were civilians.[1]

Captivity shielded the prisoners of war from combat but not from some of its consequences. The captives shared fully the hardships war brought to every Russian village, town and city, to virtually every Russian family. They shared the fruits of disorder in the all-pervasive bureaucracy, and every peril and discomfort generated by weakened facilities of transportation, production, and finance. They lived, suffered, and many thousands died in alien ghettos concentrated in hastily improvised camps, or as foreign lodgers in Russian towns, villages and households. When the tsarist government collapsed, the POWs, being wards of that government, were utterly helpless. When revolution swept across Russia, it pervaded the prisoners' lives. When civil war divided and confused the Russian people, it drew Russia's captives into its many conflicts. When foreign states intervened, prisoners of war became engaged in many capacities on every side. By the time peace came to Russia in 1920 and repatriation of the last captives became feasible, time and events had so altered the prisoners and their homelands that simple postwar adjustment was no longer possible. Most of them had to begin new lives.

The prisoners bore the marks of confinement in Russia throughout their lives. They also left the traces of their labor on the Russian land in return, and their ideas, their knowledge, their corpses, and not a few of their children remained with the Russian people. Several thousand of them remained themselves to make careers on farms, in factories, or in political activity begun during their captivity.

The civilian prisoners were businessmen, immigrant or seasonal workers, persons with family connections or property in Russia, vacationers, other travelers, and their dependents. Russian authorities detained some 200,000 Germans and Austro-Hungarians of various nationalities in this category. The reasons for detainment were not always clear. Most of the men were subject to military service at home, while others lived uncomfortably near the war zone, or behaved suspiciously, or were perhaps thought to be useful for future bargaining with the enemy. Immediately after war began in 1914 such alien civilians were registered and, as arrangements were made, assigned new locations where they were required to report frequently to police authorities. Slavic aliens were often allowed to remain in the larger cities of western Russia, but non-Slavs were transported to remote towns or villages.[2]

Strictly speaking, these interned civilians were exiles rather than prisoners. They rented private quarters in the homes of Russian residents or in hotels, and moved about freely within the confines of their assigned towns or villages. Those who had families in Russia were allowed to bring them to the villages and to live together with them at their own expense. Some who came without families married in the villages and established new homes. Many had marketable professional skills, and they sometimes prospered in captivity and became valued members of their new communities. While those with means could live in comfort, others had to find work or seek aid from charitable agencies or their home governments.

Those who failed in this lived or perished in desperate circumstances. United States diplomatic and consular officials reported that conditions among the less fortunate civilian prisoners were much worse than among their military counterparts, and that relief was more difficult to arrange because of the decentralized nature of the system.[3]

The home government of each military POW routinely received notification of his capture and the detaining power supposedly made an effort to sustain him with food, shelter and clothing. Furthermore, relief agencies at home dispatched packages of food and clothing whenever possible, and by reciprocal agreement these were allowed to pass through the postal system without cost. Officer prisoners were supposed to receive regular salaries from the captor. Except in unusual cases, civilians had none of this. They usually had to find ways to establish contact with their home governments and to prove that they were loyal subjects being held against their will in Russia, that they needed and deserved financial aid, or that they had financial resources at home which might somehow be made available to them. All of this could be extremely difficult to negotiate from a village located a hundred or more miles from a railroad station, especially since Russia had no direct communications with enemy governments. Everything depended on the cooperation and efficiency of Russian administrative officials, financial and postal facilities, and the effectiveness of neutral diplomatic and consular establishments and charitable societies. Unfortunately, few of these agencies earned a reputation for efficiency during the early part of the war.

Military prisoners, unlike civilians, continued to be captured until December 1917. Between 160,000 and 180,000 German soldiers surrendered during this period. About twelve times that number of Austro-Hungarians fell into Russian hands: estimates vary from 1,500,000 to 2,300,000. Although the Russians never took great numbers of German soldiers in a single battle, probably most of the Austro-Hungarian prisoners were taken in great "catches" in Galicia in the autumn of 1914, at Przemysl in 1915, and in the Carpathians in 1916.[4]

The Russians usually handled the small trickle of captives taken during quieter periods in an orderly fashion as they brought them from the front lines to interrogation places and then to the rear. But the large-scale operations strained Russian resources at the front and disordered the rear. When hundreds of thousands of weary, bewildered, wounded, or disaffected POWs were suddenly fed into the detainment system it became clogged and chaotic. The Russians could neither provide for them in the combat zone nor transport them promptly to the rear. Many thousands died in the aftermath of combat from their wounds or the stresses encountered during their removal. Those who survived often endured great suffering en route to the interior of Russia.[5]

Russian behavior toward prisoners was as humane in intention as that of their enemies. They ordinarily treated wounded prisoners the same as their own wounded. Where possible they moved them to the rear in trains to military hospitals; otherwise they were left in field hospitals. But there were seldom enough trains or doctors, nurses, beds, bandages, or medication at the times they were needed most. There were cases of cruel treatment of wounded POWs, and Germans and Austrians often complained of the low level of sanitation even in the better hospitals, and of the high rate of thievery among hospital personnel. But some accounts commend the Russians for treating prisoners as well as their own soldiers.[6]

Unwounded or walking wounded prisoners usually had to march to the rear, sometimes for days and weeks, until they could make connections with rail transportation. POW columns seldom had field kitchens. Instead, each prisoner was supposed to be paid twenty-five kopecks a day to purchase food along the route. But they did not always get their money, and when they did, they often found food prices inflated because civilian refugees, who also clogged the roads during and after the great battles, also wanted to buy food.

When they reached a railroad station that was not already filled with men, they were packed into modified boxcars called *teplushki.* Officers were sometimes separated from enlisted men and transported in third- or fourth-class passenger coaches, although it was not unusual for them to be transported in *teplushki* as well. Their first destinations were usually hospitals or assembly camps at or near Petrograd, Moscow or Kiev. Here they waited for unpredictable lengths of time until they could be transported to eastern Russia, Siberia or Turkestan.

Although Slavic-speaking prisoners were often allowed to remain in the west or to settle in privileged locations such as the propaganda camp at Tyumen,[7] most prisoners who survived the first period of captivity found themselves being transported rather too frequently about the vast Russian land – usually just ahead of their mail.[8] Although eager to get out of the overcrowded assembly camps, they were rightfully apprehensive about their future places of confinement.

The journey to camps on the White Sea, the River Kama, the Middle and Lower Volga, or other areas of European Russia could take many days and taught the prisoners what they all had to learn: to wait while distant officials decided what to do with them. The journey into Turkestan or Siberia could last for weeks or even months. Thirty or forty men were packed into each *teplushka* with two rows of unpadded wooded bunks along the sides, an iron stove in the middle, and a latrine bucket at one end. Between stations the doors were rolled shut and often locked from the outside. Prisoners in transit frequently spent days at a time waiting on railroad sidings, sometimes without food or other necessities. By the time they reached their destinations, the POWs were exhausted, filthy, tormented by insects and other vermin, diseased, and stripped of personal belongings by unscrupulous railway personnel, guards and fellow prisoners. Not a few of them died en route, and if the ground was frozen too hard to bury them, the corpses were left beside the railroad tracks for others to look after in a milder season.[9]

Prison camps in the classic mold, with barbed wire, guard towers, and wooden barracks, housed hundreds of thousands of men. In European Russia the camps held 2,000 to 10,000 men apiece. In the Urals and Siberia larger camps were the rule, some of them holding as many as 35,000 prisoners.[10] But there were never enough of these camps, and several hundred thousand captives were housed in every sort of improvised quarters, many not designed to accommodate permanent residents at all. Prisoners were kept in former army camps, logging camps, migratory-farmhand camps, in abandoned factories, schools, churches, theaters, circus buildings, and in jails. Since Russia had prohibited the manufacture of alcoholic beverages, many breweries and distilleries were available for conversion into prisons. It was also very common for military as well as civilian prisoners to live in private households, especially farms.[11]

Even though Siberia produced large crops during the war years, food was often scarce in the camps, especially after a rapid influx of inmates. Water sources in improvised camps were inadequate, and fuel stocks in areas suddenly flooded by thousands of captives fell perilously low. Lighting was almost never satisfactory, a matter of great concern where winter daylight lasts only a few hours. Soldiers who surrendered during late summer or autumn campaigns had to meet the fierce winter without heavy clothing, because the Russians were themselves short of winter apparel and issued none to POWs. Low standards and lax enforcement of sanitary regulations rendered these difficulties hazardous, with predictable results. Typhus, typhoid fever and other epidemics broke out in many camps and threatened to spread throughout the countryside. Thousands of prisoners perished in the winter of 1914-1915 and again the following year, especially at Omsk, Totskoye, Novonikolayevsk (now Novosibirsk), and Sretensk.[12]

Sretensk was especially notorious. Here on a remote spur of the Trans-Siberian railway east of Lake Baikal an evacuated summer camp was suddenly reactivated in late November 1915, when between 9,000 and 11,000 prisoners arrived without any equipment or preparation. The camp was actually in two parts. Over 6,000 men were crowded into military barracks in the town, where a much smaller peacetime military unit had been stationed. The rest were assigned to the summer barracks on a promontory across the Shilka river where immigrants were accustomed to wait for travel connections during the season when the Amur river steamers were in operation. These drafty wooden buildings were as "indescribably filthy" as the men who were put there with "ridiculously inadequate" facilities for washing. The only source of water was the steep-banked river which was, of course, frozen over. The latrines were unspeakable. The only hospital building burned down shortly after the inmates arrived, and of the rooms fitted out as an infirmary only one was heated. Patients were so crowded that they touched one another and only about a third of them had beds. Two POW doctors with some "primitive" hospital supplies were unable to cope with the typhus epidemic which lasted through January 1916 and killed an appalling proportion of the camp population.[13]

Russia, Germany and Austria-Hungary had some common understanding about the treatment of prisoners of war, since all three of them had ratified the 1907 Hague convention on the laws and customs of land warfare. Chapter II of that convention set general guidelines for the treatment of prisoners of war. They were considered to be in the power of the detaining government rather than the individuals or corps which captured them. They were to be treated humanely and allowed to retain private property except arms, horses, and military papers. They could be interned in a restricted area such as a town, fortress or camp, but not closely confined except in emergencies. Their labor could be employed under conditions to be discussed later, and the captor government was responsible for their maintenance. Prisoners were subject to the laws of the captor's army and could be punished for breach of regulations. They were bound to give their true name and rank when asked, but the convention is silent on other information they might willingly or unwillingly supply. Prisoners of war could be released on parole. An office was to be established by each government to provide specific information, and inquiries and the prisoners' own mail were to be transmitted postage-free. Relief societies could work with prisoners under authorization of the captor government, and gifts from abroad were to be admitted duty-free. Officers were to be paid the same as officers of equivalent rank in the captor's army, with the home government ultimately refunding this cost. Prisoners were to enjoy freedom of religion, the right to make wills, and to have death certificates issued in accordance with the captor's law. After the war prisoners were to be repatriated promptly.[14]

The Hague principles were not adequate guides for detailed administration, a fact that led to the more thorough Geneva convention of 1929. The status of communication between enemies, however, limited the chances for further positive agreement during World War I. Russia communicated with Germany and Austria-Hungary through neutral powers or through quasi-official representatives on neutral territory. By such indirect means procedures for repatriation of disabled prisoners or their internment in neutral countries were agreed upon at a series of conferences in Copenhagen, Stockholm and Kristiania (Oslo) in 1916 and 1917. Neutral channels were also used to obtain reports on conditions and treatment of POWs in enemy territory.[15]

During the period of American neutrality, the United States represented Austro-Hungarian and German interests in Russia, while Spain did the same for Russia in the central empires. This involved a number of tasks for which the United States officials in Russia were not well prepared. Civilian internees flooded the embassy and consulates, seeking intervention and financial support. Foreign service officials found themselves heavily involved in forwarding mail, lending money provided by the German and Austrian governments and various charitable agencies, arranging transportation and travel permits, checking on the property of aliens, locating temporary housing, and meeting payrolls on behalf of foreign employers.[16] They did as well as they could – especially since many United States officials spoke little Russian or German – but they fell hopelessly behind in this work, and became involved in continuous disputes with the Russian authorities and misunderstandings with the Central Powers.

Inspecting the camps throughout the vast Russian land was a formidable and nearly thankless task which required the knowledge of a soldier, physician and sanitary engineer, the skills of a seasoned diplomat, and the stamina of an athlete. The staff, however, consisted mostly of junior officers from the embassy and consulates, and a few Red Cross specialists brought in from China or the United States. When they reported satisfactory camp conditions, the Germans and Austrians accused them of ignoring reality. When they reported bad conditions, the Russians became offended and restricted their work.[17] Germany and Austria-Hungary urged the United States to demand corrections, but the Americans regarded themselves as messengers, not as the Central Powers' champions.[18] To Germany and Austria-Hungary this was a hostile attitude. When the inspectors did recommend improvements, the Russians demanded reciprocation from Berlin and Vienna. But United States officials in those cities were not in charge of Russian interests and found it difficult to work with the Spanish who did represent Russia there. The Americans were unwilling to vouch for the reporting of Spanish prison camp inspectors in Germany and Austria.[19]

The Americans were eager to provide relief for prisoners in Russia, and tended to consider the tasks of inspecting camps, delivering relief supplies, and administering emergency medication as closely related activities. But the Russians regarded them as distinct and separate types of work, each of which would require separate authorizations. As a result, camp inspectors or the officials who processed their reports found that they had to strike a fine balance between excessive truthfulness and suppression of evidence. When inspection reports were unfavorable, difficulties seemed to occur in deliveries of relief supplies, and hospital administrators became more sensitive about American Red Cross medical teams giving inoculations and sanitation training in their districts. John K. Caldwell, the American consul general in Vladivostok, expressed the problem in terms of territory. He reported: "By avoiding any protests to the officials of the other parts of Siberia, I will probably be able to supply money to the prisoners and assist them in various ways during the war."[20]

Dr. William Warfield, an American Red Cross officer on assignment as a special Department of State representative, was not so cautious as Caldwell. Between September 1915 and January 1916 Warfield inspected a number of camps in eastern Siberia and filed reports which exposed horrifying conditions, including the typhus epidemic at Sretensk. In vain he criticized Russian refusal to improve nutrition and sanitation in these camps. He hounded the authorities to issue permits to allow an American Red Cross medical team, already in Siberia, to work with him in the infected camps. In January 1916 two of his telegrams stirred up a great deal of excitment. On the twelfth he wired Ambassador George Thomas Marye that the Germans fed prisoners better than the Russians did. Marye delivered this message to the Russian Foreign Office with an appeal for improvement. Warfield suspected that the Russians might interfere with his second telegram, so he sent his assistant to Harbin, whence he cabled it to Secretary of State Robert Lansing with a copy to Petrograd on January 17. The message vividly described the crisis at Sretensk and requested the United States to "bring pressure on the highest imperial authorities" to permit the entry of the Red Cross team "without formality or delay." Marye sent a copy of this one to Foreign Minister Sergei Sazonov with a supporting memorandum.[21]

The Russian Foreign Office was sympathetic, but the military reacted furiously and forced Sazonov to demand Warfield's recall.[22] The Department of State did recall Warfield and reprimanded Marye, who subsequently resigned. This episode brought all other official United States programs on behalf of prisoners of war to a halt, including regular inspection work and a special Red Cross mission which had grown out of a personal agreement between President Woodrow Wilson and Tsar Nicholas II.[23] For several months there was only one authorized American official inspecting the camps. The new United States ambassador, David R. Francis, managed to restore and even expand the inspection program, largely through the "discreet reporting" ordered by Washington.[24] Even so, Russian bureaucratic dissimulation frustrated other American relief activities.

The fate of one project is indicative. The good offices of the United States were enlisted to arrange distribution of a large shipment of clothing, shoes and other personal necessities to German and Austro-Hungarian prisoners in eastern Siberia. These supplies had been collected, and their shipment funded, by German residents in China (with help from the German government) through Elsa von Hanneken's *Hilfsaktion* organization in Tientsin. After much difficulty a similar shipment had been partially delivered the previous year.[25] When Ambassador Francis formally requested permission to import the shipment into Russia duty-free in the spring of 1916, he was confident that delivery would take place well before the following winter. He received no reply, however, and since a second request was still unacknowledged in September when the materials began arriving at the frontier, he became concerned. Francis went in person to the Foreign Office, where he learned that no action could be taken before the approval of the military authorities had been obtained. At length general permission was granted and Francis requested authorization for specific shipments, but again two applicantions went unheeded before he secured a reply. He was then advised to take up the matter with the Russian Red Cross. He did so, only to learn that the Red Cross could authorize shipments across the Rumanian and Swedish frontiers but not across the Chinese border. It took some time to discover which official was responsible for the Chinese frontier, but after finally obtaining consent from him, Francis learned that the consulate in Vladivostok had gathered the wrong data on the supplies. While the correct information was being collected, the ambassador appealed to the minister of ways and communications for railroad cars to transport the goods. By then it was mid-November. A week later Francis discovered that the army general staff had not received proper notification of the shipment, and the project had to wait again for approval. November and December passed and no spare railroad cars could be found. Francis tried another approach. He went to the minister of finance and said he understood that the Chinese Eastern Railway was under the minister's control. "After investigation," the minister acknowledged that Francis was indeed correct. However, his control was only nominal since most of the cars had been taken over by the military authorities, he told Francis. He referred the ambassador back to the minister of ways and communications.

Despairing of any hope for the project, Francis recommended that the supplies be shipped from Vladivostok to Sweden, turned over to the Swedish Red Cross, and transported thence to Russia. The State Department overruled him, and the supplies remained undelivered when the United States severed diplomatic relations with Germany and Austria-Hungary, and ceased to represent their interests in Russia. The supplies were then turned over to the Swedish Red Cross and eventually delivered according to Francis's plan, but too late, of course, for the winter of 1916-1917.[26]

Despite this sort of difficulty POWs' conditions in general had improved somewhat by the end of 1916, although many suffered privation in the great wave of overcrowding that followed the Brusilov offensive.[27] More relief supplies came into the country, especially through the Swedish and Danish Red Cross organizations, and Russian distribution procedures became more dependable, despite the apparent practice of assigning less competent officers to war prison administration. Besides, large numbers of the most burdensome prisoners – the wounded, crippled, and sick – had died.

Able-bodied prisoners of war, excepting officers, were expected to work, but some time passed before large-scale arrangements could be made. By the end of 1915 plans to exploit POW labor began to take shape, and by October 1916 an estimated 1,500,000 men were employed. Although their labor did not begin to compensate for the some 15,000,000 Russian subjects who had been called from civilian pursuits into the armed services by mid-1917, working prisoners of war did have an impact on specific areas of the economy.[28]

The Hague convention permitted the captor to use POW labor according to rank and aptitude, "officers excepted," providing the work should not be excessive nor connected with war operations. Prisoners could work in public service, for private persons, or on their own. Reimbursement for state employment was to be at rates paid the captor's soldiers for similar work. Labor for private persons or other branches of public service was to be arranged in agreement with the military authorities. Wages should go toward improving the prisoners' position, with the balance paid them upon release "after deducting the cost of their maintenance."[29]

The Russian military authorities apparently ignored the Hague convention mandate that such work "shall have no connection with the operations of the war." Late in 1916 they were employing between 440,000 and 500,000, about one-third of all working prisoners, on constructing roads and fortifications within zones of military operations. Over half of all military prisoners of war were in provinces adjoining the front area.[30] Their work released large numbers of Russian service troops for combat, which may have influenced the outcome of any number of engagements. On the other hand, the Central Powers were doing the same thing, and in most engagements they – especially the

Germans – captured more prisoners than the Russians did.

Another 600,000 to 800,000 POWs were put to work on farms in European Russia, and 200,000 to 300,000 in Siberia and Turkestan. In some regions they replaced most of the agricultural workers conscripted into the army. At first they were simply placed in villages under police supervision. Here they were offered to peasant landholders who selected workers very much as they might choose other livestock – for their health and strength. More systematic methods were introduced in due course. Local zemstvos were put in charge of prisoners assigned to their territories, subject to control by the provincial governor and the army. The zemstvos either employed the prisoners on roads and other public facilities, or allocated them to farms on a contract basis.

About two-thirds of the farming prisoners went to the politically influential large estates, which were willing and able to complete the required paperwork, and which had difficulty replacing workers conscripted into the army. The financial incentive for employers was significant, as free farm labor in wartime was expensive. For example, Russian field workers in Taurida province received four rubles a day, while prisoners could be employed for eight rubles a month. Smallholding peasants got a lesser share of the captive labor and they complained bitterly about it. Directors of large estates countered with the argument that peasant families did not need many prisoners, as they could through family loyalties draw in women, children, and old or partially disabled men.[31]

Prisoners on farms had to work hard but usually had plenty of food and on small farms were often treated as family members. Those with agricultural backgrounds were often highly regarded and well treated in the villages. Germans were especially prized. Not a few such men found new careers and wives there, or temporarily replaced husbands who were away with the Russian army.[32]

Industrial production and construction projects occupied the other one-third of the POWs by late 1916. At mid-year 1917 prisoners of war made up about 30 percent of the foundry workers, 60 percent of the iron ore miners, 28 percent of the peat extracters in Russia. This amounted to 27 percent of the total industrial work force of the

Moscow-Tula, Donets, Urals, and western Siberian mining districts.[33] At first the Russians enlisted them rather indiscriminately in large construction projects where they could be herded into easily guarded gangs of unskilled workers. They built irrigation facilities in Samara and Saratov provinces, and in Siberia and elsewhere they supplied maintenance crews to repair roads, railroads and canals. In Omsk they put up the Trans-Siberian Railway's new office building, the tallest in Siberia. They helped construct the Black Sea and Murmansk railroads. It was the great loss of life on the Murmansk railroad that brought about a series of reprisals and counterreprisals between Germany and Russia in 1915.[34]

As Russian administrative machinery found ways to identify industrial needs and to locate the labor to meet them, trained craftsmen were put to work. They produced leather goods, metal products, electrical equipment, paper, textiles, small implements, large machines, and munitions.[35] During the civil war some isolated areas became dependent on prisoners of war for essential production. In 1919 POWs made up 50 to 80 percent of the skilled workers in Adm. Aleksandr Kolchak's Siberia. A similar condition existed in Turkestan.[36]

Many camps developed their own workshops, which sometimes became substantial factories. In Siberia their growth was stimulated by Kolchak's government contracts for supplies of military equipment, hospital implements, brushes, saddles, textiles, cigarettes, and alcholic beverages. POW businessmen organized themselves into makeshift corporations, sold stock, opened camp banks and clearing houses, printed their own notes, taxed profits for common welfare projects, and operated a credit union. At Kansk they opened a marketing association which controlled the quality of products and regulated prices.[37]

Formal and informal social structures emerged quickly after the opening of each camp. With the passage of time, the camps became clusters of immigrant subcommunities with their own leaders, class systems, microeconomies, cultural orientations, and behavioral traditions. Life depended on the cruel rhythms of Russian climate and the less regular will of the captor state, which fluctuated wildly during this revolutionary era. Hardships, however, often proved the necessity, and reinforced the growth, of community organization.

Nationality groups usually kept together, guarded their own interests, clashed with other nationalities, and worked out their own methods of passing the time. Slavic-speaking groups were probably less exclusive than others because they could more easily mix with the Russian people, as they were encouraged to do.[38] On the other hand, many of them joined exclusive political or military organizations such as the Polish or Czechoslovak Legions. Magyar prisoners were probably more dependent on their national groups since their language was completely foreign to captors and fellow prisoners alike, and their services as farmers and workers were not highly esteemed by the Russians. They probably remained clustered more firmly in the camps than other groups, which may help explain why a few Hungarian Bolsheviks were able to spread their appeal so rapidly among them. German prisoners had not only a language barrier but had also to face several waves of official anti-German agitation, which stiffened their group identification within the camps. Their general level of technical training and educational experience was high, however, and they were in demand on farms and in factories outside the camps. Large numbers of Germans became individually involved in nonprison life before the mayhem of revolution made Russia's crisis their own.

Microcosmic political bodies took shape as camp inmates selected or came under the dominance of spokesmen who represented their interests to the Russians, as they established kitchen and barracks committees to husband their common resources, and as they chose councils to resolve disputes. Where prisoners remained loyal to their home governments, or for other reasons preserved familiar military structures, their own officers or noncommissioned officers took charge. Tsarist authorities refused to recognize the authority of captured officers by depriving them of their insignia of rank. After many complaints registered on behalf of officer prisoners through neutral diplomatic channels, the Russians accepted a compromise which enabled captured officers to keep their insignia but not to wear them. Then the Russians enforced their policy of separating officers from lower ranks to prevent hostile organization. When the Bolsheviks came to power, they simply treated officers as class enemies and encouraged prisoners to struggle against them.[39]

Captured military chaplains, and medical or sanitation personnel were usually involved in the leadership unless deemed untrustworthy by their fellow inmates. The rest of camp politics, being heavily oriented toward personalities, was less predictable. Personal loyalties and enmities reached eccentric proportions during long confinement, and factions, parties, coalitions and petty federations formed and dissolved frequently. Political issues chiefly involved matters of immediate concern, such as distribution of relief supplies, improvement of housing, quantity and quality of food and clothing, enlargement of personal privileges, camp discipline, and the like. Prisoners held elections or met in camp assemblies, and sometimes met with delegations from neighboring camps to discuss matters of mutual concern. After the October revolution they even held all-Russian prisoner of war congresses.[40]

The politics of the world at large seldom dominated camp politics before 1917, except where the Russians tried to lure Slavic, Magyar, or Trentino Italian captives from old political loyalties, or where outside work had brought prisoners into contact with Russian political factions or labor organizations. After the February revolution, however, prisoners became increasingly involved in Russian affairs, including revolutionary activity.

The cohesiveness of camp social life slackened during the summer months. Then most inmates were sent out in large numbers to satellite camps and farms to work, leaving a reduced core of prisoners at the main camps. Many of these were unable to work because of wounds, illness, or disciplinary confinement. The rest of the summer camp crews occupied themselves with the repair and maintenance of camp facilities, gardening, preparation of food and clothing for winter, outdoor entertainments such as hiking, swimming, and athletic competitions, or intriguing to obtain the best jobs or other favored treatment. For a bold few, summer was the time to escape, but not many succeeded in covering the great distances before winter forced them to surrender or perish.

When the seasonal workers returned to the main camps, so did the delineations of community structures. These were not pleasant or even willing communities. In time the men became thoroughly tired of each other's company, especially as the long, dark winters forced them indoors to a cramped existence characterized by idleness, unchanging diet, and the lack of privacy or the attractions of the opposite sex. Even where conditions were most comfortable, winter encouraged "barbed-wire disease," a lethargic condition interrupted sporadically by outbreaks of extreme hostility, morose pessimism punctuated by occasional flights of unrealistic optimism, and a reduced ability to concentrate one's thoughts. Lacking the accustomed stimuli of genuine responsibilities, prisoners gradually replaced them with reveries, exaggerated routines, petty quarrels, and the cultivation of rumor. Time lost meaning in personal life. Habits of procrastination grew until many gave up lifelong habits of grooming and personal hygiene. Some lost all initiative, even to struggle against boredom, but most made an effort to overcome their own apathy and the burdens of excessive leisure.[41]

Prisoners employed every pastime they knew and invented others. They conversed, told stories, played cards and other games. They took physical exercises, wrestled, boxed, lifted weights. They carved wooden figures, molded clay pottery, fashioned personal utensils, and developed every handicraft they could get equipment for. They sang, danced, played musical instruments, formed choruses and orchestras, and sometimes became local entertainers. In more than one case POW orchestras went on tour. Prisoners read aloud, made speeches, organized debates, and established theatrical groups. There were, for example, at least 46 German theatrical groups in Russian camps, some of which became professional repertory companies.[42]

Prisoners read whatever came into their hands, and many who arrived illiterate learned to read and write before they left. Over 50 camps compiled substantial libraries of western-language books, especially after a Danish book commission imported a large supply from Scandinavia and Germany.[43] The American Young Men's Christian Association (YMCA) was active in establishing libraries and kept 73 "secretaries" circulating among the camps to supervise recreational and personal-improvement activities.[44] Inmates published camp newspapers and journals, which reduced the power of sheer rumor and sometimes attained respectable levels of local journalism. Fifty-nine German-language papers and journals appeared, including sixteen dailies and six weeklies.[45] Other papers were occasionally available from the commercial press of nearby towns or from Russian indoctrination programs. The Bolsheviks were especially active in this regard, and by 1920 had encouraged the printing of some 200 newspapers in 12 languages (24 in German) by foreign Internationalists.[46]

Formal education was one of the most remarkable POW activities. Dozens of camps organized schools, and veritable universities flourished at Skobelev near Tashkent and at Kazan, Tomsk, Krasnoyarsk, Berezovka, Sretensk and elsewhere. Berezovka had a business college with a sophisticated curriculum based on the Austrian model, a qualified faculty, reserved class space, regular schedules of lectures and examinations, and a printed bulletin.[47] Foreign languages and commercial subjects were most popular, with legal, professional and cultural topics following. In a number of cases, studies undertaken in the camps were validated by university examinations after the war.[48]

News of the February revolution excited these prison communities with hope. The new Provisional Government eased restrictions for a while on the POWs' movements, and granted them some of the rights that the revolution had established for Russians. Prisoners here and there joined labor unions, formed POW associations, and participated in public demonstrations, including May Day parades. Some of them participated in labor disputes and strikes for higher pay and improved working conditions.[49]

Hopes that the revolution would lead to freedom, peace and repatriation were soon shattered. Rampant inflation eroded the value of POW wages and stipends, and cuts in the percentage of their earnings they could keep reduced many prisoners to deep poverty. Moreover, as the government under Aleksandr Kerenskiy intensified Russia's war effort during the summer of 1917, it assumed a hard line toward POWs, especially Germans. Strict confinement in camps was restored, and newspaper agitation against the Central Powers led to unpleasant incidents. One case involved a lynching of more than a dozen prisoners in the town of Laishchev near Kazan.[50]

One group of prisoners prospered during this time, however. On March 24, 1917, the Russian government authorized an independent Czecholovak Legion to function as the armed force of Tomas Masaryk's Czechoslovak National Council in Paris. By midsummer the legion had recruited and trained over 30,000 prisoners and resident aliens, who fought impressively in Russia's last offensive in Galicia, and subsequently retained organizational stability while most of the Russian army disintegrated. The number of troops in the Czechoslovak Legion rose to over 60,000, and its impact on the history of Russia and Czechslovakia is well recognized. It was to play a special role in the lives of all prisoners of war in Siberia in 1918 and 1919.

The October revolution again raised hopes for liberation and repatriation, and again it crushed them – at least for the prisoners of war in Siberia and Turkestan. Lenin's new government offered freedom and promised peace, but delivered neither in a form beneficial to most prisoners. POWs received full rights as citizens of the Soviet state and guards were removed from the camps. Large numbers of civil and military prisoners, however, had become financially dependent on the government-supported camp system, and on charity packages and funds from abroad. When the Soviet government failed to deliver funds to support the camps and left the prisoners to subsist on the Russian economy, it worked a special hardship on the nonworking officers receiving government stipends and on prisoners employed by former camp administrations.[51]

Prisoners working in industry and agricultural also encountered new problems. Russian soldiers were leaving the army and taking the available jobs, so that little employment was left for the POWs. The Soviet government initiated peace negotiations with the Central Powers but refused to allow POWs to leave the country before the conclusion of negotiations. The upshot was that hordes of prisoners of war, many of them officially authorized to beg in the streets, wandered the countryside looking for work or a means of escape to the west.[52]

Negotiations at Brest-Litovsk proceeded rapidly by diplomatic standards, but not rapidly enough for these trapped men. The eventual treaty did not resolve the detailed procedures for prisoner exchange. By mutual agreement, this matter was negotiated by separate commissions, first in Petrograd then in Moscow. These talks were not properly underway until April 28, 1918, nearly two months after the Soviets signed the treaty.[53]

The issues were complicated and the Soviet negotiators were in no hurry. Their best hope for concessions was delay, which would also serve as an acceptable response to Entente pressures against the transfer of able-bodied Germans and Austrians to the west. The Brest-Litovsk treaty had established the right of Germany and Austria-Hungary to send relief and repatriation commissions into Russia to facilitate the exchange. The Russians, however, did not have the reciprocal privilege to send delegates to the camps of Germany and Austria-Hungary. Soviet negotiators agitated fervently for this privilege. German negotiators remained adamant on the point, because they were certain that the Bolsheviks wanted to use such delegates to spread propaganda.[54]

The most difficult problem stemmed from the disparity in numbers of military prisoners to be exchanged. Germany held over 1,400,000 Russians, while only 167,000 Reich Germans had surrendered to Russian forces. Predictably, the Germans were unwilling to accept a simple "all for all" exchange of POWs. They called instead for a "head for head" exchange, which would leave them a million or so Russians to use for further bargaining, and to satisfy Junker landlords and other employers who wanted to delay the loss of cheap POW labor. The Russians demanded a collective exchange of all prisoners immediately. After ingenious maneuvering on both sides, the matter was resolved not by the negotiating commissions in Moscow, but through diplomatic exchanges in Berlin on June 24. The head-for-head formula was accepted, but modified by further talks on July 12 with the proviso that, after all Germans had been repatriated, the remaining Russians would be repatriated at the same tempo as the regular exchange. In other words, the quicker the Russians returned the Germans — who were needed on the western front—the sooner their own men would be repatriated.[55]

All of this had taken time. Another Russian winter had passed, taking its toll among desperate men; springtime only accelerated the building of forces that would tear Russia apart. Every delay increased the number of prisoners of war who would have to share Russia's agony. And there was more delay when Count Mirbach, the German ambassador and chief commissioner for prisoner of war negotiations in Moscow, was assassinated on July 7 by Socialist Revolutionaries in an effort to overthrow the Bolsheviks. The plot failed, but it slowed down repatriation while the Bolsheviks dealt with the "counterrevolutionaries." It also intensified the efforts of two organizations of armed former prisoners to impede the work of the German and Austrian repatriation commissions. Despite the detainment of prisoners by Internationalist organizations of pro-Bolshevik prisoners and other aliens, the commissions worked with Soviet authorities to evacuate almost all of the prisoners from European Russia by October 1918,[56] The Czechoslovak Legion, however, stopped the exodus from Siberia of any prisoners who might be useful to the Central Powers.

The Bolsheviks formally launched the Internationalist movement early in 1918 to use prisoners of war to defend the Soviet government while they remained in Russia, and to spread revolution in central and eastern Europe when they returned to their homelands. Bolshevik leaders had been interested in the political potential of war captives as early as 1915,[57] and local Bolshevik organizations had been in contact with leftist prisoners in some areas as early as mid-1916. A few war prisoners took part in the October revolution, and by December 1917 large numbers were willing to volunteer for service in Red Guard units and to participate in revolutionary organizations of their own. In January and February 1918, the Bolsheviks promoted several regional conferences of POW delegates in preparation for an All-Russian Congress of Prisoners of War in Moscow in April. That congress announced a new policy of military recruitment among POWs and alien residents. Henceforth, large multinational units — regiments or brigades — would be formed by combining smaller units made up of Hungarians,

South Slavs, Czechs, Germans, and other nationalities. Although some of the previously formed national Red Guard units continued to function and many prisoners enlisted in regular units of the Red Army, the large Internationalist unit became standard, and by the summer of 1918 had been established in Moscow, Petrograd, Tver (now Kalinin), Voronezh, Penza, Samara (now Kuybyshev), Tsaritsyn (now Volgograd), Orenburg and Irkutsk.[58]

In May the Bolsheviks, who now called themselves Communists, formed a new organization to coordinate political education and military recruitment among war prisoners. This was the Federation of Foreign Sections of the Russian Communist Party. Under its president, the Hungarian POW Béla Kun, the federation had successfully established Internationalist political groups in Moscow, Petrograd, Tver, Voronezh, Penza, Samara, Tsaritsyn, Orenburg and Irkutsk.[59]

All of this was going on while the prisoner exchange negotiations were taking place in Moscow. Soviet negotiators denied that the government had any control over the Internationalists, and declared that in any case only a few of them were German. Only under heavy pressure did the Soviet regime order the German Internationalists disarmed.[60] The remainder of the Internationalists took control of many camps and forced the "liberated" nonpolitical prisoners back into them, subjecting them there to great pressure to "volunteer" for the Red Guard.[61]

The other force blocking repatriation in the summer of 1918 was the Czechoslovak Legion. The legionaries were mostly desperate men who, having forsworn Austro-Hungarian allegiance, dared not return to their homelands while the Habsburg monarchy remained intact. They insisted on continuing their war against the Central Powers after the Treaty of Brest-Litovsk removed Russia from the conflict. Under direct orders from the Czechoslovak National Council in Paris, the legion attempted to withdraw eastward through Siberia to Vladivostok and thence by sea to France.

The legionaries despatched advanced units by the Trans-Siberian Railway to Vladivostok. Finding few ships there, they began to return westward, but not before Czech and Slovak troops were spread along the entire Trans-Siberian line. The legion's uneasy detente with the Bolshevik government collapsed after an incident between legionaries and local soviet authorities at Chelyabinsk on May 14-16, 1918. When Moscow ordered the legionaries disarmed and confined to prisoner of war camps, they revolted and seized the railway stations from Samara to Irkutsk to secure their own communications. This action escalated anti-Bolshevik resistance activity in Siberia, and closed the Siberian lifeline to any traffic that the Czechoslovak Legion did not approve.

The legionaries forced the other prisoners back into the camps, and behaved as cruel overlords until the end of World War I. Thereafter they ceased to consider the Germans and Magyars as enemies and treated them more humanely. Cut off from their homelands, the hapless prisoners, when not under Czech control, were subject to perils and harassments visited on them by Internationalists and other Bolsheviks, Cossack and White military contingents, and a variety of bandits. In short, they shared with the Russian people the agonies of the civil war while losing the protection and support of their own governments.

POWs became actively involved in every aspect of the struggles and in every geographical area. They fought for and against Gen. Anton Denikin in the Caucasus and the Ukraine, Gen. Petr Wrangel in the Caucasus and the Crimea, Gen. Nikolay Yudenich in the Baltic, and Adm. Kolchak and Gen. Grigoriy Semenov in Siberia. Some even joined the Chinese bandits on the Ussuri river.[62] For a time, the Czechoslovak Legion allied itself with Adm. Kolchak and fought in his 1919 drive to the northwest. After their break with Kolchak, legionaries arrested him in 1920 and handed him and his trainload of tsarist gold over to the Bolsheviks. The Internationalists fought in many campaigns, but their numbers were seldom large and their contribution to the Bolshevik cause was limited.[63]

POWS were not only involved in foreign interventionist activities, but to some extent they – or rather Allied notions about them – were causes of intervention. In the spring of 1918 the French needed the Czechoslovak Legion on the western front and arranged for its withdrawal through Siberia. The British were especially interested in reopening the eastern front, and encouraged the Czechoslovaks to move northward toward the White Sea area to link up with a British force there. At the same time the British put heavy pressure on the Americans to enter Siberia. President Woodrow Wilson resisted until a false description of conditions among POWs in Siberia gave such action an ethical appearance. Despite clear and valid information to the contrary, Wilson subscribed to the rumor that the Czechoslovak Legion was being menaced by an army of rearmed German and Austrian prisoners under German command. Japanese interventionists used the same excuse. In August 1918 seven thousand American soldiers entered Siberia, ostensibly to guard the communications of over 50,000 well-armed Czechoslovak veterans. Historians are still debating the degree of guile involved in the American and other interventions.[64]

Although Germany and Austria-Hungary suspected that the Soviet government was unnecessarily lenient with local soviets and Internationalist units that restrained the movement of prisoners of war, Moscow did cooperate in evacuating the Central Powers' POWs. But the sheer logistical problems would have impeded their work, even if there had been no civil war and all parties had worked together efficiently and in good faith. When the Soviets lost political control of the middle and lower Volga, the Don, the Kuban, the Caucasus, the Ukraine, Turkestan, and most of Siberia in 1918, they lost access to the prisoners in these areas. When they regained these regions, transportation and communications were in worse condition than before, and registration of the prisoners of war had practically ceased. The situation was not simplified by the collapse of the Central Powers in October and November 1918.

Many of the evacuees were in the process of being repatriated when the German and Austro-Hungarian empires fell and the machinery of repatriation ceased to operate. Even before their defeat, the German and Austro-Hungarian armies had been extremely reluctant to permit escapees from Russia to pass through their front lines. Now the successor states, instead of welcoming their returning soldiers, restricted repatriation while they worked out new procedures for customs, passports, postal matters, and medical authorizations. The evacuation commissions which Germany and Austria-Hungary had despatched to Russia no longer had authority to act, and the Soviets recognized a "soldiers' council" made up of former POWs as representing all German interests in Russia. The new German government refused to recognize this council, an act that slowed repatriation even further. Berlin feared communism, and tried to avoid infiltration by indoctrinated revolutionaries in the guise of returning prisoners of war. The identity of individual returnees was extremely difficult to establish as most of the long-term POWs had lost their papers, and their physical appearance had usually changed during capitivity. Moreover, the record-keeping apparatus of Russia and their homelands had been disrupted. The solution was to confine the returnees to special camps to wait for identity clearance. Loyalty was even more difficult to establish, since the new successor states had not even existed when the prisoners had departed. Now the returnees had been exposed to Bolshevism, which openly attempted to use former prisoners of war to spread revolution. Even after establishing their identity and securing medical clearance, returnees were regularly detained for weeks in special quarantine camps to prevent the spread of political as well as clinical disease.[65]

Returning POWs did in fact cause problems. Some of those brought home before the end of the war were given short furloughs and then ordered back into the war zone. They proved to be most unwilling soldiers and a source of trouble. In several places in Austria they mutinied.[66] After the armistice some of the dedicated Internationalists returned to construct new communist parties or to bolshevize Social Democratic parties in their home countries. The greatest immediate success came to Béla Kun in the spring of 1919 when he established a short-lived revolutionary government in Hungary. Ernst Reuter became general secretary of the German Communist party and became alienated from Russian tutelage. Such alienation came much later in the career of Josip Broz, who returned to work his way up in the communist party of Yugoslavia.[67]

Even after it became possible to leave Russia, shortage of ships and money remained barriers to repatriation. Political and military difficulties with Poland and the Ukraine kept the overland transportation routes closed, and the Soviet government could not be expected to pay for transportation beyond ports of exit. The new German Republic offered to pay the costs of repatriating German military and civilian evacuees, but the successor states to Austria-Hungary were unable to obtain foreign exchange to defray these costs. Former prisoners who arrived at Petrograd, Narva, or Valdivostok without passage money were stranded and often had to return to the camps to survive. Even with money, most were stranded by the lack of passenger vessels, especially out of Vladivostok. Outside support was necessary to solve these problems.[68]

The Allied governments were willing, but not particularly eager, to provide passenger space for former enemies. They were slow in developing a plan for the Baltic ports, and agreed to move former enemy prisoners out of Vladivostok only after all Allied units and supporters had been evacuated. The American expeditionary force and the Czechoslovak Legion remained there until 1920, and even then the matter of costs had not been resolved.

By 1920 there were still over 425,000 prisoners of war in Russia. Several international charitable associations were involved in efforts to arrange for repatriation while helping to sustain the prisoners. The most important of these was the International Committee of the Red Cross, which laid the groundwork for the final repatriation. The turning point came on April 11, 1920, when the Council of the League of Nations appointed a high commissioner to coordinate activity and to rally worldwide support for the effort. The council appointed Professor Fridtjof Nansen, the renowned polar explorer and Norwegian delegate to the league, to serve as high commissioner. He was aided by Gustav Ador, president of the International Committee of the Red Cross and a league delegate from Switzerland.

Nansen raised funds, and solved the sort of bureaucratic problems that had bedeviled POW affairs from the outset. Many useful ships, for example, were not available for repatriation service because they were to be handed over to the Reparations Commission. Nansen persuaded the commission to put them at his disposal for special charter work, providing he could raise the money to pay for the service. He also persuaded several governments to donate money to the International Committee on Relief Credits for the repatriation. When the British government pledged a sizable contribution on a matching basis, but refused to pay until other governments had contributed their share, Nansen appealed to the league to raise the other half.

His work was remarkably successful. Within a month the first ship left Narva for a German port, and by midsummer 1920 a fleet of fifteen ships was in operation. During August and September 180,000 prisoners were exchanged. To fund repatriation from Vladivostok, Nansen turned to the American Red Cross, which had joined other organizations to form the Siberian War Prisoners Repatriation Fund. This group worked with Nansen to charter ships that brought several thousand evacuees from Vladivostok to Europe.[69] Nansen found it more difficult to repatriate or even to contact prisoners in Turkestan, but by March 1922 he was able to report that only about 4,000 POWs – some of them unwilling to return – remained in all of Russia. His project restored 427,386 persons of 26 nationalities to their homelands.[70] In recognition of this accomplishment he was awarded the Nobel Peace Prize for 1922.[71]

Fridtjof Nansen eloquently summarized the tragic experience of the prisoners of war in Russia in these words:

> The sufferings of these men have been far greater than I can describe. Not only have they undergone the ordinary mental anguish of the prisoner of war, they have also suffered in every conceivable way from cold, hunger, disease, neglect, and overwork. The conditions of the camps in many parts of Russia were, during part of the last four years, almost too terrible to think of, and the mortality among the prisoners has been almost inconceivably great.[72]

NOTES

1. It is hazardous to mention any totals, since official statistics and studies based on them disagree. Official Russian statistics show 1,961,333 prisoners of war taken by September 1, 1917. SSSR Tsentral'noye Statisticheskoye Upravleniye, Otdel' Voyennoy Statistiki, *Rossiya v mirovoy voine 1914-1918 goda (v tsifrakh)* (Moscow, 1925), table 33. An analysis is in Stanislas Kohn, *The Cost of the War to Russia: The Vital Statistics of European Russia during the World War* (New Haven, Conn., 1932 [Reprint, New York, 1973], pp. 37-41. German estimates run substantially higher. Margarete Klante reports a total of 2,497,378 in "Die deutschen Kriegsgefangenen in Russland," in M. Schwarte (ed.), *Der grosse Krieg 1914-1918* (Leipzig, 1932), X, 182 n. Elsa Brändström apparently used Swedish Red Cross as well as German files to arrive at 2,322,278. See *Unter Kriegsgefangenen in Russland und Sibirien* (Berlin, 1927), p. 16. Ivan Völgyes in his "Hungarian Prisioners of War in Russia 1916-1919," *Cahiers du monde russe et soviétique,* XIV (1973), 54 n., uses Hungarian as well as Russian studies to estimate only about 1,500,000 Austro-Hungarian captives. He does not give totals for Germany, Turkey or Bulgaria, but they could not bring his total higher than 1,750,000 or almost 750,000 below Klante's figure. The safest method is that chose in A. Klevanskiy, "Voyennoplennye tsentral'nvkh derzhav v tsarskoy i revolyutsionalisty Rossii (1914-1918 g.)" in M. Birman *et al.* (eds.), *Internatsionalisty v boyakh za vlast' Sovetov* (Moscow, 1965), p. 23. Klevanskiy simply states the ranges of estimates he finds credible. He estimates that Russia took between 2,000,000 and 2,300,000 soldiers and officers, including 160,000 to 180,000 from Germany and 1,600,000 to 2,100,000 from Austria-Hungary.

The number of civilian prisoners in even less clear. Some may be included in statistics for military POWs. The Russians counted some of them along with refugees from the war zones, and did not always distinguish between enemy citizens and Germans and Jews of Russian nationality who had been removed from the war zone. See Kohn, op. cit., p. 34. Many civilian prisoners kept family members with them who were not, strictly speaking, prisoners. American diplomatic officials responsible for protecting civilian prisoners of war estimated that 200,000 German and Austro-Hungarian civilians were interned in Russia. See *New York Times* October 15, 1916, (III:1).

2. *New York Times,* June 4, 1916 (I:20). Personal reminiscences published during the war and for a while thereafter provide useful knowledge of life among civilian prisoners in Russia. These include G. Jonck, *Meine Verschickung nach Sibirien: Erinnerungen und Erlebnisse eines rigaschen Buchhandlers* (München, 1916); Bruno Lachmann, "Tagebuch eines deutschen Metallarbeiters aus russicher Gefangenschaft," *Kriegshefte der süddeutschen Monatshefte,* March, 1916, pp. 926-946; Erna Leibfried-Kügelgen, *Deutsche Mutter in Sibirien: Schicksal einer Familie* (2nd ed.; Leipzig, 1935): Eduard Schmidt-Lötzen, *Von Masuren nach Sibirien: Ein Jahr in russischer Kriegsgefangenschaft* (Schwerin/Mecklenburg, 1916); B. Voss, "Erlebnisse eines Arztes in russischer Kriegsgefangenschaft," *Süddeutsche Monatshefte,* March, 1916, pp. 903-925.

3. George Thomas Marye (Petrograd) to Secretary of State, July 10, 1915; John K. Caldwell (Consul General, Vladivostok) to Secretary of State, July 21, 1915; W.P. Cresson's report on the condition of military and civilian prisoners in Volga region, enclosed in Charles S. Wilson to Secretary of State, September

13, 1915; William Warfield's report of conditions in Siberian prisoner-of-war camps, June 20, 1916. These documents are in the Department of State serial file (Record Group 59, U.S. National Archives) No. 763.72114, suffix numbers 671, 713, 818 and 1702 respectively. This file number refers to all World War I matters relating to prisoners of war. Hereafter cited as 763.72114 plus suffix number.

4. Richard G. Plaschka, "Contradicting Ideologies: The Pressure of Ideological Conflicts in the Austro-Hungarian Army of World War I," in Robert A. Kann, *et al.* (eds.), *The Habsburg Empire in World War I* (New York, 1977), pp. 105-121, describes some of the sources of low morale and inefficiency in the Habsburg forces which contributed to mass surrenders.

5. Brändström, *op. cit.*, pp. 16-85, vividly describes the suffering which resulted from Russian inability to care for large numbers of prisoners.

6. *Ibid.*, pp. 16, 26-30; Ernst Johann Faber, "Elf Monate in russischer Kriegsgefangenschaft," *Suddeutsche Monatshefte* (October, 1915), pp. 65-92; Karl Scharping, *Kulturelle und wirtschaftliche; Leistungen der deutschen Kriegsgefangenen in Russland 1914-1918* (Berlin 1939), pp. 26-29; Hans Weiland and Leopold Kern, (eds.), *In Feindeshand: Die Gefangenschaft im Weltkriege in Einzeldarstellungen* (2 vols., Wien [Vienna], 1931), *passim*.

7. Roman Dyboski, *Seven Years in Russia and Siberia (1914-1921)* (Cheshire, Conn., 1970), pp. 19-29; Heinrich Raabl-Werner, "Der Einfluss der Propaganda unter den Kriegsgefangenen in Russland auf den Zusammenbruch Oesterreich-Ungarns," *Militärwissenschaftliche Mitteilungen*, LIX (1928), 776-777; Margarete Klante, *Von der Wolga zum Amur: Die tschechische Legion und der russiche Bürgerkrieg* (Berlin, 1931), p. 72.

8. Extremely poor postal service was one of the POW's major problems in Russia, Voss, *op. cit.*, p. 910; Cresson Report and Marye to Secretary of State, January 18, 1916, 763.72114/818 and 1261.

9. See the following personal accounts on the rigors of the prisoner's journey into the interior: Wilhelm von Bülow, *Durch Stacheldraht und Steppe: Die Flucht eines Neunzehnjährigen aus russischer Gefangenschaft* (München, 1937), pp. 1-25; Victor Nowak, *Bilder aus der Erinnerungen eines Austrauschinvaliden: Erlebnisse, Beobachtungen und Leiden in russischer Kriegsgefangenschaft* (Wien [Vienna], 1917), pp. 28-40; Hereward T. Price, *Boche and Bolshevik: Experiences of an Englishman in the German Army and in Russian Prisons* (London, 1919), pp. 105-109, 120-121; Joseph Scholz, *Erinnerungen, Erlebnisse und Flucht: Aus meiner Kriegsgefangenschaft in Russland (Münsterberg/Schlesien, 1923),* pp. 1-54; *Rudolf Stenzel, Kriegsgefangenschaft in Sibirien* (Wien [Vienna], 1918), pp. 1-10.

10. Brändström, *op. cit.*, p. 45, Stenzel, *op. cit.*, p. 26, has a diagram of a large camp at Omsk.

11. Brändström, *op. cit.*, p. 45. Georg Hahn, *Kriegsgefangen in Russland 1915-1920* (Mainz, 1926) is one of many interesting accounts of POW life among the peasants. W.H. Braun, *Unter Zarenherrschaft und Sowjetstern* (Graz, 1930) shows the urban side.

12. Brändström, *op. cit.*, pp. 65-67; Price, *op. cit.*, Ch. VII; Klante, *"Die deutschen Kriegsgefangenen,"* p. 187; William Warfield, "Reports on Prison Camp Conditions in Eastern Siberia, 1915-1916," Washington, June 20, 1916, 763.72114/1702; Paul P. Gronsky and Nicholas J. Astrov, *The War and the Russian Government* (New Haven, Conn., 1929), p. 244.

13. Four of the best witnesses of conditions in Siberia were at Sretensk at

this time, each viewing the troubles from a different perspective. Price, an Englishman in the German army who later became an outstanding Shakespeare scholar, was one of the prisoners. *Op. cit.*, pp. 127-130. Magdalene von Walsleben was a German nurse whom the Russians permitted by reciprocal agreement to tour the camps. *Die deutsche Schwester in Sibirien* (Berlin, 1919), pp. 149-162. William Warfield was an American Red Cross professional on assignment as special representative of the US Department of State charged to inspect prison camps. See his "Report on Camp for Military Prisoners at Sretensk, Irkutsk Military District, Siberia," January 20, 1916 and despatches to Secretary of State on January 1 and 17, 1916, 763.7214/1487, 167 and 1277. The Swedish Red Cross nurse Elsa Brändström, writer of the most comprehensive and influential account of prisoners of war in Siberia, was also there. Indeed, she became infected with typhus herself while working among the sick at Sretensk. *Op. cit.*, pp. 71-75. See also Eduard Juhl *et al.*, *Elsa Brändström: Weg und Werk einer grossen Frau in Schweden, Sibirien, Deutschland, Amerika* (Stuttgart, 1962), pp. 74-80.

14. James B. Scott, *The Hague Conventions and Declarations of 1899 and 1907* (New York, 1915), pp. 108-15.

15. Franz Josef Scheidl, *Die Kriegsgefangenschaft von den ältesten Zeiten bis zur Gegenwart: Eine völkerechtliche Monographie* (Berlin, 1943), pp. 98-100 lists all international agreements concerning prisoners of war. Texts of proceedings are in *Procès-verbal signé à Stockholm le 13 Mai 1916* (Stockholm, 1916); Konference om Krigsfangesager, *Conférence de Copenhague, Octobre-Novembre 1917* (Copenhagen, 1917); and Conférence concernant les prisonniers de guerre, Oslo, 1917, *Procès-Verbaux des séances de la Conference concernant les prisonniers de guerre, tenue à Kristiania du 9 au 1 November 1917* (Kristiania [Oslo], 1917). Efforts to arrange prisoner exchanges through neutral channels began in 1915, following the appeal of Pope Benedict XV for repatriation of disabled captives. See Burián to Penfield, April 28, 1915, 736.72114/527.

16. [J.C. White], "Memorandum on Care of German and Austro-Hungarian Interests in Russia," April 15, 1916, 763.72114/1603 and Penfield to Secretary of State, December 8, 1914, 361.63/12; *The New York Times,* June 4, 1916 (I:20).

17. Some complaints about American services are in *Neue Freie Presse* (Vienna), January 23, 1915; Dumba to Secretary of State, January 28, 1915, 763.72115/456; *The Times* (London), January 29, 1915 (7c); Edmund Schmid, "Bei Kriegsbeginn in Südrussland," *Kriegshefte der Süddeutschen Monatshefte* (März. 1916), p. 986; Klante, "Die deutschen Kriegsgefangenen," p. 193.

18. Bryan to diplomatic and consular officers entrusted with the interests of foreign governments at war, August 17, 1914, *Foreign Relations of the United States, 1914 Supplement* (Washington, 1928), pp. 740-741.

19. United States consuls did represent Russian interests in Budapest, Prague and Trieste, but they had no authority to make diplomatic representations about prisoners in Austria-Hungary to the Vienna government. Lansing to Bryan, March 16, 1915, 763/72114/534; Penfield to Secretary of State, August 8, 1915, *ibid.*/1811; Francis to Secretary of State, May 24, 1916, *ibid.*/1701.

20. Caldwell to Secretary of State, January 18, 1915, *ibid.*/243.

21. See Warfield's summary report in note above and the following communications in 763.72114 (suffixes supplied below): "Austrian and German

Prisoners in the Irkutsk Military District," October 28, 1915, -/1088; "Report on Camps in Priamur District," Novermber 8, 1915, -/977; Warfield to Marye, January 12, 1916, -/1278; Warfield to Secretary of State, rec'd January 22, 1917, -/1167 and -/1277. See also Siler Report, February 21, 1916, -/1526; Marve to Secretary of State, January 29, 1916, and Marye to Sazonoff, January 28, 1916,-/1280.

22. Marye to Secretary of State, March 15, 1916, *ibid.*/1352.

23. At the request of Austrian Ambassador Dumba, Wilson, "not as the chief official of my Government, but only as a servant of humanity," appealed to the tsar to permit some trusted persons to distribute much needed supplies to prisoners in Siberia. Nicholas replied that he would permit such distibution, subject to reciprocal treatment by the Central Powers. Wilson to Emperor Nicholas II, March 18, 1915. *ibid.*/534 and 551. See also George Thomas Marye, *Nearing the End in Imperial Russia* (Philadelphia, 1929), p. 125. The upshot of this was the creation of an American Red Cross team to work with German prisoners in Russia, with a similar team working among Russian prisoners in Germany. The Russians were unable to finance the one in Germany and unwilling to permit the one in Russia to function without reciprocation. See *ibid.*/971, 1035, 1065, and 201.

24. Department of State to all embassies concerned with prisoner of war inspection, April 17, 1916, and Fred Morris Dearing (chargé d'affaires, Petrograd) to Secretary of State, April 19 and 22, 1916, *ibid.*/1463, 1470, and 1550. Examples of Department of State censorship of inspection reports are in Secretary of State to Francis, May 24 and September 27, 1916, ibid./1513 and 1901.

25. Paul S. Reinsch, *An American Diplomat in China* (Garden City, N.Y., 1922), pp. 162-163, and Department of State correspondence in 763.72114/271-618.

26. Francis to Secretary of State, December 14, 1916, January 1 and 5, 1917, *ibid.*/2348, 2280, and 2463. See also Klante, "Die deutschen Kriegsgefangenen," p. 193.

27. Brändström, *op. cit.*, p. 57.

28. Kohn, *op. cit.*, p. 41; Peter D. Liashchenko, *History of the National Economy of Russia to the 1917 Revolution* (New York, 1949), pp. 758-768, belittles the relief brought by POWs.

29. Scott, *op. cit.*, p. 109.

30. Kohn, *op. cit.*, pp. 37-39; S.O. Zagorsky, *State Control of Industry in Russia during the War* (New Haven, Conn., 1928), pp. 51-52; Klevanskiy, *op. cit.*, pp. 24-25, suggests roughly the same proportions as Zagorsky; Tikhon J. Polner *et al.*, *Russian Local Government during the War and the Union of Zemstvos* (New Haven, Conn., 1930), p. 155; and Alexis N. Antsiferov *et al.*, *Russian Agriculture during the War* (New Haven, Conn., 1930), p. 12, have lower estimates for the numbers employed in agriculture.

31. Polner, *op. cit.*, pp. 154-155; Antsiferov, *op. cit.*, p. 268; "Chernov's Instructions to the Land Committees" in Robert P. Browder and Alexander F. Kerensky (eds.), *The Russian Provisional Government 1917: Documents* (Stanford, Cal., 1961), II, 559.

32. Georg Hahn's book cited above is an excellent account of a German prisoner's life with a Russian peasant family. Josip Broz recalled that he received a marriage offer from a Russian peasant on behalf of his daughter, apparently because the peasant admired his mechanical skills. Vladimir

Dedijer, *Tito Speaks* (London, 1953), pp. 30-31. Many prisoners married, which caused problems at the time of their repatriation. See Henry Baerlein, *The March of the Seventy Thousand* (London, 1926), p. 141 and Reinhold Messner, "Liebe in der Gefangenschaft," in Weiland, *op. cit.*, I, 145-147. Price, *op. cit.*, pp. 171-172, recalls that the girls around Sretensk tended to adopt the political views of their POW lovers. Lachmann, *op. cit.*, p. 939, shows some difficulties which resulted from this sort of thing.

33. Zagorsky, *op. cit.*, p. 54; Klevanskiy, *op. cit.*, p. 24.

34. Brändström, *op.cit.*, pp. 177-178; Klante, "Die deutschen Kriegsgenfangenen," pp. 194-195; George Montandon, *Im Schmelztiegel des fernen Ostens: Geschichte der sibirischen Mission des Internationalen Komitees vom Roten Kreuz zu Gunsten der österreichischen und ungarischen Kriegsgefangenen (März 1919 bis Juni* 1921) (Wien [Vienna], 1923), p. 304.

35. Lachmann, *op. cit.*, pp. 944; Klevanskiy, *op. cit.*, p. 24 n.

36. Brändström, *op. cit.*, p. 222.

37. *Ibid., pp. 219-222; Nachrichtenblatt der Reichszentralstelle für Kriegs- und Zivilgefangene,* No. 18 (Oktober, 1919, p. 6, and No. 19 (Oktober, 1919), p. 5; *Leopold Kern, "Lagerindustrie," in Weiland, op. cit.*, I, 123-127.

38. Raabl-Werner, *op. cit.*, p. 777; Dyboski, *op. cit.*, pp. 21-29.

39. Penfield (Vienna) to Secretary of State, June 3, 1915 and Pierce to Marye, September 1, 1915, 763.72114/537 and 820; Klante, "Die deutschen Kriegsgefangenen," p. 192.

40. V. Kopylov, "Vserosiyskiy s'ezhd voyennoplennykh sotsial-demokratov internatsionalistov (aprel 1918 g.)," in Birman *et al.* (eds.), *op. cit.*, pp. 66-89.

41. The expression "barbed-wire disease" *(Stacheldrahtkrankheit)* was coined by a Swiss physician, but all prisoners knew it and had a word for it. See A.L. Vischer, *Barbed Wire Disease: A Psychological Study of the Prisoner of War* (London, 1919). An excellent example of the behavior and attitudes associated with "Stacheldrahtkrankheit" are in Burghard Breitner, *Unverwundet gefangen: Aus meinem sibirischen Tagebuck* (Wien [Vienna], 1921), pp. 132-134, 163, 170, 179-180, and 232. Gustav Krist, *Poschol Plenny!* (Wien [Vienna], 1936), pp. 42-43, comments on its effects in Turkestan. Hans Bayer used POW newspapers and literary journals as well as Vischer to describe it in *Presse und Nachrichtenwesen der im Weltkrieg Kriegsgefangenen Deutschen* (Berlin, 1939), pp. 9-19, 76-80.

42. Hermann Pörzgen, *Theater ohne Frau: Das Bühnenleben der Kriegsgefangenen Deutschen 1914-1920* (Königsberg, 1933), pp. 157-164; Franz J. Hentschel, *Auf Tamerlans Spuren: Des Ostens Dämmerung oder Aufstieg? Selbsterlebtes aus Turkestan und Russland* (Leitmeritz [Litoměřiče], 1924), pp. 16-17, 27-29, 55.

43. Klante, *op. cit.*, p. 194; Theodore W. Koch, *Books in the War: The Romance of Library War Service* (Boston, 1919), p. 267.

44. Frederick Harris *et al.* (eds.), *Service with Fighting Men: An Acount of the Work of the American Young Men's Christian Associations in the World War* (New York, 1922); Ethan T. Colton, "With the YMCA in Revolutionary Russia," *Russian Review,* XIV (1955), 133; Roger Ames to Richard T. Evans, February 22, 1916, 763.72114/1526.

45. Bayer, *op. cit.*, pp. 62-74.

46. A. Strizhkova, "Pechat' inostrannykh internatsionalistov v Sovetskoy Rossii (1917-1920 gg.)," in Birman *et al.* (eds.), *op. cit.*, p. 371; A.W. Tregubow [Tregubov], "Über die Presse der Sozialdemokraten-Internationalisten in Sowjetrussland (1918)," *Beiträge zur Geschichte der Arbeiterbewegung*, XIV (1972), 268-283.

47. Price, *op. cit.*, p. 128; Dyboski, *op. cit.*, p. 36; Hentschel, *op. cit.*, pp. 28-29; Anton Schreinert, *Die Kriegsgefangenen-Handelsschule in Beresowka (Sibirien)* (Aussig, 1920). The YMCA published a guide for this sort of activity. See J. Gustav White, *Educational Activities for War Prisoners: A Manual . . . with Plans of Study and Examination Questions* (Geneva, 1918).

48. Klante, "Die deutschen Kriegsgefangenen," p. 199.

49. *The New York Times*, April 29, 1917 (I, 5:2); V.R. Kopylov, "Kak voyennoplennye v Rossii prazdnovali 1. maia 1917 g.," *Istoriya SSSR*, III (May-June 1967), No. 3, 32-37; Wilhelm Vogel, *Zwischen Weissen und Roten: Sibirische Erlebnisse* (Berlin, 1929), pp. 16-25; Popov, *op. cit.*, pp. 76-87.

50. *The New York Times*, September 11, 1917 (I:7); Ernst Streeurwitz, "Der Brand von Laischew," in Weiland, *op. cit.*, I, 271.

51. Völgyes, *op. cit.*, p. 65.

52. F.M. Bailey, *Mission to Tashkent* (London, 1946), p. 8; Hentschel, *op. cit.*, p. 37; Anne-Marie Wenzel, *Deutsche Kraft in Fesseln: Fünf Jahre deutscher Schwesterndienst in Sibirien (1916-1921)* (Potsdam, 1931), pp. 44-47.

53. Winfried Baumgart, *Deutsche Ostpolitik 1918: Von Brest-Litowsk bis zum Ende des Ersten Weltkrieges* (Wien [Vienna], 1966), p. 258 n.; Brändström, *op. cit.*, p. 195.

54. Karl von Bothmer, *Mit Graf Mirbach in Moskau* (Tübingen, 192), pp. 10-14.

55. *Ibid.*, pp. 64, 91; Baumgart, *op.cit.*, p. 253 n.; Edward H. Carr, *A History of Soviet Russia: The Bolshevik Revolution 1917-1923* (New York, 1950), II, 22 n. The text of the agreement is in Scheidl, *op. cit.*, p. 139.

56. Brändström, *op. cit.*, p. 198.

57. Olga H. Gankin and H.H. Fisher, *The Bolsheviks and the World War: The Origin of the Third International* (Stanford, Cal., 1940), p. 214.

58. Soviet and socialist-bloc authors emphasize the Internationalists as the only significant aspect of the prisoner-of-war experience, other than the foreign interventions. Cf. V.R. Kopylov, "International Units of the Red Army," in *Great Soviet Encyclopedia: A Translation of the Third Edition* (New York, 1976), X, 343; A.A. Struchkov, "Internatsional'nye gruppy RKP (b) i voinskiye formirovaniya v Sovetskoy Rossii (1918-1920 gg.)," *Istrorischeskiy Arkhiv*. 1957, No. 4, pp. 3-36; and Birman *et al.* (eds.), *op. cit.*, contains twelve articles by separate authors. Studies emphasizing Germans include Konstantin L. Selesnjow [Selesnev], "Deutsche Internationalisten im Kampf um die Verteidigung der jungen Sowjetmacht (1917-1921)," *Zeitschrift für Militärgeschichte*, IV (1967), 167-177; N.A. Sabajew [Subayev], "Deutsche Internationalisten in Tatarien (1917-1920)," *Beiträge zur Geschichte der deutschen Arbeiterbewegung*, VII (1955), 290-297; and I.M. Kulinitsch [Kulinich] and M.M. Koschik [Koshik], "Die revolútionäre Tätigkeit der deutschen kommunistischen Gruppe Spartakus in der Ukraine im Jahre 1919," *Beiträge zur Geschichte der deutschen Arbeiterbewegung*, I (1959), 577-593.

59. Rudolf L. Tökés, *Béla Kun and the Hungarian Soviet Republic: The Origins and the Role for the Communist Pary of Hungary in the Revolutions of 1918-1919* (New York, 1967), p. 71 and *passim;* Völgyes, *op. cit.*, pp. 67-85; Struchkov, *op. cit.*, p. 5.

60. James Bunyan, *Intervention, Civil War and Communism in Russia, April-December 1918* (Baltimore, 1936), pp. 93-94.

61. Raabl-Werner, *op. cit.*, p. 782; Völgyes, *op. cit.*, p. 84; A.H. Brun, *Troublous Times: Experiences in Bolshevik Russia and Turkestan* (London, 1931), p. 78. Others insist that hunger or self-defense against bandits or mob violence were the chief motives for enlistment. See Rudolf Köstenberger, *Sechs Jahre in Turkestan* (Graz, 1923), p. 36; Hentschel, *op. cit.*, p. 44. Christian Schmitt, *Schwert und Kosakenpeitsche: Erinnerungen an die mehr als 5-jährige Kriegsgefangenschaft des Fabrikarbeiters Christian Schmitt in Russland, Kaukasien und Sibirien* (Eberbach-am-Neckar, 1921), insists that he enlisted during the Russo-Polish war in the hope of getting through the Polish lines.

62. Vogel, *op. cit.*, p. 42; Dimitry V. Lehovich, *White against Red: The Life of General Anton Denikin* (New York, 1974), pp. 220-222.

63. Klante, *Von der Wolga*, pp. 98-99; D.J. Footman, *Civil War in Russia* (London, 1961), p. 138 n.

64. A recent profile of this debate is in Eugene P. Trani, "Woodrow Wilson and the Decision to Intervene in Russia: A Reconstruction," *The Journal of Modern History*, XLVII (1976), 440-461, See also Baumgart, *op. cit.*, pp. 54-56.

65. Renée-Marguerite Cramer, "Repatriement des prisonniers de guerre centraux en Russie et en Sibérie et des prisonniers de guerre russe en Allemagne," *Revue international de la Croix-Rogue*, II (1920), 549-550; *The New York Times* March 13, 1918 (2:1), *ibid.*, May 22, 1918 (3:1); "Gefangenenheimschaffung aus Russland," *Nachrichtenblatt der Reichszentralstelle für Kriegs- und Zivilgefangene*, No. 27 (März, 1920).

66. *The New York Times*, August 28, 1918 (1:4); Richard G. Plaschka *et al.*, *Innere Front: Militarassistenz, Widerstand und Umsturz in der Donaumonarchie 1918* (Wien [Vienna], 1974), I, 278-290.

67. Tökés, *op. cit.*, *passim; The New York Times*, September 30, 1953 (1); Julius Deutsch, "Otto Bauer," *Neue österreichische Biographie* (Wien [Vienna], 1957), X, 209-218; Didijer, *op. cit.*, pp. 30-35.

68. Cramer, *op. cit.*, p. 539, 542-543; Gaston Lichtenstein, *Repatriation of Prisoners of War from Siberia: A Documentary Narrative* (Richmond, Va., 1924), p. 55-58; Lansing to Polk, August 16, 1919, in Suda L. Bane and Ralph H. Lutz (eds.), *Organization of American Relief in Europe 1918-1919* (Stanford, Cal., 1943), p. 674.

69. Lichtenstein, *op. cit.*, pp. 14-18.

70. League of Nations, *Official Journal Records of the First Assembly Plenary Meetings*, Microfilm reel 37 [402], pp. 136-144 (November 18, 1920); League of Nations, *Official Journal Records of the Assembly, 1922*, Part 1, Microfilm reel 41 [406], "Report Submitted to the Assembly by the Fifth Committee," pp. 144-145.

71. E.E. Reynolds, *Nansen* (Harmondsworth, England, 1949), pp. 214-223.

72. *League Official Journal*, November 18, 1920, reel 37 [402], p. 137.

THE CZECH LEGION IN ITALY DURING WORLD WAR I

Rowan A. Williams

Despite their propensity to settle in foreign parts – substantial colonies existed in Russia, France, and The United States – only about three hundred Czechs and Slovaks were resident in Italy when that state declared war on Austria-Hungary on May 23, 1915.[1] Officially nominated "Austrians" by the Italian government, these unfortunates were either interned or placed under house arrest. The outstanding exception was the Czech Karel Veselý, who had resided many years in Brescia. On his own initiative and working alone at his own expense, Veselý rented an office in Rome, which he named "The Bohemian Office," and set about the creation of a new Czech image in the Italian press. One of Veselý's projects was the translation and publication of Edvard Beneš's *Bohemia Against Austria-Hungary.*[2] As secretary general of the Czech National Council in Paris, Beneš seized upon the occasion for a journey to Rome.

At the very same time (June 1917) the president of the council, Tomáš G. Masaryk, was in Russia trying to form a Czech national army to fight against the Central Powers. As early as 1915 Masaryk had declared: "Neither the Allies nor Vienna will be able to pass us by in silence if we have soldiers. Without a decisive military struggle we shall obtain nothing from anybody."[3] The council was particularly interested in the Czech and Slovak prisoners of war in Italy, and as political a mentality as that of Edvard Beneš could not have resisted the opportunity to approach the Italian authorities on the question.[4]

The third member of the triumvirate who made up the council was its vice-president Milan Rostislav Štefánik, a proven friend of the Italians. A naturalized French citizen, Štefánik had been born at Bratislava in 1880. He had volunteered for the French Army at the outbreak of war in 1914 and had seen action as a pilot on the Aisne and near Ypres. On a flight over the Italian front in the spring of 1916, Štefánik had observed a large enemy formation, entirely undetected by the Italians, moving into a threatening position. Štefánik immediately informed the Italian supreme command and the gathering offensive was crushed.[5] This was the man who in April 1918 became, in addition to his other duties, head of the Italian representation on the Czech National Council.[6] Although Štefánik was only a lieutenant colonel, the French promoted him to acting brigadier general the following June.

The long-range plan of Masaryk and his young friends was to recruit a Czech national army in Russia, Italy and France, and have it concentrated in France.[7] In the initial phases after Italy entered the war, about a thousand Czechs and Slovaks had deserted to the Italians. Their number was appreciably augmented following the Italian victory at Gorizia (August 1916) and during the eleventh Battle of the Isonzo (August 1917).[8] There was a strong undercurrent of leftist revolt among the enlisted men in Italy's POW camps.[9] At one of them, Santa Maria Capua Vetere, in January 1917 the men organized themselves into a body calling itself "The Czecho-Slovak Volunteer Corps." Their initiative spread with astonishing speed and branches were soon formed elsewhere.[10] The one in the camp at Salerno even formally declared war on the Austro-Hungarian Empire. In the camp at Padula, south of Salerno, were concentrated 10,229 men.[11] Encouraged by local agents of the Czech National Council, they published a monthly journal, *The Struggle,* in which they expressed their wishes. Above all, they wanted to fight the Austrians alongside the Italian army. Failing this, they declared their willingness to fight in France. And they wished to act as a national army of occupation in their homeland.[12] Clearly, the leadership in Paris was obliged to respond to this call from the camp, which it had itself largely inspired.

Beneš and Štefánik were in constant close touch with the French government, which was increasingly distressed at the high casualty rate in the trenches. As early as the spring of 1916 it had asked the Russian government to send an expeditionary force to be deployed in France.[13] Now it was apparent that if the Czech National Council were in a position to supply trained men, it might well demand recognition of cobelligerency. September of 1917 found Beneš again in Rome to negotiate the release of Czech and Slovak prisoners who wanted to volunteer for a Czech formation to fight in France.[14] Almost every day Beneš discussed the project with the Italian military authorities, and met with only frustration. General Montanori, the deputy foreign minister, was totally under the influence of his superior, Baron Sidney C. Sonnino. Gen. Gaetano E. Giardino, the war minister, was a firm believer in the Hague convention of 1907.[15] Gen. Baron di Spingardi, president of the Royal Prisoners' Commission, whom Beneš judged an Austrophile, was a stickler for the Hague stipulations about not using prisoners of war to fight against their homeland.

The Italians' initial lack of cooperation is understandable. Sonnino was prejudiced against Slavs because of Italian rivalry with the South Slavs over Trieste and the Istrian peninsula. He would scarcely at this point be anxious to accede to the wishes of the Czechs and Slovaks, the South Slavs' most steadfast friends and ethnic cousins.[16] Sonnino told Beneš that the Austro-Hungarians had so many Italian prisoners that he was compelled to abide by the Hague convention. He doubted whether he could liberate the Czech and Slovak prisoners, much less send them to France. The Austrians might retaliate by sending thousands of Italians to Syria or Turkey "Where they would perish wholesale."[17] Agile diplomatist that he was, Beneš at once challenged the objection. Surely if the prisoners were formed into a section of a Czecho-Slovak national army to fight in Italy there would be no grounds for deporting Italian prisoners to the east. Ultimately it was agreed that a military force would indeed be recruited from among Italy's prisoners, but it would be employed in Italy under the direct authority of the

Italian supreme command, though it would be recognized as a part of the projected Czech forces in France and Russia.[18] This monumental decision having been reached, Beneš boarded a train for Paris on 10 October.

Disillusionment soon followed. The Italians had agreed only on "employment," never imagining the prisoners in a combatant role.[19] A formal note from Gen. Giardino spelling out the Italian position reached Paris on October 14:

> 1.The Italian government would recognize the authority of the Czech National Council.
>
> 2.It would free the prisoners and establish a joint control over them with the Czech National Council.
>
> 3.It would form the prisoners into semimilitary detachments which would not serve at the front but in the communications zone.
>
> 4.The liberated troops would not be subject to military discipline but rather to the discipline of prisoners of war.[20]

Obviously, since Masaryk's "decisive military struggle" could not be realized with picks and shovels, further persuasion was needed. The Italians began to implement the "agreement" in September, releasing prisoners and forming them into labor companies.

It was at this point (October 24) that the Italian proponents of intervention were rudely shocked by the disaster of Caporetto. A force of thirty Austro-Hungarian divisions, bolstered by seven German, smashed into the Italian Second Army.[21] Not until they reached the Tagliamento river were the Italians able, even partially, to regroup. Whole divisions had been surrounded and cut off. Of 400,000 Italians lost, 350,000 were taken prisoner.[22] Immediately the Italians appealed to the British and French for emergency support. In the longer run, the Italian need for trained military personnel was now obvious to all, which made the recruitment of prisoners of war a more attractive course.[23]

By February 1918 enough Czechs and Slovaks had been set free to form seven battalions; these were deployed near Mantua working on defensive positions.[24] From Russia, where he had been working to organize the largest contingent of the Czech Legion, Masaryk tried to influence the situation. He urged his warm friend the Italian ambassador to advise his government to form the Czechs into combat units.[25] In February Captains Šeba and Chalupa left Russia for Italy to help organize a Czech legion modeled on the army corps in Russia.[26]

Attached to the Italian supreme command was a Czechslovak officer, Captain Hlaváček, Štefánik's liaison officer.[27] It was Hlaváček who informed Štefánik of the intention to move the Czech labor units north from Mantua toward the combat zone. Štefánik immediately hurried off to Rome. A long audience with Vittorio E. Orlando proved fruitless. Though the Italian prime minister was sympathetic, he would make no commitment on paper. Gen. Armando Diaz, now chief of staff, was concerned about such difficulties as language and organization, but he admitted the weakness of Sonnino's position.[28] By the middle of April Štefánik had overcome all Italian reservations and misgivings.[29] Gen. Diaz forthwith directed Gen. Andrea Graziani to proceed with the creation of a Czecho-Slovak army division in Italy. Establishing his training center at Foligno in Umbria, Graziani and the Czech rank and file embarked on an instant love affair.[30]

A soldier's general, Graziani was tough, vigorous, impatient of staff work, and sported a ferocious forked beard. Though he epitomized the combat commander, the Czech officer corps resented his determination to emphasize military professionalism to the virtual exclusion of a Czechoslovak imprint on the legion.

The formal agreement that at long last founded the Czech Legion in Italy was signed April 21, 1918, at the Braschi Palace in Rome by Orlando, his new war minister, Gen. Zupelli, and Gen. Štefánik.[31] The document established that the freed prisoners would fight side by side with the Italian Army on an equal basis. Although it left the internal organization and disciplinary statutes to a subsequent accord, the agreement stipulated that the Czechs and Slovaks would serve jointly under officers appointed by the Czech National Council and Italian officers. The overall command would rest with an Italian general.[32]

The Italians believed that the Czech contribution would be most meaningful in the intelligence area. Small reconnaissance detachments were to be organized and dispersed along the entire front. Dressed in enemy uniforms, their mission included intelligence, propaganda, and sabotage. That this work was dangerous in the extreme did not deter volunteers; eventually, 2,000 men were involved.[33] Since these reconnaissance and commando units suffered a much higher casualty rate than normal combat troops, the Czech leadership was justifiably dissatisfied. Their contribution to the Allied war effort was being hopelessly diluted by submerging the Czechs in an ocean of Italian manpower. To satisfy the political leadership, therefore, the small units were amalgamated as the 39th Regiment. In actuality, however, they continued to function as separate units.

The nucleus of these small units was made up of a group of Czech and Slovak officers and men under the command of a Slovak, Dr. Privko. They had been positioned on the Austrian front line when they decided to desert to the Italians in June of 1917. They crossed over, bringing with them the detailed plans for an offensive aimed at Trent.[34]

The 39th Regiment appears again and again in the records, usually fighting as commando units of one company or less. In June 1918, the Seventh Company fought at Monte Asolone. With the First Company they held an important position at Cima Tre Pezi, south of Trent. Here they took a hundred prisoners and seven machine guns. By far the most remarkable achievement of the 39th was the capture of "almost an entire headquarters." The commando succeeded in infiltrating the Austrian lines individually, using their knowledge of the language and wearing the imperial uniform. Among the prisoners were several high-ranking officers.[35]

Much of the recruiting and organizing for the main force was accomplished by Capt. Šeba, who had done similar work in Russia. Organization and training were centered in Umbria, with the largest concentration at Foligno. Other regiments were stationed at Perugia, Spoleto, and elsewhere. By May 5, 1918, there were 17,000 Czech and Slovak prisoners of war. Of these, 14,000 responded to the first call for volunteers, 11,500 of whom were formed into the First Division.[36]

The appeal to the prisoners was based on anti-German nationalism. The ghost of 1848 continued to have influence before the outbreak of war in 1914, but it existed more as a "general sentimentality" than as a pragmatic political movement. The overall majority of prisoners were apathetic to the national appeal, and wary of an uncertain future in the military ranks of an ephemeral state. Representing more than 80 percent of the Czech prisoners in Allied custody, they elected not to join the Czech formations.[37]

On June 3 the division was redesignated the Sixth. While the legion continued to grow in numbers and to gain proficiency with the Italian No. 91 rifle and the unfamiliar dagger, others set about trying to regularize the status of these combat soldiers without a country of their own.

What was the status of the Czechoslovak soldier? There was no *corpus iuris,* civil or military, since there was no governing constitution. The individual legionary was not subject to Italian, or Russian, or French law. The Italian answer was to recognize the oath to the Czech National Council as establishing a foundation of legality. The two parties signed a convention to that effect June 30, 1918. On July 13 a Czech-Italian military tribunal was established.[38]

General Štefánik and his aides accelerated their recruiting efforts. On June 10 the Sixth Division received 600 legionaries from France. Eight hundred more were found in the prisoner cages behind the Salonika front.[39] Thomas Nelson Page, the United States ambassador to Italy, was a keen observer of Czech fortunes. He reported to United States Secretary of State Robert Lansing on May 9 that the Czechs had mustered about 12,000 men, and had been equipped from French and Italian stores.[40] Two weeks later Page recommended that the United States aid the legion by "encouraging their co-nationals in America to volunteer in the Czecho-Slovak Legion now acting in Italy with the Italian Army; they number 12,000 or, as they claim, 17,000."[41] The result was a statement issued by the United States War Department declaring that, at the direction of President Woodrow Wilson, Yugo-Slavs, Czechoslovaks and Ruthenians could be sworn into a Slav Legion. No one subject to American conscription was permitted to enlist, nor were

Slavs from coal-mining areas. Candidates were to be between the ages of 18 and 45, qualified for general military service, and loyal to the United States. Officers were to be of the same "race" and were to be trained at the Central Officers' Training School at Camp Lee, Virginia.[42]

These developments in the military sphere found reflection in both the political and intellectual areas. In the early stages of the war the Allies had sought to divide Austria-Hungary from Germany. Gradually, under the influence of Wilson's Fourteen Points and the active propaganda of a plethora of "national councils," policy veered toward a destruction of the Habsburg state. The Italian government permitted a meeting in Rome April 8-11 of representatives of the subject nations of Austria-Hungary.[43] Calling itself the Council of Oppressed Races of Austria-Hungary, this body passed many resolutions, one of which pleaded for the recognition of the Czech prisoners as combatants.[44] The press in this spring of 1918 was avid in its support. Gaetano Salvemini, in his *Unità,* and Zanotti-Bianco in *La Voce del Popolo* fervently endorsed the Czech cause. One publishing house produced a pamphlet, *La Storia di Bohemia,* while a mixed Italo-Czech committee worked on another entitled *La Nazione Cecoslovacca.* There was even an elaborate ceremony honoring Jan Hus, with the key note address given by Italian Senator Rizzini. The prestigious *Corriere della Sera* on this occasion published a special edition dedicated to the religious reformer's memory.[45]

The Czech National Council was particularly anxious that the division should be employed as an integral unit. With Graziani's hearty support, Štefánik continually insisted on this point in his dealings with the Italian supreme command. Graziani, in fact, exuberantly proposed an offensive on the Piave that would have Prague as its objective. The overworked officers at the supreme command were not amused. Nevertheless they did assign the division's 33rd Regiment to the Italian Third Army, commanded by the Duke of Aosta.[46]

The enemy high command was delighted to see the return of campaign weather to the Italian front. They had been unable to follow up the crushing defeat at Caporetto the previous October in the teeth of an Alpine winter. The

Austro-Hungarians nursed only contempt for the Italian army, believing it undermanned and demoralized.[47] In contrast Austro-Hungarian troop morale was high, for all agreed that the major enemy of the Habsburg Empire was Italy, and "were enthusiastic to fight Italian pretensions."[48] The Habsburg high command decided to strike on the Piave with the seizure of Venice, Verona, and Brescia as the ultimate objective. Fifty-three infantry and five cavalry divisions were available.[49]

At the Italian supreme command, Gen. Diaz fully expected an attack, but was determined to surrender no more Italian soil to the enemy. Nevertheless, he fortified the river lines in the area: the Adige, the Brenta, and the Po. Large areas along the latter two waterways were to be flooded by breaching the levees, if necessary.[50] Initially Diaz had planned to concentrate his forward strength against the forbidding heights of Austro-Hungarian held Monte Grappa. However, unexpected intelligence arrived at the Italian supreme command. A Czech officer named Stinny deserted to the Italians with news of the Austro-Hungarian plan in time for Italian troops to be diverted to a more southerly concentration on the Piave.

The Austro-Hungarian offensive lunged southward on June 15. Although the first battalion of the 34th Regiment received the full brunt of the attack on the high ground at San Dona di Piave, it managed to throw back the enemy. At Forsalta the first battalion of the 33rd Regiment also fought off the Austro-Hungarian offensive. The two battalions suffered 181 casualties: 62 killed, 18 missing, and 101 wounded. A "certain number" were taken prisoner, 11 of whom were executed as traitors at Oderzo.[51] The third company of the 33rd Regiment did not fare so well. They were surrounded by the enemy and, though they defended themselves for more than six hours, ultimately had to surrender. Of 40 men, 18 were killed and 15 captured. After a brief court martial all 15 were executed at Conegliano in Veneto. Their bodies were exposed for six days, each bearing a placard on which was written in six languages "Traitors to the Fatherland."[52]

The valor of the Czecho-Slovaks was proved beyond question in the eight days of fighting on the Piave.[53] The

Duke of Aosta, as commander of the Third Army, specifically commended the first battalion of the 33rd Regiment, while Masaryk telegraphed the legion, jubilantly proclaiming, "All Czechs are *condottieri*"[54] After the successful repulse of the offensive, King Victor Emmanuel III, with Štefánik present, decorated 33 Czech and Slovak soldiers at Nove di Bassano.[55]

In no way does it detract from the bravery of the Czechs and Slovaks to note that they knew very well that death awaited them if they were captured. In the Piave engagement, 37 of them were taken prisoner; all were executed. It is an easy matter to cry "atrocity" at the killing of any prisoner of war, but the bald fact was that a body of men such as the Czech Legion could find no sanction in law.

Furious, Štefánik had leaflets dropped over enemy lines promising that for every legionary executed, ten Austro-German and Magyar prisoners would be killed. It did not take the other side long to respond with their own leaflets. They pointed out that the legionaries were traitors according to international law, and that they would retaliate on the basis of ten Italian prisoners for each Austro-Hungarian killed. For their part, they declared, they were acting according to Austrian law and international law. "Who," the message concluded, "is Lt. Col. Štefánik?"[56]

Following the battle on the Piave, the division moved to Monte Baldo, near Verona, for rest and recuperation.[57] The commandos of the 39th Regiment, meanwhile, continued their operations. One four-man patrol crossed Lake Garda under cover of darkness to accomplish "a delicate and secret mission." The patrol arrived at their destination in good order only to find the enemy waiting for them. One Czech was killed in the ensuing skirmish, one escaped in the darkness (and lived to tell the tale), and two were taken prisoner. These two were executed at Geotta di Riva on July 6.[58]

After a long rest period, on August 15 the division relieved the XIII and XVII Groups of the Italian Alpine troops along a twelve-mile stretch of the front line from Lake Garda to the Adige River. Brig. Gen. Sapienza commanded the division's second brigade, which was positioned in the line, while Brig. Gen. de Vita commanded the first brigade, the division reserve.[59] The bulk of the second brigade was concentrated at lofty Monte Dosso Alto, the lynchpin of the whole defense line. Here were 12,500 men under the command of some 300 Italian and Czech officers. All was calm for several days, but on August 29 the enemy attacked in force. The 34th Regiment held its position. Next, on September 9 the Austro-Hungarians concentrated against the 33rd Regiment. Again the line held, as infantry threw back the attackers at Dossa Casina. There followed a general outbreak of artillery duels and exchanges of small-arms fire all along the line, reaching its maximum violence on September 21.[60] Following an intense artillery and gas preparation, a superior Austro-Hungarian force, singing the Czech national anthem, moved toward the legion. Desperately the defenders clung to their position, throwing hand grenades at close quarters. After two hours the Austro-Hungarians succeeded in occupying the high ground. Less than an hour later, the first brigade launched a counter-attack, and regained the crucial terrain by 5:30 a.m.[61] This action at Monte Dosso Alto was the most significant engagement of the Czechs and Slovaks in Italy. Again the Czech National Council wired its hearty congratulations, and on October 3 Prime Minister Orlando spoke in the Italian parliament in favor of Czechoslovak independence.[62]

Although Austro-Hungarian troops still stood on Allied soil, all was far from well with the empire's cause. Bulgaria surrendered September 30, causing near panic in Budapest. The political leaders were justly fearful that French and Serbian troops along the River Sava would invade from the south. The Allied army on this front numbered some 627,000 men, organized into 29 divisions.[63] The Hungarian politicians put pressure on the imperial high command to release Hungarian units to defend the homeland.[64] The first transfers were effected on the Piave front, where improvised Austrian units were hastily thrown into the line. To keep out subversive propaganda and revolutionary agitation, the high command created an isolating pocket between the front line troops and the interior. Nevertheless, there were desertions and mutinies in October.

Austria-Hungary's September proposal for a general peace conference, together with the collapse of Bulgaria at the end of that month, augured well for the plans of the Czech National Council. Already in September Beneš had obtained Masaryk's approval of his plan to constitute a government and proclaim the Czechoslovak Republic. All that obstructed this course was the failure of the Italian government to recognize the council. Beneš therefore decided on a third journey to Rome, and in the course of it, to visit the Czechoslovak division in the field. Beneš recounts in his memoir:

> I started from Verona for the front by Lake Garda, and it is still with emotion that I remember the sight of the Alps occupied by our troops. Our cars passed through places where suddenly on the slopes there appeared hundreds of green uniforms and Italian hats with the red-white cockade. Farther on we unexpectedly passed from the mountain defile into a broad cavity above which, in an ampitheater were assembled about 2,000 of our troops in a deluge of flags and waving hats. There was a long outburst of cheering, and I was then deeply moved as they intoned the strains of our national hymn.[65]

Beneš inspected the very site where the Czechs had defended themselves with hand grenades. After visiting the wounded in a Verona hospital, he attended a conference with the ranking Czech officers at Spezzia. Here all the grievances against Graziani were aired; his refusal to allow a distinctively Czechoslovak stamp to the division and his stubbornness were particularly stressed. Shortly thereafter Graziani was relieved by Gen. Luigi Piccioni, presumably as a result of Beneš's personal intervention. Ironically, this change occurred the very day before the great general offensive.

After Dosso Alto the Czech division moved into Castelfranco Veneto, northeast of Padua, prepared to play a part in the final offensive. The main Italian thrust was in the direction of Belluno, with a secondary attack by the VIII and X Armies, which were to cross the Piave almost due north of Venice.[66] To deceive the enemy, the bersaglieri struck first in the area of the secondary attack on October 20. The Czechs supported this diversion, losing six killed and twenty-four wounded.[67]

On October 24, a year to the day after Caporetto, the great Italian offensive exploded along the entire front from the Alto Adige to the Adriatic. Fifty Italian, three British, two French, and one Czechoslovak divisions threw themselves against the enemy.[68] For two days the Austro-Hungarian army held, then the troops took affairs into their own hands. Hungarian, Czech, Croat, Slovene, Ruthene, Polish, Serb, and even Austrian units refused to fight, mutinied, and demanded to be sent home. If necessary, they fought their officers and those units that remained loyal.[69] By November 2 the Austro-Hungarian army "ceased to be a military instrument." Officers of the imperial headquarters received armistice terms from Gen. Armando Diaz on November 2.

For the Czechoslovak Legion new challenges lay ahead, but for the moment there was time for a parade before King Victor Emmanuel. At Padua, where the division was now stationed, the king, together with the Count of Turin and Gen. Diaz and Pietro Badoglio, took the review and presented colors to each of the four regiments.[70] Though they had fought on a limited front, the Czechs and Slovaks nevertheless lost 300 killed, 60 executed, and thousands wounded or frozen to death. The troops won 16 Silver Medals for Military Valor and 18 bronze, in addition to 10 war crosses.[71] Later the Italian government inscribed a large boulder, which can still be seen at Rovereto, the scene of the last Czech engagement. The inscription reads:

> To the Czech legionaries who heroically died on our front, champions of the dream as we were. Supporters of liberty and justice. Italy forever salutes them in sacred remembrance.

NOTES

1. Emo Egoli, *I Legionari cecoslovacchi in Italia 1915-1918,* (Rome, 1968), p. 18.

2. Beneš's pamphlet first appeared in Paris in 1916 under the title *Detruisez l'Autriche-Hongrie!* The English and Italian translations appeared the following year.

3. Thomas G. Masaryk, *The Making of a State* (London, 1927), p. 109.

4. Edvard Beneš, *My War Memoirs* (London, 1938), pp. 170-171. Vesely had furthered the establishment of an "Italian Committee for Czechoslovak Independence" which shepherded into the Italian press a periodic journal with articles and news items penned in Prague and

funneled through Switzerland to Italy. It was entitled *The Czechoslovak Nation in the World War.* Egoli, *op. cit.*, p. 23.

5. Masaryk, *op. cit.*, p. 109.

6. Giulio C. Gotti-Porcinari, *Coi legionari cecoslovacchi al fronte italiano ed in Slovacchia* (Rome, 1933), p. 33.

7. Masaryk, *op. cit.*, p. 109.

8. Egoli, *op. cit.*, p. 20.

9. Officers were confined in two separate camps. Numbering about 1,000 in 1917, they were located in the Termini Imerese (Palermo) and Cittaducale (Rieta). The officers did not share the troops' revolutionary zeal. The struggle to the enlisted men was not simply to establish a nation, but also to effect far-reaching social reform. Most officers, especially those from the regular army formations, made it obvious that they considered themselves a privileged class. Egoli, *op. cit.*, p. 42.

10. Karel Pichlik *et al., Cerveno, bila a ruda,* [Red, White and Crimson] (Prague, 1967), p. 316.

11. Pichlik *et al., op. cit.*, p. 319.

12. Egoli, *op. cit.*, pp. 26-27.

13. Beneš, *op. cit.*, p. 123. Ultimately, 10,000 Russian soldiers arrived in France, among them an obscure soldier named Rodion Malinovskiy, later marshal of the Red Army, scourge of Slovakia, and Soviet minister of defense.

14. *Ibid.*, p. 203.

15. The Hague Convention states that the capturing power "may utilize the labor of prisoners of war," but that such labor "shall have no connection with the operations of the war." C.I. Bevans (ed.), *Treaties and Other International Agreements of the United States of America 1776-1949,* Vol. 1 (Washington, D.C., 1968).

16. Only reluctantly did Masaryk and Beneš relinquish their scheme of a corridor physically connecting Czechoslovakia and Yugoslavia. Cf. Peter Pastor, *Hungary Between Wilson and Lenin* (New York, 1976), p. 85. Sonnino was so suspicious of Slavs that Leonido Bissolati, a dedicated foe of the Austrians, was brought into the government as minister without portfolio to balance him.

17. Beneš, *op. cit.*, p. 205.

18. Gotti-Porcinari, *op. cit.*, p. 35.

19. Egoli, *op. cit.*, p. 22.

20. Beneš, *op. cit.*, p. 214.

21. Cyril Falls, *Caporetto, 1917* (London, 1965), p. 34. Present were two officers destined for fame in a later war: Captain Erwin Rommel and General Pietro Badoglio. *Ibid.*

22. *Ibid.*, p. 141.

23. Pichlik *et al. op. cit.*, p. 321.

24. Gotti-Porcinari, *op. cit.*, p. 35.

25. Masaryk, *op. cit.*, p. 135.

26. *Ibid.*, p. 181.

27. A lieutenant in the Austro-Hungarian army, Hlaváček had deserted to the Italians in 1916 with important documents. Promoted by his "captors," he was decorated by them and assigned to their supreme command. Egoli, *op. cit.*, p. 75 n.

28. Chief, French Military Mission to Minister of War, March 10, 1918, in Ludovit Holotík, *Štefánikovská legenda a vznik CSR* [The Štefánik Legend and the Origin of the Czechoslovak Republic] (Bratislava, 1960), p. 443. Beneš later wrote of Štefánik's mission that it was "his greatest success during his war-time activity." *Op. cit.*, p. 290.

29. French Ambassador Berrère so wired his foreign minister. Holotík, *op. cit.*, p. 451. He later rhapsodized Štefánik's "brilliantly accomplished mission." Berrère to Foreign Minister, 6 June, 1918. Holotík, *op. cit.*, p. 455.

30. Gotti-Porcinari, *op. cit.*, pp. 35-36.

31. Egoli, *op. cit.*, p. 26.

32. *Ibid.* Supreme Command Circular No. 6500-0 immediately followed this understanding, approving "The Czechoslovak Volunteer Corps." *Ibid.*, p. 32.

33. *Ibid.*

34. Characteristically, the Austrian press screamed to the echo. The Austrians nourished an expectation of desertion and mutiny long before the war, and were hypersensitive on the issue. Cf. Gunther E. Rothenberg, *The Army of Francis Joseph* (West Lafayette, Ind., 1976), p. 184. The Italians probably would not have been so impressed with Privko's desertion had the *Reichsrat* and the Austrian press not exploded over the incident.

35. Egoli, *op. cit.*, p. 45.

36. Beneš, *op. cit.*, p. 296. It comprised four regiments: the 31st, 32nd, 33rd, and 34th. This same day the first battalion of the 33rd regiment moved into the Piave front. Egoli, *op. cit.*, p. 38. The first major Czechoslovak formation committed against the enemy, the 33rd, was attached to Gen. Grazioli's assault army. Gotti-Porcinari, *op. cit.*, p. 45.

37. Jonathan Zorach, "The Czecho-Slovak Army 1918-1932" (Doctoral dissertation, Columbia University, 1975), p. 16.

38. Egoli, *op. cit.*, p. 34.

39. *Ibid.*, p. 40. Those prisoners declining to join the legion were concentrated at Badia di Sulmona and Avanzano. *Ibid.*

40. Page to Secretary of State, 7 May, 1918. *Foreign Relations of the United States: 1918 (here after cited as FRUS), Supplement 1: "The World War," I, 803.*

41. Ibid., May 18, 1918, *loc. cit.*, p. 806.

42. *Ibid.*, pp. 827-828.

43. Pichlik *et al.*, *op. cit.*, p. 324.

44. *Ibid.*, p. 324.

45. Egoli, *op. cit.*, p. 38.

46. *Ibid.*, p. 41.

47. Girard L. McEntee, *Italy's Part in Winning the World War* (Princeton, 1934), p. 96.

48. Norman Stone, *The Eastern Front, 1914-1917* (New York, 1975), p. 243.

49. Francis Deák, *Hungary at the Peace Conference* (New York, 1942), p. 9.

50. McEntee, *op. cit.*, p. 94. "If the new trench work had been placed end to end it would have almost reached from New York City to Salt Lake City." *Ibid.*, p. 95.

51. Egoli, *op. cit.*, p. 42. Among those killed was Captain Jan Čapak, the president of the executive committee of the volunteer corps. He had been heading an infantry assault unit.

52. *Ibid.* p. 43 n.

53. "A legend has sprung up that the British and French troops saved the Italian Army. Be advised that of the fifty-six Allied divisions on the Italian front, fifty of them were Italian, three British. . . two French. . . and one Czechoslovak division. It will be at once obvious that the six

divisions of the Allies, as opposed to the fifty of Italy's, is a small proportion of the whole." McEntee, *op. cit.*, pp. 96-97.

54. Gotti-Porcinari, *op. cit.*, pp. 47.

55. Egoli, *op. cit.*, p. 43.

56. Gotti-Porcinari, *op. cit.*, pp. 47-49.

57. Egoli, *op. cit.*, p. 43.

58. *Ibid.*, p. 44.

59. Gotti-Porcinari, *op. cit.*, p. 47. On their committal, the British government issued a proclamation addressed to Austria-Hungary declaring that the legionaries had been recognized as cobelligerents by England. It was useless in stopping the executions.

60. Egoli, *op. cit.*, p. 45.

61. *Ibid.*, pp. 45-46; Gotti-Porcinari, *op. cit.*, p. 52.

62. Egoli, *op. cit.*, p. 46. The Italian government was remarkably late in recognizing the Czech National Council as a provisional government. France took that step June 29, England on August 14, and the United States on September 3. Italy did so only on October 24. *Ibid.*

63. M. Larcher, *La Grande Guerre dans les Balkans* (Paris, 1929) cited in Bogdan Krizman, "The Belgrade Armistice of 13 Nov. 1918," *The Slavonic and East European Review,* XLVIII, No. 110 (Jan., 1970), 77 n.

64. Thomas Cuninghame, "Between the War and the Peace Treaties," *The Hungarian Quarterly,* V (1939), No. 3, 414. Of the 58 Austro-Hungarian divisions deployed in Italy, almost half (27) were either Hungarian army units or militia-type Hungarian *honvéd* units. Deák, *op. cit.*, p. 9.

65. Beneš, *op. cit.*, pp. 428-429.

66. McEntee, *op. cit.*, pp. 104-105.

67. Egoli, *op. cit.*, p. 46.

68. McEntee, *op. cit.*, p. 116. Rothenberg differs, listing 51 Italian, three French and one Czechoslovak division. *Op. cit.*, p. 217. Troops of the 39th Regiment supported the Italians, entering the town of Rovereto with them. Egoli, *op. cit.*, p. 47. One regiment (the 332nd) of the U.S. 83rd Division participated in the offensive.

69. Rothenberg, *op. cit.*, p. 214.

70. Gotti-Porcinari, *op. cit.*, p. 63.

71. Egoli, *op. cit.*, p. 47.

CZECH AND SLOVAK PRISONERS OF WAR IN RUSSIA DURING THE WAR AND REVOLUTION

Josef Kalvoda

In mid-May 1917, a British intelligence officer, William Wiseman, reported to his superiors that there were 220,000 "Bohemian prisoners of war who surrendered to Russia, over 50% of whom are expert mechanics." Wiseman, the head of the British intelligence group (Secret Service – MI 1c, now known as MI 6) operating in the United States, from where he organized his intelligence work in Russia, advised his "Chief" to send "the leader of the most important CZECH secret society in America" to organize "the Czechs and Bohemians in Russia." Furthermore, "A similar leader from the chief SLOVAC [sic] Society in America would proceed to Petrograd and work on similar lines."[1] According to Wiseman, all 220,000 prisoners of war were almost "entirely reliable from the Allied point of view. If these prisoners could be released, they, with the other Czechs now in Russia, would form the nucleus of one of the most important and most bitterly anti-German societies."[2]

In the same report Wiseman claimed: "The Germans have managed to secure control of the most important secret societies in Russia, and it is necessary that this German influence should be exposed and counter-societies organized, if necessary."

In the summer of 1917 the leader of "the most important CZECH secret society in America", Emanuel V. Voska, whose code name was "Victor" and who was the head of

Professor Tomáš G. Masaryk's "private intelligence," financed and controlled by Wiseman since 1916, went to Russia together with other Czechs and one Slovak to conduct propaganda and gather intelligence.[3] Officially he and his group were members of the Committee of American Citizens of Slav Origin. This was, however, merely a cover for their work, and they reported to Wiseman's chief agent in Russia, the well-known writer W. Somerset Maugham.[4] Masaryk himself was dispatched by the British to Russia in May 1917. His task was to conduct propaganda aimed at keeping Russia in the war, and to recruit Czech and Slovak prisoners of war into the Czecho-Slovak army.[5]

Another memorandum written by Wiseman on June 30, 1917, stated that the Russian government had authorized the formation of "an independent Czecho-Slovak army which probably will number 250,000 men. This army consists of Czecho-Slovak prisoners who originally were drafted into the Austrian Army, but surrendered to the Russians as soon as the first opportunity afforded itself. The permission to organize an independent Bohemian army in Russia," the memorandum continues, "is tantamount to a recognition of Bohemian independence, which at least implicitly is also recognized in the Flag Day speech of President [Woodrow] Wilson."[6]

The data on the number of Czech and Slovak prisoners of war in Russia and the expected size of the Czecho-Slovak army in the Wiseman report came from his Czech agents operating in the United States, led by Voska, who in turn had their own informants and confidants in Russia.[7] The figure of 220,000 Bohemian prisoners of war may be fairly accurate, since "Bohemians" could also have been German-speaking prisoners of war from the Czech lands. However, to expect the formation of an army of 250,000 from among the Czech and Slovak prisoners of war in Russia was unrealistic, to say the least.

The relatively large number of Czech POWs in Russia was due, in part, to defections to the Russians during the early stages of the war. On one occasion a whole Czech regiment went over to the Russians. Among the reasons for those defections were pro-Russian sentiment among the Czechs and Slovaks, and the expectation of an early Russian victory in the war. Indeed, not only many Czech leaders but also some Allied government officials expected the Russians to reach the Czech lands before Christmas 1914.[8] The advancing Russian army, however, was stopped by the Germans, and the POWs had to stay in Russia for three years or more. As it happened, the Czech Legion, as the Czecho-Slovak army in Russia was usually called, left Siberia only in 1920.

There are no exact statistics on how many Czech and Slovak POWs were in Russia in 1917. Some of those who called themselves Bohemians were either bilingual or spoke merely German. Similarly, some of the Slovak POWs were bilingual. There were political differences among the Czech as well as among the Slovak prisoners of war, and only a minority of them joined the Czecho-Slovak army. Many of the POWs were apolitical and glad to be out of the war, or preferred a prisoner's life to soldiering. Some of them kept their oath of loyalty to the emperor and equated joining of the legion with treason. Indeed, more Czechs died for Austria-Hungary than joined the legion. Monuments in Czech towns and villages erected to those who lost their lives during World War I testify to it.

The building of the Czecho-Slovak army in Russia has to be placed into a broader political context. Already before the war Czech settlers in Russia had their associations and kept in touch with some Czech political leaders in Austria-Hungary, most notably Dr. Karel Kramář, the leader of the Young Czech party in the Vienna parliament, whose wife was Russian and who often visited Russia and his villa in the Crimea.[9] Members of the Czech associations in Kiev also maintained contacts with such Czechs as Dr. Lev Borský, one of the leaders of the State-Rights Progressive party, the only Czech political party that openly advocated the Bohemian kingdom's independence in its prewar program. Kramář rejected such a program, suggesting that only "political children" could talk about Czech independence in view of the fact that the Czech lands border on Germany. Yet shortly before the war he himself had drafted a constitution of an All-Slavic Federation to which the Bohemian kingdom would also belong. The Tsar of Russia would be its emperor. (It was modeled on the German Empire.) In all secrecy Kramář transmitted the document to the Russian foreign minister,

Sergey Sazonov, but Masaryk learned about it from a Russian intelligence officer early in 1915. Kramář knew Sazonov and many other Russian leaders and diplomats personally. When the war started, the Czech leader expected the "Czech question" to be solved by the victory of Russian arms.

The British, rivals of the Russians, closely watched the activities of Czech political leaders in the Vienna parliament and elsewhere. They knew of Kramář's pro-Russian orientation.[10] In their pursuit of policy of balance of power, they tried to prevent the hegemony of Russia or any other state in Europe.[11] Russian control of the Czech lands and the Slovak areas of Hungary would undoubtedly upset the balance of power in Europe. Austria-Hungary had its place in the European balance: it was a buffer against both Russia and Germany. The establishment of an independent Poland and the cession of some provinces of Austria-Hungary, promised by secret treaties in 1915 to Italy and Rumania, would still leave the Danubian empire a great power in Central Europe. Without the Czech lands and Slovakia, however, Austria-Hungary would cease to be a barrier to either German or Russian hegemony in the Balkans. Moreover, with Bohemia, Bulgaria, Poland and Serbia within an All-Slavic Federation headed by Russia, as proposed by Kramář, Russian hegemony in Europe would be accomplished. Control of the pivotal Czech lands and Slovakia was the key to the future organization of Europe. From the British point of view, Czech independence was a lesser evil than Russian hegemony in Europe.

Since both the British and Russian governments were interested in that key area, the orientation of the leadership of the Czech independence movement abroad during the war was of utmost importance to them. The presence of a large number of Czech and Slovak POWs in Russia, and the pro-Russian feelings of the Czechs and Slovaks, placed the Russian government in a better position to help to liberate the two nations, and to influence their future state's orientation in foreign affairs. Fully aware that their British and French allies would frown on any attempt to incorporate this crucial Central European region into a Russian-led federation, the Russian government decided in 1916 to support Czecho-Slovak independence.[12] It did not lose any of its interest, however, in who would be at the helm of the new state and who would formulate its policies.

It was the view of an Austro-Hungarian expert in the Russian ministry of foreign affairs that to annex the Czech lands and Slovakia to Russia would be unwise in view of the fact that too many non-Russians already lived in Russia. Besides, the Czechs were Roman Catholics and had a "German" culture. For these and other reasons it would be better if they were to have an independent state of their own, but friendly toward Russia. Since Masaryk was pro-Western, anti-Russian, and most likely under British material influence, the expert advised, it was important to prevent him from gaining control of the Czecho-Slovak independence movement in Russia or of the armed force that was to be formed in accordance with proposals made by the Alliance of Czecho-Slovak Associations in Russia and the Russian military.[13]

The Russian government was well acquainted with Professor Masaryk, a deputy in the Vienna parliament, who arrived in England in 1915. They knew that some Czechs in Russia were under his leadership and received instructions from him. In order to offset Masaryk's influence, the Russian government decided to bring to Russia another exile deputy, Josef Dürich, who had been sent abroad by the Maffie, a secret Czech organization dedicated to the cause of Czech independence, and leaders of the Young Czech party (Kramář), the Agrarian party (Antonín Švehla), and others.[14]

A member of the Agrarians, the largest Czech party in the Vienna parliament, Dürich was pro-Russian, and had been selected by Kramář for work in Russia. He was vice-president of the Czech National Council, established by agreement between him and Masaryk in Paris in February 1916. Masaryk was the council's president, and Dr. Edvard Beneš its secretary.[15]

In the conflict within the Czecho-Slovak independence movement in Russia and the struggle for its control toward the end of 1916 and in the early months of 1917, the big prize was the more than 200,000 Czech and Slovak prisoners of war. Their loyalties and leadership would influence both the orientation of the future Czecho-Slovak state and the organization of Central Europe. The protagonists in this little understood and hardly known contest were the "two deputies" from the Vienna parliament, Masaryk and Dürich. The latter had the support of the tsarist government, and the former was suspected by the same government of the "British connection." It was neither Masaryk nor Dürich, however, who was responsible for the establishment of the Czech military unit in Russia. The latter was the result of the efforts of the Czech settlers in Russia and their organizations.

The Czech *Družina* had been founded by the leaders of the Czech colony in Russia in August 1914, and its inauguration took place in Kiev, the center of the Czech associations in Russia.[16] Representatives of the Czech colony in Russia had been given an audience by the tsar, who was sympathetic to the idea of Bohemian independence, and to their request to establish a Czech military unit that would fight shoulder to shoulder with the Russian army that was expected to liberate the Czech lands. The *Družina* represented Czech solidarity with the Russians, and had propaganda and military value.

Members of the *Družina* were sent on reconnaissance to division commands on the front, where they demonstrated both their bravery and their ability to elicit intelligence from enemy soldiers. Speaking Slavic languages, they knew the mentality of the Czechs and Slovaks in the Austro-Hungarian armies. They brought in prisoners from night patrols, and induced Czech and Slovak soldiers to defect to the Russians. Their work was such a great success that the Russian military commanders requested that more Czechs should be allowed to serve in the Russian army as volunteers. They urged the release of prisoners of war for military duty in Czech units that would be attached to the Russian army.

Since it was a novel idea to recruit soldiers from among POWs, the Russian government hesitated to approve the requests of the Czech associations in Russia and the Russian military for the release of POWs for military duty. At first it insisted that the POWs accept Russian citizenship before their enlistment in the *Družina.* But since naturalization was a lengthy process, noncitizens were eventually accepted. The *Družina* grew into a battalion, then a regiment, and on April 17, 1916, by order of Gen. Mikhail V. Alekseyev, chief of staff of the Russian army, it was transformed into a brigade consisting of two regiments.[17] The Russian military acceded to the requests of the Alliance of the Czecho-Slovak Associations in Russia and its leader, Vácslav Vondrák, to enlarge the unit and ultimately form an army from among the volunteering POWs.

Shortly after the establishment of the Czech brigade, the Alliance of the Czecho-Slovak Associations in Russia held its second congress in Kiev (April 25–May 1, 1916) at which it elected a new leadership with Dr. Vondrák at its helm.[18] Two resolutions adopted by the congress charged the new leadership with the task of "forming a Czecho-Slovak army," and levying a war tax and national tax, to be paid by the members of the associations and the working POWs. General Alekseyev endorsed the idea of building a Czecho-Slovak army on August 23, 1916, but stipulated that it would have to come under the control of the main administration of the general staff assisted by a military commission to be headed by the Czech-Russian Maj. Gen. Jaroslav Červinka, who spoke Czech and was well acquainted with Czech national aspirations.[19]

The Russian government agreed with the military's recommendation to assemble a Czecho-Slovak army, but it did not want to have it under the influence of an organization with headquarters outside Russia–the Paris Czecho-Slovak (as it had been renamed) National Council whose president was Masaryk. To facilitate building the army the Russian government insisted on the establishment of another national council, this one in Russia, headed by Deputy Dürich. The council was to have largely advisory functions on matters concerning the army, POWs, and political-diplomatic affairs. Half the council's membership was selected by Deputy Dürich who represented the Czechs at home, and the other half was selected by the Alliance of the Czecho-Slovak Associations in Russia.[20]

The establishment of the council led to an open break between Dürich and the Paris council under Masaryk. Eventually, Milan R. Štefánik, a French army officer of Slovak origin, came to Russia on a French government mission to negotiate the transfer of Czech POWs to France. A co-opted member of the Paris council, Štefánik delivered the notice that Deputy Dürich had been expelled as its vice-president.[21]

Despite Štefánik's campaign against Dürich, the Russian government recognized the Dürich-led council on March 6, 1917. On April 6, 1917, the Russian War Council approved the plan to form a Czecho-Slovak army as drafted by Gen. Červinka.[22] In the meantime, however, the tsarist government had collapsed, and the arrangements made by Dürich, Alekseyev and Červinka were in limbo. Because Dürich refused to resign as head of the new council, the Russian Provisional Government dissolved it in mid-April 1917. Later, Masaryk summed up the situation succintly in a letter to an acquaintance in the United States: "The revolution buried absolutism, its Slavic policy, and hence also our colleague Dürich."[23]

Dürich and his followers were not even allowed to attend the third congress of the Alliance of the Czecho-Slovak Associations in Russia convened in Kiev on May 6, 1917.[24] At this congress the statutes of a Russian branch of the Czecho-Slovak National Council were adopted. Control of the Czechoslovak independence movement in Russia passed from the Czech-Russians to revolutionary émigrés–POWs from the Austro-Hungarian monarchy, and Masaryk was recognized as its leader. From then on Masaryk and the Czecho-Slovak National Council in Paris were the official spokesmen for the Czecho-Slovak independence movement.[25]

While tsarist officers had highly valued the work done by the volunteers of the Czech brigade, many Russian government officials believed the POWs were more useful in industrial enterprises and agriculture than in military formations. Russia had plenty of manpower but was short of military hardware and foodstuffs. Skilled Czech mechanics were therefore extremely valuable in factories. In Taganrog, for example, large numbers of Czech POWs worked in munitions factories. They had their own organizations that looked after their interests. The Czechs were seen as excellent workers by their employers, whereas some Hungarian and German POWs, according to the Russian press, were involved in espionage and sabotage.[26]

Although the Russian government approved the formation of a Czecho-Slovak army corps, recruitment of volunteers proceeded slowly. The recruiters could not convince the majority of the more than 200,000 Czech and Slovak POWs in Russia that they should join the army. According to a Czech source published shortly after the war and quoting official figures,[27] from the beginning of the war to February 1915, 1,433 volunteers (1,155 Czech-Russians and 278 POWs) joined the *Družina.* Between March 1915 and March 1916, a mere 869 volunteers (804 Czech-Russians and 65 POWs) joined the unit. And between March 1916 and the May 1917 congress of the Alliance of the Czecho-Slovak Associations in Russia, 6,947 volunteers, of whom only 17 were Czech-Russians, joined the Czecho-Slovak army.

Masaryk arrived in Russia in the second half of May 1917, carrying a passport issued to him by the British Foreign Office under the name Thomas George Marsden.[28] His original purpose in Russia was to conduct pro-Allied propaganda and recruit POWs into the existing Czecho-Slovak army, which by then consisted of 7,273 volunteers from among the POWs and 1,917 Czech-Russians, of whom close to 800 were actually Russian citizens who had been mobilized into the Russian army at the outset of hostilities and requested transfer to the Czech *Družina.*[29]

While in Russia, Masaryk tried to give new impetus to the formation of the Czecho-Slovak army corps. Aleksandr Kerenskiy's government, however, frowned upon the Czech attempt to recruit POWs into the legion, as the army was usually called, believing that the POWs should remain in agriculture and industry. It was feared the legion might set a dangerous precedent for the non-Russian peoples living in the empire, especially the Ukrainians. Since the Czech troops were stationed in the Ukraine, the Ukrainians might get ideas about establishing their own legion and eventually secede from Russia. Kerenskiy therefore stopped the recruitment of POWs, and even decided to disband the legion, though the decision was not implemented immediately.[30]

The turning point in the history of the Czecho-Slovak army in Russia was the battle of Zborov during the Kerenskiy offensive. Although the offensive failed, the Czech brigade fighting in the Zborov region was cited for bravery in the Russian army report of July 3, 1917. The Czechs captured 62 officers, 3,150 soldiers, 15 pieces of artillery and many machineguns, most of which were then turned on the enemy.

Kerenskiy immediately visited the sector, promoted the officer commanding the brigade to the rank of general, and promised full cooperation in building a Czecho-Slovak army.[31]

After the battle of Zborov, the Russian branch of the Czecho-Slovak National Council sent more than three hundred agitators into the provinces to find POWs, gather them into larger groups whenever possible, inform them about the situation in their homeland and the independence movement, and, of course, urge them to join the army. Recruitment of the POWs still ran into many difficulties.[32] Some employers did not want to release their POWs, basing themselves on government regulations according to which the agitators had the right to recruit only unskilled workers, and skilled ones only if they first found substitutes for them. In many places the local soviets objected to recruitment, claiming that the war had already been ended by the decision of "Russian democracy," that there would be no more fighting, and that there was to be peace without annexations or indemnities. These soviets saw recruitment as a counterrevolutionary act, a manifestation of Czech chauvinism that wanted to prolong the war for selfish reasons.[33]

There were likewise differences of political opinion among the Czech and Slovak POWs, and their attitudes toward the legion varied. Some POWs were eager to serve in the legion; others refused to talk or even listen to the agitators. Prisoners' attitudes depended on many factors, not least their former social position and political background, upbringing, place of birth, and satisfaction or dissatisfaction with their present occupations. While skilled mechanics earned good wages and some prisoners enjoyed village life, unskilled workers and former students could expect their position to improve by joining the army.

Statistics on the results of the four separate recruitment drives conducted between May 1917 and May 1918 are interesting, but do not tell the whole story. According to the Czech source quoted earlier,[34] in the first recruitment drive conducted during the months of May through September 1917, the emissaries tracked down 3,385 local groups with 83,328 Czechoslovak POWs, 21,760 of whom volunteered for service in the legion. In the second drive during the last three months of 1917, the 149 emissaries visited 4,090 groups, containing 124,000 Czech and 26,000 Slovak prisoners of war, and enlisted 9,780 volunteers. The third recruitment drive of January-February 1918 located 5,128 groups, but there were only 137,193 prisoners among them, and the six emissaries were able to enlist a bare 1,500 volunteers. When the legion was on its way to Vladivostok, during March-May 1918, 34 emissaries recruited 5,131 prisoner soldiers.

This source added to the results of the four recruitment drives 7,273 volunteers who had joined the army before Masaryk assumed political leadership, and 1,000 volunteers in the Serbian army corps and arrived at a total of 46,450 volunteers. According to this estimate, "A good half, perhaps two-thirds, of our people in Russia did not comply with their national duty."[35] It would perhaps be more realistic to say that between one-fourth and one-fifth of the POWs volunteered for service in the legion. This can be only a speculative estimate, since the exact number of Czech and Slovak POWs in Russia is not known, and kept changing. As a result of the exchange of POWs after the signing of the Treaty of Brest-Litovsk in March 1918, some Czech and Slovak POWs went home and were among the 500,000 prisoners who had returned to Austria-Hungary by the end of June 1918.[36]

During the campaign in Siberia in the summer of 1918, an additional 15,000 men enlisted in the legion, according to the same Czech source, which lists the total number of legionaries at 61,450.[37] A contemporary British intelligence estimate puts the number at 42,000 in mid-March, when the Soviet government formally decided to honor the agreement it had made with Masaryk and let the legion travel to France via Vladivostok.[38] An official United States source, dated December 10, 1918, reports that from June 1 to November 15, 1918, the total of Czecho-Slovak troops engaged in the anti-Bolshevik campaign was 49,709 soldiers and 1,600 officers.[39]

The social background of those who joined the legion is a subject of conjecture and dispute. A Czech communist source cites estimates made by Czechoslovak communists living in Russia during the revolution, according to which the legionaries were "almost 70 percent workers, 10 percent petit bourgeois elements, and 10 percent kulaks."[40] Edvard Beneš in a letter of July 29, 1919, breaks down the legion's social composition as 20 percent farmers and farm workers, 20 percent students, including university students, 5 percent employees of banks and trade, 20 percent factory workers, 25 percent artisans, and 10 percent small businessmen.[41]

These data do, however, indicate that the legionaries came from all walks of life; the whole political spectrum, as it had existed in prewar Czech politics, was represented in the legion. The motives of individual POWs for joining the army ranged from staunch patriotism, especially on the part of those who joined the Czech *Družina,* to opportunism and search for material advantage. Needless to say, those who possessed certain skills, the mechanics and engineers, earned good wages; those without marketable skills, especially students and untrained workers, suffered hardship in the prison camps.

There was a relatively large number of Social Democrats among the legionaries, despite their party's formal commitment to the preservation of a federalized Austria-Hungary. The left-wing among them were susceptible to Bolshevik agitation. Indeed, polarization of the forces of the Czecho-Slovak independence movement in Russia began to be noticeable after the battle of Zborov. A company of Czechs served in the "Kornilovtsi" battalion loyal to the Russian commander in chief, Gen. Lavr G. Kornilov, whose fondness for the Czechs stemmed from a Czech soldier who helped him escape from captivity in Austria-Hungary. Upon his return to Russia, he became a national hero to many as well as anathema to others. The Czech "Kornilovtsi" guarded his headquarters and eventually, after the October revolution, followed him to the Don region where they fought alongside the Volunteer Army.[42]

Some left-wing Social Democrats sympathized with Lenin and found their way into the Red Guards and, later, the Red Army. These Red Czechs, whose number has been estimated between 5,000 and 10,000,[43] separated themselves in due course from the mainstream of the Czecho-Slovak independence movement, and established their own political organ, the Czechoslovak Communist party, in May 1918.[44]

While Masaryk insisted on maintaining neutrality in Russia's internal affairs, and the legion remained neutral both during the "Kornilov affair" and the October revolution, the Czech Bolsheviks insisted it was the duty of all socialists to help the new Russia ushered in by the Bolshevik revolution. At the opposite end of the political spectrum were those who acknowledged Czech indebtedness to Russia, which was the first of the Allies to raise the flag of Czecho-Slovak independence, and who wanted to help the national and democratic Russia whose very existence was in danger.[45] As it happened, the polarization of the Czechs in Russia was a great factor in the Czechoslovak Legion's clash with the Bolsheviks toward the end of May 1918.

In Russia on June 13, 1917, Masaryk made an agreement to transfer 30,000 Czech POWs from Russia to France with the visiting French minister of armaments and munitions, Albert Thomas.[46] Yet only two small transports of legionaries left Russia in 1917 and arrived by way of Russia's northern ports to France. Among the reasons for the failure to transfer a larger number of legionaries and prisoners of war were diplomatic complications, little progress in recruiting volunteers to go to France, transportation difficulties, the severe winter in the Russian north, changes in the command of the Russian army, and political chaos in Russia after the October revolution.

Why did Masaryk want the legion or the larger part of it in France? He was a "westerner," and would have liked the Czech lands liberated by armies coming from the West. He also believed the war would be decided on the Western Front. As he wrote in his memoirs, the plan was for the legion to invade Germany with the Allied armies from the west, and travel home through Berlin and Dresden.[47] Furthermore, if he wished to be recognized as the leader of the new state instead of Kramář or some other domestic politician who had played a much more prominent role in Czech politics before the war than he had, and if the new state was to have a "western" and Protestant outlook, these could be more easily accomplished if the Czechs were liberated from the west rather than the east.[48]

The tsarist government was aware of the Catholic nature of Czech culture, and implicit recognition of it was reflected in the names of the two regiments that formed the first Czech brigade. The first regiment had been named after St. Wenceslas, the second after Sts. Cyril and Methodius.[49] While still in Russia, Masaryk, a Protestant, was probably already thinking about the future cultural revolution he was to launch at home in 1919 under the slogan "Away from Rome." This seems indicated by the renaming of the army units early in December 1917 to reflect Hussite tradition. The first regiment became the Master John Hus Regiment, the second the George of Podebrady Regiment. The Czechoslovak Legion's third regiment and artillery brigade were named for Jan Žižka, the fourth regiment for Prokop Holý, and the whole first division became the Hussite Division.[50]

After the Bolshevik revolution the Eastern front began to disintegrate. Yet Masaryk did not want the legion taken either to the Rumanian front, to prevent the latter's collapse, or to the Don region, where it would serve as a liaison between the Volunteer Army and the Rumanian and other Allied forces.[51] He insisted on its transfer to France, and eventually early in March 1918, Masaryk arranged with the Soviets for the legion to depart Russia through Valdivostok. He then left Russia, telling the troops that he was going to France to be their quartermaster there.

The legion became a part of the Czecho-Slovak army in France, that is, of the French army, by the joint decision of Masaryk and the French government in January 1918; in February the French government approved its transfer to France. [52] The Czecho-Slovak army corps was stationed in the Ukraine when the latter decided to secede from Russia, and was in turn overrun by Bolshevik troops. The Ukranian *Rada* then appealed to the Germans for help. With the German entry into the Ukraine, the legion had to leave its territory.[53] As the troops, hourses and equipment loaded on seventy trains were moving eastward, the units covering the army's withdrawal from the Ukraine engaged in a skirmish with an advanced German column at Bakhmach, a railroad junction.[54] This was the only time the legionaries fought alongside the Bolsheviks against the advancing Germans, and had the opportunity to observe the behavior of their temporary allies. The Red Guards were composed mainly of rabble, who fled the battlefield the instant they came under fire. Since the Czechs were able to halt the Germans, they were able to collect large amounts of military hardware and equipment left behind by the fleeing Red Guards. This and other war materiel, including almost all the legion's heavy artillery, were turned over to the Kursk soviet, earning the legion Bolshevik praise. [55]

On March 15 and 16, 1918, Lenin formally consented to the army corps leaving Russia by way of Vladivostok. He may well have been glad to have the corps out of the way, since it was the only combat-ready military force in Russia at that time. A few days later, however, Leon Trotsky, commissar of war, injected himself into the picture. He wanted to use the legion as a nucleus for building the new Red Army.[56] His request was rejected by the Czech political and military leadership, and new agreements were made in subsequent negotiations for the depature of the troops. These agreements were subjected to various interpretations by local soviets as the trains crawled toward their destination in the Far East.[57]

The ratification of the Peace of Brest-Litovsk by the Soviets placed the legal status of the legion in doubt, to say the least. The troops on the trains became targets of Bolshevik propaganda and agitation, conducted, if not principally, at least in part, by Czech Bolsheviks, who insisted that all proletarians had a duty to defend the new Russia. Trains were stopped, derailed, departures were delayed, and eventually the Soviets began to insist on the troops' complete disarmament.[58] Internationalists harassed the legionaries who, according to the former, were going to France to fight for the capitalists. Bolshevik duplicity, aggravation caused by the Czech Bolsheviks' agitation and efforts to induce the legionaries to enlist in the newly establihed Czechoslovak Red Army at Penza, and the fact that many Internationalists were Germans and Hungarians, created an anti-Bolshevik mood among the legionaries.

Several of the first troop trains had arrived in Vladivostok, others were en route on the Trans-Siberian Railway or were still in European Russia, when early in May 1918 the trains west of the Ural Mountains were notified that they had to proceed to Russia's northern ports rather than the Far East.

The legionaries saw in this a Bolshevik plot to dismantle the legion, and refused to go to the north of Russia even when the Allies instructed them to do so.[59] The rank and file urged their military leaders to stop surrendering weapons to the Soviets and to press on to Vladivostok by the legion's own efforts, shooting their way through if necessary.

The Soviet government's decision to put the Czech Bolsheviks in Moscow in charge of Czechoslovak affairs in Russia early in May 1918 was another important development affecting the legionaries' fate.[60] The Czech Bolsheviks constantly drummed into Trotsky's and Lenin's ears the idea that there were at least 15,000 proletarians among the legionaries, and that these proletarians could be enlisted into the Red Army. In Penza, as legionaries were turning over their weapons to the Soviets, Red agitators tried to persuade them to join the Red Army, but their effort produced meager results. Since the Czech Bolsheviks failed to convince the legionaries that they should stay in Russia "whom they should love," they urged the Soviet government to take drastic steps to enable the Czech Bolsheviks to seize power with the Czecho-Slovak independence movement in Russia and bring about the disbanding of the legion.[61] The activities of the Czech Bolsheviks and their decision to form the Czechoslovak Communist party in Russia played a significant role in the legionaries' uprising late in May 1918.

The incident had many causes, but this is not the place for detailed description and analysis of all the events that led up to the legion's revolt. A few questions may be raised, however, to indicate some of the explanations or interpretations of the revolt and the insistence of the legion's political leadership on neutrality in Russian domestic affairs.[62]

Were the legionaries afraid of the German army, or did they believe the Bolsheviks were merely agents of the Germans? Was the uprising the result of a plot concocted by the Allies and counterrevolutionary Czech officers? Was it a reaction to the activity of the Czech Bolsheviks in Russia and their misguided tactics? Were the legionaries clear-sighted enough to recognize the Bolshevik threat to the entire world already in 1918?

Communist historians in general follow Lenin's analysis of the revolt made in June 1918. As Lenin put it, the legion's action was an attempt, supported by Anglo-French imperialism, to overthrow the Soviet government.[63] Part of Lenin's thesis was accepted by the German military and government: it was an Allied plot to seize control of Siberia.

The basic facts in the case were as follows.[64] The legionaries were complying with the neutrality policy insisted on by Masaryk and traveling through Vladivostok to France. A policy of neutrality for the only well-organized and combat-ready military force in Russia, composed mostly of former POWs, however, was hardly compatible with some of the provisions of the Peace of Brest-Litovsk, such as the dissolution of the Russian army and the exchange of POWs, nor with the Bolsheviks' overall international policy objectives. In order to implement the neutrality policy, Masaryk's deputy in Russia, Prokop Maxa, made concessions to the Soviets by disarming most of the army corps and insisting on disarming the rest. This policy was expressly approved by Masaryk who advocated that the Allies recognize the Soviet regime as the *de facto* government of Russia. Appeasement of an aggressor is usually the surest way to war, and the legionaries were bound to find that out sooner or later.

In order to reach the French front where they were to fight the Central Powers, the legionaries set out for the Far East. Exposure to Bolshevik propaganda, constant delays, and harassment by the Internationalists made the legionaries suspicious of Bolshevik intentions. The confiscation of the legion's property in Moscow, the closure of the office of the Czecho-Slovak National Council and the army's recruiting office in Moscow on orders of the Soviet government on May 12, 1918, the arrest of the leaders of the Russian branch of the National Council and Masaryk's deputies in Russia, Prokop Maxa and Bohumil Čermak, in Moscow on May 20, 1918,[65] prepared the legion's leaders for worse to come. It came in the form of the Trotsky's order of May 25, 1918, to shoot to kill any armed Czechoslovak on the Trans-Siberian Railway. The Czechs were ready for this possibility. They had excellent intelligence and were able to intercept all telegrams dispatched from Moscow to soviets in Siberia.

On May 19, 1918, the commander of the Red Army unit in Penza had told two Czech volunteers confidentially that the fate of the Czecho-Slovak army corps was already settled and that Moscow had decided to disband it. From May 17 to 19 this "decision" had been an open secret in Penza,[66] where the legionaries were surrendering their weapons in accordance with the agreement negotiated by Prokop Maxa. Some young military officers were not taken by a surprise: they had contingency plans to reach Vladivostok on their own. These contingency plans, prepared by Capt. Kadlec on Capt. Radola Gajda's orders early in May 1918, were not designed to overthrow Bolshevik rule or to restore the Eastern front, but to reach Vladivostok under any circumstances.[67] When the Czechs revolted, they did so in order to get out of Russia. They pursued their eastward course until July 7, 1918.

Had the Czechs revolted to overthrow Soviet rule in Russia, they would have pursued a different strategy. They would not have abandoned the western bank of the Volga river, and they would have attempted to link up with the Volunteer Army in the south and the Allied expeditionary force in the north. They would have joined forces with the anti-Bolshevik Russians and marched on Moscow and Petrograd.

Furthermore, while the trains in European Russia and western Siberia were fighting their way eastward, some 15,000 Czech troops remained idle in Vladivostok for a whole month. Only late in June did some of those for whom weapons were available decided to go back to Siberia to help their comrades. The lack of support given the young officers who led the revolt by their senior officers already in Vladivostok, Gen. Shokorov and Dieterichs, clearly shows the legion had no plan to reestablish the Eastern front or to overthrow Soviet rule in Russia when it revolted.

However, when the legion had proved its own effectiveness and exposed Bolshevik weakness, when it gained control of the railway and deposed local soviets standing in its way, and when the local population rose against the Bolsheviks, then the Allies began to instruct the Czechs not to abandon their positions but to reinforce them, to keep their weapons and not to give them up, and to be ready for a possible westward move in order to join up with the Whites in the south of

Russia and the Allied force in Arkhangel'sk. But the decision of the Vladivostok group to break with Masaryk's policy of neutrality and go back to Siberia came too late, one Czech officer noted. According to him, "Had the Vladivostok group been transported back to the Ural Mountains in time, we would certainly have destroyed the Bolsheviks and so liberated the whole of Russia from their oppression, and this would perhaps have meant a speedy and victorious return to Bohemia for us."[68] This was speculation, he conceded, but not groundless.

After the Czechs had begun to reestablish the Volga front, the local population hailed them as liberators. Allied officers encouraged the legionaries to move west and promised them Allied help. In anticipation of the speedy arrival of Allied troops to restore the Eastern front, the Czechs took one city after another in relatively easy victories over the Bolshevik Red Guards. Their revolt, however, prompted the Soviets to speed up building the Red Army by hiring former tsarist commissioned and noncommissioned officers to train the Soviet troops and lead them in battle.[69] Units of the Red Army led by professional officers were sent against the legion, which had overextended itself in the belief that it would soon be relieved on the frontline by Allied troops. As it happened, the Allied armies never reached the Volga front, and the legion was forced to abandon city after city as it was beaten back to the east.

The retreating soldiers were exposed to Bolshevik agitation and propaganda. The demon (as one legion officer called it) of lack of confidence in themselves and their strength seized many of the soldiers, who began to subvert the army's organization by refusing to obey orders and follow discipline.[70] The officer in question, Col. Josef Švec, committed suicide. The note he left said he could no longer go on living because of the shame brought upon the army by reckless fanatics and demagogues who were destroying their own and others' most precious quality—honor.

The crisis in the legion came to a head just before the declaration of Czechoslovak independence in Prague on October 28, 1918. To relieve the situation, the French military sent Gen. Milan R. Štefánik, who was also minister of war in the newly established Czecho-Slovak Provisional government headed by Masaryk, to the troops in Siberia. The news of the collapse of Austria-Hungary, the declaration of independence, and Masaryk's telegram of November 14, 1918,[71] requiring the troops to remain in Siberia to strengthen the new state's hand at the Paris Peace Conference, temporarily arrested the decline of the troops' morale. Early in 1919, however, the legionaries retired beyond the Urals and limited themselves merely to guard duties along the Trans-Siberian Railway.

Political changes in the government of Siberia—the replacement of the regime dominated by the Socialist Revolutionaries by that of Adm. Aleksandr V. Kolchak, caused friction between the Czechs and the new Siberian leadership. The Whites tried in vain to involve the best-equipped and best-trained troops, the Czecho-Slovak army corps, in their anti-Bolshevik campaigns. The corps was now under the jurisdiction of the Czecho-Slovak government in Prague and of Beneš, who represented that government at the Paris Peace Conference. Late in 1919, after the signing of the Peace Treaties, the homesick troops were instructed to prepare to leave Siberia.[72] There was no longer any need to use them for leverage at the peace conference, since the new state had obtained international recognition of its boundaries. In addition, toward the end of 1919 the army corps leaders realized the Whites would not defeat the Soviets, and decided to come to terms with the latter.

The legion's encounter with the Bolsheviks entered its final phase on February 7, 1920, when its representative signed an armistice with the Soviets. Article 5 of the agreement stipulated that the Czechs were to leave Adm. Kolchak in Irkutsk, where he was being held in custody.[73] On the day the armistice was signed, the admiral and his prime minister were shot. As Winston Churchill put it, "The magnificent record of the Czechoslovak army corps has been marred by the surrender of Kolchak."[74]

After the armistice the Czech troops withdrew to Vladivostok where they waited for ships to take them home. Their encounter with the Bolsheviks and, especially, their behavior in Siberia after they withdrew from the front early in 1919, have been a subject of controversy at home and abroad.[75] That controversy will continue as long as there is interest in the saga of the Czechs who fought in Russia and Siberia, the last of whom sailed from Vladivostok in September 1920.

NOTES

1. "Russia" (Report under file "R" [May 18, 1917 ?], Wiseman, General *L*1, William Wiseman Papers in E.M. House Collection, Yale University Library, New Haven, Conn. [hereafter cited as WWP]).

2. *Ibid.*

3. "Committee, of Slav Origin, for Russia" (Memorandum of June 30, 1917, in file "S", WWP).

4. Zdeněk Hruban, "Hovory s Josefem Martínkem" [Conservations with Josef Martínek], *Americké Listy, April 6, 1979. Josef Martínek was a member of the group sent to Russia.*

5. Report of W. Somerset Maugham, December 7, 1917, Polk Drawer 73, E.M. House Collection, Yale University Library, New Haven, Conn.

6. See note 3 above.

7. Report of Rotenberg, "Russia" [May 15, 1917 ?], WWP.

8. Henry W. Steed, *Through Thirty Years, 1892-1922* (Garden City, N.Y., 1924), II, 43-44; Karel Pichlík, *Záhraniční odboj 1914-1918 bez legend* [Resistance Abroad, 1914-1918, Without Legends] (Prague, 1968), pp. 90-91; "Paměti kapitána Em. V. Vosky" [Memoirs of Captain Emanuel Victor Voska], published in serialized form in *Jas* (Vols. VII, VIII, IX, and X [1933-1936]. No. 18, 1933.

9. For details see Malada Paulová, *Dějiny Maffie; odboj Čechu a Jihoslovanu za světové války, 1914-1918* [History of the Maffie: Resistance of the Czechs and Yugoslavs during the World War, 1914-1918] (Prague, 1937-1938). The text of the constitution of the All-Slavic Federation is in *ibid.*, I, Appendix, 635-640. See also Pichlík, *op. cit.*, pp. 31-32.

10. There is a wealth of documents about the Neo-Slavic movement in the Public Record Office, London; some of these are cited in Paul Vyšný, *Neo-Slavism and the Czechs, 1898-1914* (London, 1977). Karel Krámár was a leading Neo-Slav.

11. Sir Eyre Crowe: From Memorandum on the Present State of British Relations with France and Germany, January 1, 1907, *British Documents on the Origins of the War, 1914-1918,* ed. G.P. Gooch and Harold Temperley, III (London, 1928), 402-403.

12. See three long memoranda drafted by M. Priklonsky of the Russian ministry of foreign affairs: "Confidential Memorandum of the Ministry of Foreign Affairs on the Czecho-Slovak Question" (September 19, 1916), "Addendum to the Secret Note on the Czecho-Slovak Question" (October 3, 1916), and "Russia, England, and the Question of Czechoslovak State. Conditions for a Genesis of This State" (October 30, 1916) in Czech translation in Jaroslav Papoušek, *Carské Rusko a naše osvobození* [Tsarist Russia and Our Liberation] (Prague, 1927), pp. 120-144 and 147-155.

13. *Ibid.*, pp. 73-77.

14. *Ibid.* Also Josef Dürich, *V českých službách; vypsání mého pobytu za*

hranicemi, 1915-1918 [In Czech Service: A Description of My Sojourn Abroad, 1915-1918] (Klášter nad Jizerou, 1921), p. 31.

15. Dürich, *op. cit.*, pp. 16 ff.

16. Czech literature on this subject is very extensive. One may mention V. Vondrák, *Z doby bojů o samostatnost Ceskoslovénskeho vojska* [From the Time of Struggle for the Independence of the Czechoslovak Army] (Prague, 1925); František Steidler, *Československé hnutí na Rusi* [The Czechoslovak Movement in Russia] (Prague, 1922); and J. Kudela, *Přehled vývoje čsl. revolučního hnutí na Rusi* [An Overview of the Development of the Czechoslovak Revolutionary Movement in Russia] (Prague, 1923). Significant studies are J.F.N. Bradley, *La Legion tchecoslovaque en Russie, 1914-1920* (Paris, 1965), and Gerburg Thunig-Nittner, *Die tschechosowakische Legion in Russland* (Wiesbaden, 1970).

17. Eduard Beneš (ed.), *Světová válka a naše revoluce: Documenty* [The World War and Our Revolution: Documents], III (Prague, 1928), 656.

18. Pichlík, *op. cit.*, pp. 193-194.

19. Papoušék, *op. cit.*, pp. 104-105.

20. *Ibid.*, pp. 169-171; Beneš, *op. cit.*, III, 606-609; and Dürich, *op. cit.*, pp. 41-47.

21. Dürich, *op. cit.*, pp. 48-56.

22. *Ibid.*, pp. 51; Benes, *op. cit.*, III, 608; Papoušek, *op. cit.*, pp. 180-181.

23. Dürich, *op. cit.*, p. 72.

24. *Ibid.*, pp. 54-60, 73-74.

25. Zdeněk Václav Tobolka, *Politické dějiny československého národa od r. 1848 až do dnešní doby* (Political History of the Czechoslovak Nation from 1848 till the Present Time] (Prague, 1932-1937), IV, 184-185; also Pichlík, *op. cit.*, p. 240.

26. Josef Kudela, *S našim vojskem na Rusi: V době příprav* (With Our Army in Russia: During the Time of Preparations] (Prague, 1922), pp. 42-45.

27. *Ibid.*, p. 6.

28. Josef Kalvoda, "Masaryk in America in 1918," *Jahrbücher für Geschichte Osteuropas*, Vol. 27 (1979), No. 1, p. 93.

29. Kudela, *Přehled vývoje...*, p. 71.

30. *Ibid.*, p. 76.

31. *Ibid.*, pp. 77-78; Thunig-Nittner, *op. cit.*, pp. 23-28.

32. Kudela, *Přehled vývoje...*, pp. 78-80.

33. *Ibid.*, p. 79.

34. *Ibid.*, pp. 80-81.

35. *Ibid.*, p. 81.

36. Pichlík, *op. cit.*, p. 413.

37. Kudela, *Přehled vývoje*, p. 81.

38. J.F.N. Bradley, "The Allies and the Czech Revolt against the Bolsheviks in 1918," *The Slavonic and East European Review*, Vol. XLII, No. 1 (June, 1965), p. 284.

39. The report from Siberia by the U.S. Consul to the Secretary of State lists also the number of dead and wounded legionaires. For these and other data pertinent to the legion see Josef Kalvoda, *Czechoslovakia's Role in Soviet Strategy* (Washington, D.C., 1978), pp. 291-292. According to Masaryk, the fighting strength of the legion in Russia was 92,000 men. This is an exag-

geration. See Thomas G. Masaryk, *The Making of a State: Memories and Observations, 1914-1918* (London & New York. 1927), p. 288.

40. Jan Kvasnička, *Československé Legie v Rusku, 1917-1920* [The Czechoslovak Legions in Russia, 1917-1920] (Bratislava, 1963), p. 321.

41. *Ibid.*

42. Pichlík, *op. cit.*, pp. 289, 302 and 461.

43. Thunig-Nittner, *op. cit.*, pp. 88-90; Jindřich Veselý, *O vznik a založení* KSC (On the Genesis and Founding of the Communist Party of Czechoslovakia] (Prague, 1952), p. 55; and Theodor Syllaba, *T.G. Masaryk a revoluce v Rusku* (T.G. Masaryk and the Revolution in Russia] (Prague, 1959), p. 193.

44. Details are discussed in Veselý, *op. cit.;* and Jindřich Veselý, *Češi a Slováci v revolučním Rusku 1917-1920* [Czechs and Slovaks in Revolutionary Russia, 1917-1920] (Prague, 1954).

45. Among these Czechs were Josef Dürich and those who fought beside the Volunteer Army.

46. Pichlík, *op. cit.*, pp. 257 and 269.

47. T.G. Masaryk, *Světová revoluce: Za války a ve válce 1914-1918*. [The World Revolution: During the War and in the War, 1914-1918] (Prague, 1925), p. 19.

48. To the dismay of many, including Kramář, Masaryk launched a "cultural revolution" under the slogan "Away from Rome" in 1919.

49. Alois Navrátil, *Katolicismus a úcta svatováclavská v čsl. legiích* [Catholicism and the Cult of St. Wenceslas in the Czechoslovak Legions] (Prerov, 1930); and same author, *Svatý Václav a čsl. legie* [St. Wenceslas and the Czechoslovak Legions] (Přerov, 1929).

50. Kvasnička, *op. cit.*, pp. 66-67.

51. Bradley, "The Allies..."; and Pichlík, *op. cit.*, pp. 304-312.

52. Beneš, *op. cit.*, p. 631-633.

53. *Ibid.*, p. 634.

54. M. Klante, *Von der Wolga zum Amur* (Berlin, 1931), pp. 130-132; Radola Gajda, *Moje paměti; československá anabase; zpět na Urál proti Bolševikum — Admirál Kolčak* [My Memoirs; the Czechoslovak Anabasis; Back to the Urals against the Bolsheviks — Admiral Kolchak] (Prague, 1920), p. 16.

55. Beneš, *op. cit.*, p. 635.

56. *Ibid.*, pp. 636-637.

57. Details in Karel Zmrhal, *Armáda ducha druhé míle* [The Army with the Spirit of the Second Mile] (Prague [1920]), pp. 15-19.

58. Františék Šteidler, *Naše vystoupení v Rusku r. 1918* [Our Uprising in Russia in 1918] (Prague, 1923), p. 11-25.

59. Pichlík, *op. cit.*, pp. 395-397; Zmrhal, *op. cit.*, pp. 23-24.

60. Pichlík, *op. cit.*, pp. 402 ff.

61. *Ibid.*, p. 415.

62. The various interpretations are found in some of the sources cited previously, e.g., Bradley, "The Allies..."; Šteidler, *op. cit.*, Zmrhal, *op. cit.*, Kvasnička, *op. cit.*, and František Polák, *Sibiřská anabase čsl. legií* [The Siberian Anabasis of the Czechoslovak Legions] (New York, 1961); Vlastimil Vávra, *Klamná cesta; Příprava a vznik protisovětského vystoupení čs. legií* [The Deceitful Way: The Preparation and Origin of the Anti-Soviet Uprising of

the Czechoslovak Legions] (Prague, 1958) Jindřich Veselý, *Češi a Slováci v revolučním Rusku 1917-1920* [Czechs and Slovaks in Revolutionary Russia, 1917-1920] (Prague, 1954); Ludevít Holotík, *Štefánikovská legenda a vznik ČSR* [The Stefánik Legend and the Origins of the Czechoslovak Republic] (Bratislava, 1958); and many others.

63. V.I. Lenin, *Collected Works,* XXVII, 465-468 and 482-484.

64. The most extensive English-language work dealing with the subject is Victor M. Fic, *The Bolsheviks and the Czechoslovak Legion: The Origin of Their Armed Conflict, March-May 1918* (New Delhi, 1978).

65. Pichlík, *op. cit.,* pp. 412-420.

66. Zmrhal, *op. cit.,* pp. 38-39.

67. Šteidler, *op. cit.,* pp. 46-81.

68. Gajda, *op. cit.,* p. 83.

69. Kalvoda, *Czechoslovakia's Role...,* pp. 291-292.

70. Josef Švec, *Deník plukovníka Švece* [Dairy of Colonel Svec] Ed. Josef Kudela (Prague, 1923), pp. 338-339.

71. *Masaryk a revoluční armáda; Masarykovy projevy k legiím a o legiích v zahraniční revoluci* [Masaryk and the Revolutionary Army; Masaryk's Addresses to the Legions and About the Legions During the Revolution Abroad] (Prague, 1921), pp. 224-226.

72. Jan Šeba, *Rusko a Malá dohoda v politice světové* [Russia and the Little Entente in World Politics] (Prague, 1936), p. 473.

73. Jaroslav Kratochvíl, *Cesta revoluce* [The Way of the Revolution] (Prague, 1922), pp. 652-656.

74. Winston S. Churchill, *The Aftermath* (New York, 1929), p. 260.

75. The number of works related to this controversy is extremely large and include those of Karel Kramář, Eduard Beneš, Thomas G. Masaryk, the Czech and Soviet Communists, and some White Russians, e.g., Konstantin V. Sakharov, *Cheshskie legiony v Sibiri* (Riga, 1930) and *Das weisse Sibirien* (Munich, 1925).

SOVIET PROPAGANDA AMONG GERMAN AND AUSTRO-HUNGARIAN PRISONERS OF WAR IN RUSSIA, 1917-1921

Arnold Krammer

When the flames of revolution crept into the Russian camps, they found in the weary and dissatisfied subjects of the Central Powers splendid nourishment. Long before the Germans at the Western Front took off their eagles and marks of distinction from their hats and uniforms, their comrades in the Siberian camps had done it. The Russian Bolsheviki threw open the gates of the prison camps and out of them poured the German, the Austrian, and the Hungarian Bolsheviki.[1]

Johan Prins, Director of YMCA Relief in Siberia, 1919.

However heinous war is, the fate of the captured soldier is particularly unfortunate. Abandoned by his home country and often despised by his captors, the prisoner of war is especially vulnerable, both physically and psychologically, to the whims of his guardians. Of the many programs to which he has been traditionally subjected (military interrogation, hard labor, excessive security, and so forth), the most odious — considering the prisoner's inability to resist — is the campaign to undermine his morale, reorient his political ideology, and finally to turn him into a willing agent against his homeland. While such manipulation of prisoners has occurred in every conflict throughout history, it was pursued with almost religious fervor during World War I. Millions of men were locked in a savage and unyielding death struggle, with each government committed to a continuing total war. The war could only grind to a bloody halt if one side or the other achieved a military victory; or if nations simply ran out of young men to feed the apparently unending demand for fresh troops; or if revolution forced the governments to bring the war to an end. With the idea, then, of hoping to undermine each others' government, each country viewed its massive numbers of prisoners of war as potential revolutionary agents who might be repatriated to work against their former countries.

The Austro-Hungarian high command, for example, however personally committed to the conservative political structure of the nineteenth century, worked tirelessly to foster socialism and pacifism among its Italian POWs, who were then repatriated to mingle with the Italian troops on the front.[2] The Italians, for their part, propagandized heavily among their Austro-Hungarian prisoners to forment revolutionary nationalism among the Serbs, Croats, Czechs, Poles, Magyars and Slovenes who comprised the majority of the empire. Germany, caught as it was in the two-front nightmare that Bismarck had so often warned against, propagandized actively among all its prisoners. Thus the Imperial German General Staff, composed largely of Junkers and landed aristocrats, embarked upon the bizarre task of creating revolutionaries. Its success ranged from the creation of a tiny (54-man) Irish "Brigade", made up of anti-English captured Tommies,[3] to the aggressive manipulation of revolutionary sentiment among its Russian prisoners to form two divisions of Ukrainian POWs for service with the German army on the Eastern Front.[4] Finally, tsarist Russia, the most firmly entrenched autocracy in the war, worked with nearly unequaled zeal to radicalize the approximately 1.6 million German and Austro-Hungarian prisoners of war held in camps across Russia.

Yet nowhere was a campaign to convert large numbers of enemy prisoners of war more aggressively undertaken, or, for that matter, more successful, than that of the new Soviet government against the 1.6 million German and Austro-Hungarian POWs which it had inherited from the fallen tsarist government. These prisoners, caught up in the chaos of the Russian revolution and the transfer of governmental power that followed, were not only subjected to the notorious hardships of Russian prison life, with any hope for early repatriation a distant and problematical prospect, but they quickly became the object of an extensive propaganda campaign to recruit them into the Red Army. Many thousands did enlist with the embryonic Soviet forces – perhaps even tipping the balance in the civil war – but equally important, many returned to postwar Germany, Austria, and Hungary to propagandize, promote local revolu–tions, and aid in the development of native communist parties.

Because of the wartime chaos, the lack of proper communications, and the enormity of the Russian countryside, there is little agreement about the number of German and Austro-Hungarian prisoners in the Russian camps. Of the nearly 2.4 million Austro-Hungarian, Bulgarian, Turkish and German men in Russian captivity, United States Ambassador David R. Francis, for example, estimated that 250,000 German and 250,000 Austrian prisoners, plus an additional 200,000 interned German and Austrian civilians, were held in 400 camps in Siberia, Central Asia and European Russia.[6] Elsa Brändström, head of the Swedish Red Cross Delegation in Russia during the same period, on the other hand, estimates that there were only 101,000 German combatant prisoners, but at least 214,000 German civilian prisoners. [7] George F. Kennan, the United States dean of Soviet history, estimates that there were no more than 160,000 German POWs, and that a higher proportion of the captive officers were Austrian and German than of the men. [8] Regarding the Hungarian captives, one authoritative source lists the number at 700,000 [9] while another states that the real number was greater than that.[10] The most accurate figures, or rather range of estimates, are that Russia took between 2,100,000 and 2,400,000 soldiers and officers, including 160,000 to 180,000 from Germany and 1,600,000 to 2,100,000 from Austria-Hungary. [11]

These prisoners of war – especially the Germans, Austrians and Hungarians among them – were already viewed by a revolutionary movement not yet in power as potential converts. Indeed, in September 1914, a month after the outbreak of the war, Lenin wrote in his famous theses on the war:

> The slogans of social democracy at the present time should be: first an all-sided propaganda spread in the army and the area of military activity of a socialist revolution and of the necessity of turning the weapons, not against brothers, hired slaves of other countries, but against . . . the bourgeois governments . . . of all countries. To carry on such propaganda in all languages it is absolutely necessary to organize illegal cells and groups in the armies of all nations.[12]

Interestingly, German, Austrian and Hungarian prisoners were already the groups of POWs most susceptible to revolutionary propaganda. Very early in the war, no later than 1915, the Russian government began an unofficial policy of differentiating among the incoming prisoners, pampering the Czechs,[13] Serbs and Slavs as fellow members of the same ethnic group. Non-Slavs did not fare well, and learned early to despise these discriminatory policies and the government that enforced them.[14] Moreover, of all the national groups of POWs they were initially the most vehemently anti-Russian; when captured, as were the 120,000 Austro-Hungarian defenders of Przemysl in 1915, the entire body often took a sacred oath to undermine the social structure of their captor's homeland at every opportunity.[15] Still other factors influencing the German, Hungarian, and Austrian POWs to take up the revolutionary cause were the nearly legendary arrogance of their officer class, who made up about three percent of the total POW community, and the chasm in treatment and living conditions between them and the vast numbers of enlisted men.[16] Finally, there was raging discrimination within the prisoner communities against their Jewish comrades – a continuation of the violent and centuries-old anti-Semitism for which Eastern Europe is notorious. Jewish prisoners were often terrorized, and certainly ostracized by the general POW population, as were the large number of nonprofessional soldiers and reservists, who were viewed as inferiors by the rgular army corps. It is no wonder that these POWs, rejected by their governments, discriminated against by policies that favored other nationalities among them, and looked down upon by their own officers from positions of relative comfort, were vulnerable to antitsarist, but more especially antiwar, propaganda.

There is little doubt that it worked. As early as the fall of 1916, hard-core socialists among the prisoners, particularly in the Hungarian camps, were already making substantial progress proselytizing their comrades. They formed Marxist study groups, and organized Russian-language classes by which thousands of POWs were given a steady diet of political indoctrination in the guise of learning to follow the war news in local newspapers. By the spring of 1917, as the tsarist government tottered, German and Austro-Hungarian prisoners turned almost routinely to local Bolshevik organizations for food, funds, and arbitration in such issues as their officers' supposed "right" to first selections from Red Cross packages, and POW orderlies' refusal to work for their officers without compensation. The takeover by the Provisional Government in March 1917 led to a complete breakdown of internal POW control. No one knew who was in authority over the camps. Guards were randomly changed, and, in some cases, simply became fed up with the chaos and went home. Their replacements were often wounded veterans, vengeful against the captives and frustrated at their new, lowly assignments. Camp conditions, if possible, worsened: food deteriorated in quality and quantity, and the ruble fell in value while the price of goods rose sharply.[17] The prisoners of war, dressed in rags and undernourished, were dying by the thousands from typhoid and dysentery — the living forced to sleep among the dead.[18] Moreover, Aleksandr Kerenskiy's new government, by continuing the war, ended any hope of reversing the growing trend among German and Austro-Hungarian POWs toward revolution. Not only was this to insure a continuation of their dismal camp conditions, but unlike the minority nationalities, these men had little to gain by the defeat and dissolution of imperial Europe. To make matters worse, the new Provisional Government continued the policy of playing up to the Slavic minorities to the disadvantage of the other prisoners, recruiting Czechs, Serbs and Slovaks to bolster the thinning ranks of its army, and so exacerbating the already existing tension between the "pampered" minorities and the non-Slavic POWs left behind in the camps. The deterioration of camp conditions and the government's pro-Slavic policies, as events sadly showed, were not the limit of their misfortune. With the intensification of Kerenskiy's war effort during the summer of 1917, public hysteria against the Central Powers often vented itself against the German and Austro-Hungarian POWs in nearby compounds. In one case, local townspeople lynched more than a dozen POWs in the town of Laishchev near Kazan.[19] By autumn of 1917, a vast majority of the POWs were ripe for revolution.

The Bolshevik victory in October was generally welcomed by the prisoners, if for no other reason than as a change of the status quo. Indeed, the revolution revealed that many groups of German and Hungarian POWs – generally socialists– in Tomsk, Omsk, Krasnoyarsk, Kazan, Ivanovo-Voznesensk and Yekaterinburg had received weapons from local Bolshevik and Menshevik groups and had become Red Guard auxiliaries during the six-week period preceding the revolution. An unknown number had even participated in the storming of the Kremlin, and units of German and Hungarian Red Guards fought with arms to establish Soviet rule in sixteen cities.[20] As will be seen, the participation of German and Austro-Hungarian POWs in the Soviet revolution was only beginning.

The new Bolshevik government quickly realized the great potential of the approximately two million prisoners of war spread throughout Russia, and moved immediately to sway them into signing on with the new regime. First, recruited German, Austrian and Hungarian prisoners would help form the backbone of the new Soviet armed forces, while simultaneously depriving the Central Powers of additional manpower. Moreover, after suitable indoctrination, the recruits could then be used as politically conscious cadres in pursuit of Lenin's model of a continuation of the revolution in Germany and Austro-Hungary. Propaganda was the key.

The first appeal to the prisoners came in a long *Pravda* editorial on December 2, 1917, followed by another in *Izvestia* on December 5. All war prisoners were declared "free citizens" with the same rights as Russians, and were urged to "support the socialist revolution . . . and come to the defense of the peace and brotherhood of all nations."[21] The following day, December 6, Karl Radek's International Propaganda Department of the Commissariat for Foreign Affairs followed up the government's appeal to the POWs with an intense propaganda blitz. A host of German- and Hungarian-language newspapers, which had long been used to appeal to enemy soldiers at the front (such as *Der Völkerfriede*),[22] were rerouted inland to deluge the newly freed captives, and the government announced the publication and free distribution of a new periodical designed just for them: *Die Fackel* (The Torch), and a sister publication for the Hungarian prisoners, *Nemzetközi Szocialista* (International Socialist). One day later, on December 7, the government announced the creation of a Prisoners of War Commission to be established within the Ministry of Military Fronts – an indication of the seriousness with which Soviet Russia viewed its inherited potential army. On December 23, *Izvestia* called upon former prisoners "to organize groups among themselves for the improvement of their legal and economic status . . . under the government of the proletariat."[23] And thousands of them did.

While a large percentage of the former POWs, now "free citizens," roamed their districts in futile search for work and food, or rushed westward in hope of escaping Russia for the hospitality of neutral Denmark or Sweden, many thousands accepted the government's advice and began electing spokesmen and representatives. These representatives were called together on January 30, 1918, at the First Revolutionary Congress of International Social Democratic Prisoners of War, held in Samara. The congress was a well-orchestrated propaganda event at which POW representatives rose to plead with the Soviet government for permission to form themselves into Red Guard units for the defense of their new socialist homeland. After a decent interval, the government agreed to allow German and Hungarian POWs to form Red Guard auxiliary units, and by February 1918 their formal organization was well under way. Numerous additional congresses were held throughout Russia: in Omsk on February 10; Moscow on February 13; Petrograd on February 19; Omsk again on March 10;

Kenishma and Kostroma on March 20; and again at Samara on March 23. From these congresses political agitators were dispatched to the camps at Yekaterinburg, Novgorod, Yaroslavl, Tver, Saratov, Penza, Borovsk, Ufa, Chelyabinsk, and Tomsk.[24] One observer at the Moscow congress described the results of the intense politicking there:

> Delegates from the two million war prisoners became so impregnated with Bolshevik propaganda and spread it so thoroughly among their men that whenever a prisoner escaped and got back into Germany he was kept in a detention camp for two weeks and fed on literature gotten out of the German government and calculated as a cure for the revolutionary fever.[25]

However politically successful its efforts to convert the most vulnerable war prisoners during its first several months in office, what the Soviet government really needed was soldiers.

Consequently, in the first week of January 1918 Trotskiy created a central organization, the All-Russian Prisoner of War Bureau, "capable of fulfilling the spiritual and material needs of the working-class elements of the prisoners of war."[26] The new bureau, placed in the hands of a party firebrand named Ivan Ulyanov, was made responsible for coordinating the various propaganda efforts toward a single goal: the recruitment of "International Social Democratic Prisoners of War" – henceforth simply called "Internationals" – into the Red Army. Almost immediately, the bureau launched an emergency enlistment campaign in the most militarily critical regions around Petrograd and Moscow, offering recruits cash rewards and guaranteed safe passage to their homelands in exchange for service in the Red Army.[27] Government-orchestrated mass meetings of Internationals took place in Moscow, Petrograd, Tver, Yaroslavl, and Ivanovo-Voznesensk throughout February and March of 1918. Enlistments soared. On March 4, the executive committee of the All-Russian Prisoner of War Bureau authorized the publication of two additional propaganda newspapers aimed at German-speaking POWs in Omsk *(Die Wahrheit)* and in Moscow *(Die Weltrevolution),* through which both Lenin and Trotskiy exhorted the faithful to join the ranks of the Red forces. Another newspaper aimed at the Hungarians, called *Szociális Forradalom* (Social Revolution) and published in an edition of 20,000 copies twice each week, was launched the following month. Next came recruiting posters which thundered:

> Comrade Internationalists! . . .
>
> Russia does not need words and empty expressions of sympathy. She needs work, discipline, organization, and fearless fighters. Have you faith in the Revolution, in the International, in the Soviet Government? If you have, join at once the International Legion of the Red Army.[28]

Then came direct pressure within the camps themselves. Representatives of the Swedish Red Cross, for example, reported encountering a massive psychological and physical propaganda campaign in every camp they visited. They found large signs everywhere announcing the government's offer of 200 rubles per month and better food for all enlistees.[29] So aggressive was this campaign that the US Consul in Khabarovsk, Douglas Jenkins, reported to Washington that the Bolsheviks had even tried to persuade the members of the Swedish inspection team to convince the interned soldiers to join the Red Army.[30]

The success of this intensive propaganda effort to recruit prisoners of war was – as might be expected – startling. Within three months, by April, 1918, enlistments rose spectacularly. It is estimated that between 18,000 and perhaps as many as 50,000 prisoners volunteered to join the newly formed International units of the Red Army.[31] Thousands more continued to enlist through the summer and autumn of 1918 – impressive results in comparison with the pathetically few enlistments by native Russians during the same period.[32] Moreover, the Internationalists outnumbered the Bolshevik soldiers, and in some areas of Russia, such as western Siberia and the territory east of Lake Baikal, ex-prisoners of war constituted the bulk of the Red forces.[33] The majority (approximately 60 percent) of the prisoner-recruits were Hungarian; the next largest group (30 percent) were German-Austrian; and the remainder (10 percent) were various Slavic minorities who had not already either responded to the preferential treatment of previous governments and enlisted in the army, or joined the Czech Legion.

Yet, more important than the number of POWs who joined the International units, their national composition, or their relative strength in various areas of Russia, was their appearance on the scene at a moment when the Soviet government's immediate future was most uncertain. They played an important role in forcing Bolshevik rule upon the Russian people, quelling scores of anti-Soviet riots, and carrying out arrests, seizures, and the requisition of property. One expert, Professor Victor Fic, states unequivocally: "If not for those foreign nationals in the armed forces of the Bolsheviks, it is very doubtful whether their regime could have survived the challenge of the opposition which began to gather momentum during April and May 1918."[34]

In evaluating the early success of the propaganda campaign, however, it must be noted that a large number of those who joined, perhaps the overwhelming majority, did so as a way out of their dismal camp conditions – an avenue made more attractive by the government's manipulation of their food supplies, and the bonus offered those who signed up. An Austrian officer who spent six years in Siberia sums up this aspect of prisoner response:

> The Red Army was our only recourse to escape starvation. That was the principal recruiting inducement with the Bolsheviki . . . . Although, like all my companions in the prison camp, I had acquired more radical ideas as time went by, we prisoners felt absolutely deserted and neglected by our own governments . . . . So after the hospital was shut up for good, and the prospect of getting food from any other source proved hopeless, we made our decision . . . . New recruits of the Red Army, previously imperial Jager officers! We laughed at the irony of fate and felt relieved to be free at last from prison life . . . . our real and only purpose.[35]

More succinctly, in the words of one German participant, "[We] didn't fight for any certain political ideal or for a stable government regime. [Our] single aim, indeed, [our] single burning wish, was to see the war to an early end, and to be finally able to return home."[36]

To those who joined the International units of the Red Army out of either revolutionary conviction or as an avenue out of the malnutrition and stupifying boredom of camp life, must be added a much smaller number – perhaps no more than several hundred men – who joined for reasons of personal ambition. Mostly noncommissioned and junior officers, they could not resist the temptation of immediate promotion in the Red Army with the opportunity to command units five or eight times larger than they could ever have hoped to lead in their own armies.[37]

The last, and smallest, category of prisoners to respond to the Soviet campaign did so, curiously, out of anti-Bolshevik sentiment. They enlisted to work against the Soviet regime from within its army, with the thought perhaps of engineering a coup against the government. While there is no way of knowing the number of men who enlisted with such intentions, or how close they may have come to achieving their goal, it is clear that the Soviet government was convinced that the threat was real. On May 23, 1918, Moscow dispatched urgent and confidential orders to all districts under government control warning that "rabid nationalists" among the Germans and Hungarians in the Red Army were planning to execute a political coup in Siberia and to seize control of the critical Trans-Siberian railroad. Local soviets were ordered to dismiss all prisoners of war from executive committees and from all important posts in the army. Considering that foreign Internationalists constituted, in May 1918, the majority of Bolshevik forces, the possibility that an unknown number of them were agents of Berlin and Vienna must have been a chilling thought to the Soviet government.[38]

Those prisoners who had resisted the Soviet recruitment campagn were often subject to harsh treatment. Their camps were placed under the virtual control of the Internationalists, who in turn initiated a propaganda campaign of their own to coerce unsympathetic prisoners. In addition to speeches, posters, mandatory political seminars and the like, recalcitrant prisoners were often subjected to severe pressure. A report by the Danish embassy (which represented the interests of the war prisoners), and confirmed by reports from Elsa Brändström in the field, stated that German, Austrian and Hungarian Internationalists randomly humiliated and brutalized "war prisoners who refused to identify themselves with the Bolsheviks."[39] The position of those who continued to resist enlistment is summed up by a former German prisoner in Siberia, Edwin Dwinger, who recalled: "Two Bolshevik officials met with the prisoners and asked me to translate 'Whoever supports the White troops will be shot, but whoever among you POWs enters our ranks at once becomes a free Russian citizen and will be given pay and arms like our soldiers'."[40]

While the government's recruitment campaign continued to draw soldiers from among the prisoners of war, the regime quietly introduced a radical new program. Not only could the prisoners be used to bolster the ranks of the Red Army in defense of the revolution, but they might also be the source of revolutionary cadres, which could return to Central Europe to found national communist parties and carry the bacillus of revolution to the capitalist enemy. To the prisoners this change had much significance. Fighting for a Bolshevik party that advocated peace was one thing, for peace would surely lead to an improvement in their wretched camp conditions and might even get them home more quickly; but to enter a new war was quite another. Several factors, however, soon gave them second thoughts. First, the massive German attack on Russia on February 18, 1918, caused men to rally to the new flag by the thousands. Then the revelation of Germany's treaty plans for territorial aggrandizement in the east galvanized the prisoners into action. Enlistments rose and revolutionary fervor blazed as the prisoners became convinced that Berlin and Vienna did not desire peace after all; that they had been fighting for an ideal no higher than the quest for territory; and that, whether Central Powers or Entente, the real war was being waged between socialism and capitalism. The second factor that influenced the prisoners to participate in the founding of the Communist International was the treatment which those among them fortunate enough to have been repatriated found waiting for them at home. Many were immediately shipped out to another front and further combat; others were thrown into new camps until their political reliability could be ascertained; and some were even refused entry into their homelands and shipped back to Russia.[41]

The final factor was the new Soviet propaganda campaign emphasizing the need to carry the flames of the revolution into the heart of Europe. The Internationalists were appealed to as the advance guard of the world revolution. Their unit names were changed to reflect greater revolutionary spirit: the Karl Liebknecht Regiment (stationed in Petrograd), the Friedrich Adler Battalion (Petrograd), the First and Second Communist International Regiments (Yaroslavl), the Karl Marx Battalion (Kazan), the Karl Marx Regiment (Novonikolayevsk), and so on. The Bureau of Revolutionary Propaganda shifted into high gear, publishing some 3 million copies of foreign-language newspapers, 800,000 of which were in German, and 900,000 in Hungarian.[42] Special prisoner-of-war congresses were convened in Petrograd on February 20, in Moscow on February 26, and again on March 14, all building toward the grand event: the First All-Russian Congress of Prisoners of War, held in Moscow from April 14 to 16. For those prisoners detained in Central Asia a simultaneous congress took place in Tashkent; for those in Central Siberia a congress met in Irkutsk; Western Siberia in Krasnoyarsk; and for those in Eastern Siberia in Kansk. The main show was in Moscow, of course, and the Soviets pulled out all the stops. Lenin himself welcomed the more than 1,000 delegates who jammed into the largest available auditorium, claiming to represent "520,426 organized prisoners of war." For the following two days, the huge audience was lashed into revolutionary frenzy by speeches in the three official languages of the congress: Russian, German, and Hungarian. "The proletariat has no homeland," the applauding delegates were reminded. "Inflame the country you are returning to, but inflame it not with hatred, but with true fire. Put an end to the state of the capitalists, priests and robber barons. Returning prisoners of war: REVOLT!"[43]

Among the numerous dramatic proclamations and resolutions that came out of the congress – all of which, naturally, pledged the lives and fortunes of the war prisoners in Russia to the new theme of carrying the revolution to Western Europe – one was especially significant. It was the creation of an organization with the cumbersome label of "Foreign Internationalist Socialist Workers' and Peasants' International Association," whose task was the education (read "propaganda") of the prisoners of war. In contrast to the various other organizations and government bureaus, however, the association was not out to enlist military recruits, but political recruits for export to revolution-ripe Germany and Austria-Hungary. The method was simple: all repatriated prisoners, en route to either country, were to be injected with large doses of revolutionary ardor. Those who elected to remain in Russia, as soldiers of the Red Army or as civilians who adopted Russian citizenship, were to be indoctrinated further. The prisoners were now officially involved in the Communist International – a fact underscored by Lenin's decision, a month later, to rename the association just created at the congress. It was simply to be called the Federation of Foreign Sections of the Russian Communist Party.

As a result of the new policy of using POWs as exported revolutionaries, the government opened a special training center in Moscow to create dedicated agents who would be dispatched to their homelands as repatriated prisoners, but would remain under Soviet control. The men were indoctrinated through a rigorous schedule of classroom lectures on Marxism, interspersed with rudimentary training in military intelligence. The center itself was divided into a German and a Hungarian section to prepare agents better for the individual problems of each country, and to lay the groundwork of embryonic communist parties. It was from this center that the German and Hungarian Soviet Republics emerged. According to Russia's suspiciously high figures, Moscow claims to have trained and exported 20,300 such operatives during the spring of 1918, 3,500 of whom were sent to Germany, and 5,000 to Hungary.[44] Another source lists the number of Hungarian agents, equally unrealistically, as 3,000.[45] Far more reasonable is the estimate that "probably no more than 100 trained agitators arrived in Hungary before the proclamation of the Hungarian Soviet Republic on March 21, 1919."[46] Nonetheless, even 100 proved to be enough.

Both Russia's allies and enemies objected to this new tactic of turning returning prisoners into germs of revolution, but the loudest denunciations came, not from the anxious Allies who still feared that the Bolsheviks were acting in Germany's interest, but from Berlin. The Treaty of Brest-Litovsk, after all, contained a clause (Article II) by which both parties had promised to "refrain" from agitation or propaganda against the governmental, public or military institutions of the other. Reacting to reports of "infected" prisoners being repatriated to Germany, the German ambassador in Moscow, Count Mirbach, now head of the German Repatriation Commission, protested angrily. While there is clear evidence that Berlin itself was heavily propagandizing its 1.5 million Russian prisoners, and that the several thousand German and Russian prisoners being repatriated daily by both sides during the spring of 1918 contained agents and agitators going in both directions,[47] Mirbach brought the matter to Trotskiy. It was a ludicrous scene. The German ambassador, whose government was equally guilty of propagandizing its POWs – though far less successfully – confronted the Soviet leader of the Red Army, whose political philosophy was grounded on the export and continuation of world revolution. As one would expect, Trotskiy placated Mirbach with several meaningless gestures. First, he assured the German representative that propaganda activities among the prisoners had ceased, as required by the Treaty of Brest-Litovsk. Any congresses or rallies held by the prisoners, he noted, were their own affair, since they now had the same rights as Russians. Then, by a decree of April 21, Trotskiy announced that official Russian citizenship had been conferred on all foreign nationals serving in the Red Army[48], and was thus able solemnly to assure Count Mirbach that not a single German, or indeed any non-Russian, citizen was serving in the Soviet armed forces. Whether or not he believed the story[49], Mirbach was forced to look on in silent humiliation the next day during a military parade in Moscow as brigades of "German war prisoners brushed by him with the banner calling on German Communists to overthrow their Kaiser as their Russian comrades had overthrown their Tsar."[50] Soviet propaganda not only continued, but increased feverishly.

Recruitment and training centers for foreign activists appeared in numerous Soviet cities, their task now widened to produce three types of POW activists: social organizers for executive positions on the Federation of Foreign Sections, or with their own communist parties when they returned home; military leaders to serve in the Red Army's Internationalist units; and recruiting officers, whose past successes in organizing prisoner enlistment had earned them the privilege of returning to the camps to persuade the hundreds of thousands of still uncommitted prisoners to join the Red Army. These schools' primary purpose was stated in their report for September 1918: "We are not training fancy orators but deeply convinced, sincere fighters for communism who. . .know in full the straight party line of class struggle – even when awakened from a deep sleep."[51] At graduation each group was pledged to travel "near and far, wherever prisoners of war work, . . . in order to carry out political agitation and propaganda."[52]

In this atmosphere of intense propaganda, coupled with the soaring optimism of an impending world revolution, and bolstered by the troops rallying to Moscow's banner in the face of civil war and Allied intervention, enlistment in the Red Army reached its peak in May 1918. While figures differ wildly, the accepted number of German, Austrian and Hungarian prisoners to join the Red Army (and these three nationalities formed the overwhelming majority of the Internationalists) was 90,000 Germans and Austrians, and 100,000 Hungarians.[53] Most eventually fought on all the internal fronts during the civil war.

For the next two years, as the Internationalists fought across Russia, repatriation of the nearly one million other prisoners moved at a snail's pace – obstructed at every turn by the Soviet government. Despite the German government's continual efforts to initiate a massive POW repatriation program –for instance, by sending negotiating teams headed by Moritz Schlesinger and Oskar Cohn of the newly created *Reichszentralstelle für Kriegs- und Zivilgefangene* (Central

Government Bureau for War and Civilian Prisoners) to Moscow[54], or by periodically releasing a batch of Russian prisoners in an attempt to elicit a like return of German prisoners there were few results. The Bolshevik government's position was manifestly equivocal: conciliatory toward Berlin's diplomatic protests, while continuing to propagandize the prisoners. The longer the prisoners could be kept in Russian hands, the longer the Bolsheviks had to indoctrinate them, a procedure that continued well into 1920.[55] As late as May 1920, in fact, the director of the Norwegian Relief Organization, Fridjof Nansen, estimated that there were still 100,000 German, Austrian and Hungarian prisoners of war left in Russia.[56] That figure was doubled by Herbert Hoover's American Relief Association.[57] In 1921 the International Red Cross stated that there were still more than 15,000 prisoners interned in the south of Russia, with many thousands more unaccounted for.[58] Many had settled down to a quiet peasant life; others had found their calling as artisans and laborers. As late as 1924, astonishingly, the American Red Cross estimated that there were still 6,773 prisoners left in Russia – 450 of whom were Germans.[59] Sadly, there is no way of knowing the true number of prisoners who never returned from the Soviet Union, and whether they did so out of personal conviction or by government control.

Better known is the impact many of the politically indoctrinated prisoners had on Germany and Austria-Hungary after they reached home. In midsummer of 1918, Germany's General Wilhelm Groener, later the successor to Erich Ludendorff after the abdication of the Kaiser, lamented "the evil state of mind – Bolshevism – which was being brought into the country from the [Eastern] front."[60] By October, a month before the Armistice, General Max Hoffmann declared helplessly:

> How can the joyful determination of our brave men to give their lives for their country – this sacred fire – be kept burning when ice-cold streams . . . are poured over the army by . . . returned prisoners of war who have been put back into the army? The worst enemy against which the army has to guard itself is Bolshevism. [61]

At the same time, the German secret service reported an influx of repatriated POWs from Russia bringing heavy trunks of what turned out to be virulent revolutionary propaganda destined for delivery to the Russian embassy in Berlin.[62] When the chaos gave way to revolution in November 1918, former prisoners of war from the Russian camps were liberally represented in the naval mutiny at Kiel,[63] as well as in the uprisings in Leipzig, Magdeburg, Hamburg, Düsseldorf, Stuttgart, Oldenburg, Halle, and Bremen.[64]

Then the hardened revolutionaries arrived. Karl Radek himself, disguised as a returning Austrian war prisoner, managed to slip through the lines to Berlin to help direct events.[65] With him was Ernst Reuter, who soon became the secretary-general of the German Communist Party (KPD).[66] In fact, many of the first leaders of the KPD – men like Leo Jogiches, August Thalheimer, Felix Wolf, Ernst Mayer, Franz Aenderl, Rudolf Rothkegel, Hermann Osterloh, Arkadij Maslow, and Fritz Dressel – received their political education in the prison camps of Russia.[67] Together with Rosa Luxemburg and Karl Liebknecht's *Spartakusbund*, the Revolutionary Shop Stewards, and the USPD, these former prisoners of war rode the German revolution to its ultimate collapse in January 1919. Before it was crushed, one enthusiastic participant exclaimed: "The success of the revolution in Germany proves that some of the German war prisoners from Russia did manage to get through!"[68] This was an expansive and unrealistic view of the causes of the upheavals in postwar Germany, to be sure, though not without at least a grain of truth.

The spark of revolution jumped to Austria where the dissolution of the Habsburg Empire provided the dry tinder for the firestorm to follow. Thousands of returning prisoners of war gravitated to Vienna where they generally supported the activities of the Social Democrats. Unlike Germany, which had developed a native communist party without reliance on Moscow, the Austrians had both funds and leadership from Russia – the latter by prisoners of war. Indeed, the Austrian Communist Party was founded by, and drew much of its early leadership from, the prisoners: Gottlieb Fiala, Johann Koplenig, and Karl Toman, to cite but three.[69]

The Hungarian socialist upheaval is curious for several reasons. It was, of course, the longest surviving postwar soviet republic (133 days). It conformed more closely than any of the other socialist experiments to orthodox Leninism. And while it was led by former prisoners of war, the majority of those back from Russia – even those who had been thoroughly trained in Bolshevik schools and were considered highly indoctrinated – simply did not participate. Most of the thousands of POWs who returned to Hungary settled down to their new circumstances, and gave no sign that their participation in the events in Russia had been the result of political conviction. On the other hand, those who did become involved in the Hungarian Soviet Republic played significant and highly visible roles. The Béla Kun regime was, in large measure, led by former prisoners: Ferenc Münnich, Tibor Szamuely, Ferenc Pozsonyi, Endre Rudnyanszky, Imre Nagy, Mátyás Rákosi, and, of course, Béla Kun himself.[70] Moreover, of the eighteen members of the Hungarian Communist Party's Central Committee, six were former leaders of the Hungarian Bolshevik prisoners of war in Russia: Kun, Rabinovics, Seidler, Vántus, Pór, and Nánássy.[71]

Whatever the ultimate fate of the *Spartakusbund,* the Austrian communists, and the Béla Kun regime, as well as a variety of prisoner-led uprisings such as those in Styria[72] or Kragujevac[73] in 1918, the fact is that the leadership was often provided by indoctrinated prisoners of war from Russia. Yet one must be careful not to over-emphasize their importance or generalize their impact. There is little doubt that the Bolsheviks recognized the value of converting the more than 2 million prisoners of war in their hands, and that due to dismal camp conditions and a variety of other circumstances, the regime wa quite successful. It is clear that the prisoners enlisted in the Red forces in large numbers – particularly those from Germany and Austria-Hungary – and that they helped tip the military balance in the Bolsheviks' favor. Indeed, one can state that these International units helped to establish the soviets in power, especially in Siberia where they made up the bulk of the Red Army. Also clear is the fact that many of the repatriated prisoners succeeded in organizing the *already fermenting* revolutions in postwar Central and Eastern Europe, and promoted Soviet influence in the development of those upheavals. One may even speculate whether their appearance and participation in these events did not fuel the rise of the right-wing nationalist groups that came in their wake. Could the strength, virulence, and anti-Semitism of the *Freikorps* or the Gyula Gombos-led Awakening Magyars, for instance, have increased in proportion to the growing strength of local communist parties, whose own growth can be traced to the returning prisoners from Russia? It would be one of History's supreme ironies to think that the Bolsheviks, by repatriating indoctrinated prisoners, inadvertantly created Fascism in Germany – since it was Germany, of course, which introduced Lenin into Russia, inadvertantly creating Bolshevism.

In the final analysis, however, it appears that the prisoners of war who became prominent in communist affairs in later years were those who already had firm convictions about socialism. However temporarily successful in the chaotic years following the end of World War I, the long-term effects of Russia's prisoners of war on the history of Central and Eastern Europe has been slight. Yet, between 1917 and 1921, in Russia, they may well have changed the course of history.

NOTES

1. Johan W. Prins, "With Prisoners of War in Siberia," *Asia [and the Americas]*, XIX (January, 1919), p. 67.

2. Charles Roetter, *The Art of Psychological Warfare, 1914-1945* (New York, 1974), pp. 74-75.

3. *To Make Men Traitors: Germany's Attempts to Seduce Her Prisoners of War* (London, 1918).

4. Erich von Ludendorff, *Meine Kriegserinnerung 1914-1918* (Berlin, 1919), p. 566. For a fascinating review of psychological warfare by various sides, see Wilhelm Ernest, *Die antideutsche Propaganda durch das Schweizer Gibiet im Weltkrieg, speziell die Propaganda im Bayern* (Munich, 1933); Hans von Hentig, *Psychologische Strategie des grossen Kriegs* (Heidelberg, 1927), Vol. IV; George Huber; *Die französische Propaganda im Weltkrieg gegen Deutschland 1914 bis 1918* (Munich, 1928); and Alfred Charles Northcliffe, *Die Geschichte des englischen Propagandafeldzugs* (Berlin, 1921).

5. See the outstanding study by Robert C. Williams, "Russian War Prisoners and Soviet-German Relations, 1918-1921," *Canadian Slavonic Papers*, IX, No. 2 (1967), 270-295; also Ernst Drahn, *Bibliographie der frontpropagandaschriften deutscher Sprache im Weltkrieg (Entente)* (Oldenburg i.O., 1919);

Ludolf Gottschalk von dem Knesebeck, *Die Wahrheit über den Propaganda Feldzug und Deutschlands Zusammenbruch; Der Kampf der Publizistik im Weltkrieg* (Munich, 1927).

6. David Francis, *Russia from the American Embassy (April 1916-November 1918)* (New York, 1921), p. 4.

7. Elsa Brändström, *Among Prisoners of War in Russia and Siberia* (London, 1929), p. 234.

8. George F. Kennan, *Soviet-American Relations, 1917-1920* (Princeton, N.J., 1958), Vol. II: *The Decision to Intervene*, p. 71.

9. Iván Völgyes, "Hungarian Prisoners of War in Russia, 1916-1919," *Cahiers du monde russe et soviétique*, XIV (Janvier-Juin, 1973), 54.

10. Rudolf L. Tökés, *Béla Kun and the Hungarian Soviet Republic: The Origins and Role of the Communist Party of Hungary in the Revolutions of 1918-1919* (Stanford, Calif., 1967), pp. 49-50.

11. A. Klevanskiy, "Voyennoplennye tsentral'nykh derzhav v tsarskoy i revoliutsionalisty Rossii 1914-1918 g.," in M.A. Birman *et. al.* (eds.), *Internatsionalisty v boyakh za vlast' Sovetov* (Moscow, 1965), p. 23.

12. V.I. Lenin, *The Imperialist War* (Moscow, 1930), pp. 61, 63. Among the prisoners, Lenin always believed that "the German proletariat is the most trustworthy and reliable ally of the Russian and proletarian world revolution." V.I. Lenin, *Collected Works* (New York, 1932), XXIII, 235.

13. Prior to the March Revolution, the tsarist government was so successful in capitalizing on the dissatisfaction of the Czech element in the Austrian prison camps, that France and Italy decided to support a similar independence movement. After March 24, 1917, the Russian government authorized an independent Czechoslovak Legion to function as the armed force of Masaryk's Czech National Council in Paris, their number eventually rising to more than 60,000.

14. Jenö Györkei and Józsa Anatal, *Magyar internacionalisták a Nagy Október Szocialista Forradalomban* [Hungarian Internationalists in the Great October Socialist Revolution] (Budapest, 1957), p. 18; and the outstanding study by Völgyes, *op. cit.*, p. 57.

15. Jenö Lévai, *Féher Cártól — Vörös Leninig: Magyar hadifoglyok szenvedései Oroszországban* [From White Tsar — to Red Lenin: The Suffering of Hungarian Prisoners of War in Russia] (Budapest, 1932), 1., füzet, p. 3.

16. "The gaping distance between the officers and men became obvious at the moment of capture," wrote the famous Hungarian novelist and participant, Lajos Zilahy, "for while the former usually had some money and valuables with which to help themselves, however sparingly . . . the soldiers existed without a penny, [and were] thrown into the greatest uncertainty." *Hadifogoly magyarok története* [The History of Hungarian Prisoners of War] (Budapest, 1930), p. 60.

17. Edwin Erich Dwinger, *The Army Behind Barbed Wire* (London, 1930), p. 250.

18. The death rate was higher in Russia's POW camps than in the prison camps of any other country in the war. Approximately 300,000 - 400,000 prisoners perished in Russia! (Völgyes, *op. cit.*, p. 58; Tökés, *op. cit.*, p. 50).

19. A. Manushevich, "Iz Istorii Uchastiya Internatsionalistov v Oktyabr'-skom Vooruzhennom Vostanii" [From the History of the Internationalists' Participation in the October Armed Uprising], *Novaya i Noveyshaya Istoriya*, No. 6, 1962, p. 43; Margarete Klante, "Die deutschen Kriegsgefangenen in

Russland,'' in Max Schwarte (ed.), *Der grosse Krieg, 1914-1918* (Leipzig, 1923), p. 200.

20. N.A. Popov, ''Revolyutsionnye Vystuplenii Voyennoplennykh v Rossii v Godakh Pervoy Mirovoy Voiny'' [Revolutionary Activities of Prisoners of War in Russia during the First World War], *Voprosy Istorii,* No. 2, 1963, p. 80; L.I. Zharov and V.M. Ustinov, *Internatsional'nye Chasti Krasnoy Armii v Boyakh za Vlast' Sovetov v Gody Inostrannoy Voyennoy Interventsii i Grazhdanskoy Voiny v SSSR* [Internationalist Units in the Red Army in the Years of Foreign Intervention and Civil War in USSR] (Moscow, 1960), p. 11.

21. G.B. Shumenko (ed.), *Voyennoye Sodruzhestvo Trudyashchikhsya Zarubezhnykh Stran a Narodami Sovetskoy Rossii, 1917-1922* [Military Solidarity of Foreign Workers with the Peoples of Soviet Russia] (Moscow, 1957), pp. 38-40.

22. Drahn, *op. cit.,* pp. 5-10.

23. Shumenko, *op. cit.,* p. 40.

24. John Bradley, *Allied Intervention in Russia* (New York, 1968), pp. 59, 62; Charles H. Briscoe, ''The POW Problem in Russia: Justification for Allied Intervention, 1918-1920,'' (Master of Military Arts and Science thesis, US Army Command and General Staff College, Ft. Leavenworth, Kansas, 1977), pp. 56-99.

25. Louise Bryant, *Six Months in Russia* (New York, 1918), p. 278.

26. Ivan Ulyanov, ''Oktyabr'skaya Revolyutsiya i Voyennoplennye'' [The October Revolution and the Prisoners of War], *Proletarskaya Revolyutsiya,* No. 7 (90), 1929, p. 96.

27. Jenö Györkei and Józsa Antal, ''Adalékok a Nagy Októberi Szocialista Forrandalomban és a Szovjetunió polgárháborúbán részt vett magyar Internacionalisták törtenétéhez'' [Data on the History of the Hungarian Internationalist Participants in the Great October Socialist Revolution and the Russian Civil War], *Hadtörténelmi Közlemények,* Nos. 3-4, 1957, p. 32.

28. *Znamya Truda,* April 19, 1918, p. 3, cited in James T. Bunyan, *Intervention, Civil War, and Communism in Russia April - December 1918: Documents and Materials* (Baltimore, 1936), p. 95.

29. Ernest Didring, (ed.), *Sveriges hjälp till Krigsfangarna, 1915-1919* [Sweden's Aid to Prisoners of War, 1915-1919] (Stockholm, 1920), p. 38; *Rapports sur les visites des camps des prisonniers en Russie et Allemagne par les délégations de Croix-rouge danoise* (Copenhagen, 1916).

30. John K. Caldwell to Secretary of State Robert Lansing, July 25, 1918, in *Papers Relating to the Foreign Relations of the United States: The Lansing Papers, 1914-1920* [hereafter cited as *Lansing Papers*], Vol. II: *1918, Russia* (Washington, D.C., 1939-1940), 302.

31. The number of Internationalists who served in the Red Army during any particular period is most difficult to estimate. During these first three months of 1918, for example, Margarete Klante states that only 18,000 men joined the Red Army *(Von der Wolga zum Amur: Die Tschechische Legion und der russische Burgerkrieg* [Berlin-Königsberg, 1931, p. 98); Ulyanov *(op. cit.)* states that 50,000 prisoners volunteered; Elsa Brändström places the figure at a rather high 90,000 *(op. cit.,* p. 239); and Louis Fischer dismisses out of hand the notion that any prisoners joined the Red Army *(The Soviets in World Affairs* [London, 1930], I, 104-105).

32. According to the files of the Supreme Military Collegium, recruitment from among Russian nationals was, as late as April 9, 1918, negligible. For example, in Nizhniy Novgorod only 174 men were pursuaded to enlist; not a single volunteer in Voronezh, or in Ivanovoznetsk; and in Irkutsk only 350 men joined. Fic. *op. cit.*, p. 116.

33. K. Yeremeyev, "Nachalo Krasnoy Armii" [The Beginning of the Red Army], *Proletarskaya Revolyutsiya,* No. 4, 1928, p. 155; N.I. Shatagin, *Organizatsiya i stroitel'stvo Sovetskoy Armii v period innostrannoy voyennoy interventsii i grazhdanskoy voiny 1918-1920 g.* [Organization of the Soviet Army during the Foreign Intervention and Civil War, 1918-1920] (Moscow, 1954), pp. 55-63; Kennan, *op. cit.*, p. 73.

34. Fic, *op. cit.*, p. 110.

35. C.S., "A Red Guardist's Narrative, I," *Living Age,* CCCV (April 21, 1920), 96-98; Gusztáv Grátz (ed.), *A Bolsevizmus Magyarországon* [Bolshevism in Hungary] (Budapest, 1921), p. 60.

36. K.I. Albrecht, *Der verrantene Sozialismus* [Treasonous Socialism] (Berlin, 1934), pp. 568-569.

37. N.A. Popov, *op. cit.*, p. 87.

38. See Fic., *op. cit.*, pp. 178-185, for additional information on this important episode.

There is also substantial evidence that Berlin did, in fact, have plans to organize such a coup with the help of German Internationalists in the Red Army, and that the German government often reminded its nationals in Russian captivity that rewards and punishments would be meted out to them at the end of the war. See Kennan, *op. cit.*, pp. 314-5; Francis to Washington, June 19, 1918, *Lansing Papers,* I, 563-4; John A. White, "Siberian Intervention: The Allied Phase" (Ph.D. Dissertation, Stanford University, 1947), pp. 311-312.

39. Brändström, *op. cit.*, p. 239.

40. Edwin E. Dwinger, *Prisoner of War: A Siberian Diary,* (New York, 1930), pp. 225, 279.

41. Ferencz Münnich, *Kun Béla a Magyar Tanácsköztársaságról* [Béla Kun and the Hungarian Soviet Republic] (Budapest, 1954), p. 541.

42. Ulyanov, *op. cit.*, p. 109.

43. *Izvestia,* April 15, 1918; *Pravda, April 16, 1918;* Völgyes, *op. cit.*, p. 78.

44. Ulyanov, *op. cit.*, p. 109.

45. Elemér Mályusz, *The Fugitive Bolsheviks* (London, 1931), p. 147.

46. Völgyes, *op. cit.*, p. 80.

47. See, for example, E. Willis, *Herbert Hoover and the Russian Prisoners of World War I: A Study in Diplomacy and Relief 1918-1919* (Stanford, 1951), pp. 11-12; Conrad Hoffman. *In the Prison Camps of Germany: A Narrative of "Y" Service Among Prisoners of War* (New York, 1920), pp. 81-83; K. Bothmer, *Mit Graf Mirbach in Moskau: Tagebuch vom 19 April bis 24 August 1918* (Tübingen, 1922); but most importantly, Robert C. Williams, *op. cit.*, who reveals that in the summer of 1918 Berlin was even exploring the possibility of organizing a Russian volunteer army composed of Russian prisoners for use against both the Bolsheviks and the Allies (pp. 275-6).

Despite these early prisoner exchanges, it was nearly two years after the Treaty of Brest-Litovsk before a large-scale evacuation started. The Bolsheviks, even more than the Germans, were suspicious of the spies and agents who might be among the returnees. Moreover, Moscow was aware that the British were planning to move against north Russia and Turkestan, and that any Internationalists repatriated from those areas would leave Siberia seriously weakened. Consequently, the Bolsheviks obstructed Danish and Swedish Red Cross attempts to negotiate major prisoner exchanges until 1920.

48. Jane Degras (ed.), *Soviet Documents on Foreign Policy* (London, 1951), Vol. I: *1917-1924*, pp. 70-1.

49. George Kennan, surprisingly, does believe the story! In *Decision to Intervene (op. cit.)* he states that "the entire effort of recruitment was, in fact, a short one . . . It was terminated at the insistence of [the German and Austrian governments], and the communist formations were broken up, as soon as the German and Austrian repatriation and welfare commissions (made possible by the Brest-Litovsk Treaty) arrived on the spot." (p. 73).

50. William Hard, *Raymond Robin's Own Story* (New York, 1920), p. 227.

51. "A Magyar Kommunista Csoport Munkája" [The Hungarian Communist Section's Activities], *Szociális Forradalom* (Moscow), No. 51 (September 21, 1918), in Mrs. Sándor Gábor (ed.), *A magyar munkásmozgalom történetének válogattot dokumentumai* [Selected Documents from the History of the Hungarian Workers' Movement], Vol. V: *November 7, 1917 - March 21, 1919* (Budapest, 1956), pp. 116-117.

52. Pál Gisztl, "Az Oroszországi Kommunista (Bolsevik) Párt Magyar Csoportja megalakulásának 40. évfordulójára [The Fortieth Anniversary of the Formation of the Hungarian Section of the Russian Communist (Bolshevik) Party], *Párttörténelmi Közlemények*, No. 2, 1958, p. 183: Völgyes, *op. cit.*, pp. 73-81.

Despite these efforts to create a horde of political cadres, the government was relatively unsuccessful. In the words of Professor Völgyes, "the Military Division was more successful in making internationalists out of the prisoners . . . than the propaganda division in making Bolsheviks out of the internationalists." *(op. cit.*, p. 81).

53. *Pravda*, March 21, 1959; Völgyes, *op. cit.*, p. 73; K.L. Selesnjow, "Unbekannte Namen 1918/1919 im Fernen Osten gefallener deutscher Internationalisten," *Beträge zur Geschichte der Arbeiterbewegung*, 3/1974, p. 448; Rudi Dix and Sonja Striegnitz, "Deutsche Internationalisten im Kampf für die Sowjetmacht 1917-1920," *Die Grosse Sozialistische Oktoberrevolution und Deutschland*, II (Berlin, 1967), pp. 9.

54. For the detailed records of these missions and negotiations, *see Victor Kopp 1920-27*, Roll 4794, Serial L. 671; *Moritz Schlesinger: 1920*, Roll 2457, Serial 4829; and *Personal Correspondence*, Roll 2458, "The Records of the German Foreign Office Received by the Department of State," Microfilm Publication T120, National Archives, Washington, D.C.; microfilm collection of the *Nachrichtenblatt der Reichszentralstelle für Kriegs- und Zivilgefange* in N.Y. Public Library.

55. See the pamphlets by Franz Cleinow, "Bürger, Arbeiter Rettet Europa! Erlebnisse im sterbenden Russland," (Berlin, 1920); Otto Friedl, "Erlebnisse eines Deutschen in der Roten Armee," (Berlin, 1919).

56. John Sorensen, *Saga of Fridjof Nansen* (New York, 1932), p. 280.

57. Herbert Hoover, *Herbert Hoover: An American Epic (Famine in Forty-*

five Nations: Organization Behind the Front 1914-1920), II (Chicago, 1960), 385.

58. "Rapport Général - Comité international de la Croix-rouge." *10e Conférence International de la Croix-rouge,* March 30, 1921 (Geneva), p. 127.

On at least one occasion the prisoners were actually used for international bargaining. That was when the Soviet government sought to free the survivors of the abortive Béla Kun regime in Budapest by declaring the large number of Hungarian officers still in Russian captivity to be hostages. See Gustav Hilger and Alfred G. Meyer, *The Incompatible Allies: A Memoir-History of German-Soviet Relations, 1918-1941* (New York, 1953), pp. 42-3; and the vitriolic exposé in Mályusz, *op. cit.*, pp. 33-34, 156-157, 258.

"Mr. Felix Warburg's Address at Meeting of the Siberian Repatriation Fund" in Gaston Lichtenstein, *Repatriation of Prisoners of War From Siberia* (Washington, D.C., 1924), p. 14.

60. Ralph Lutz, *Fall of the German Empire, 1914-1918* (Stanford, Calif., 1932), p. 113.

These words were echoed by Winston Churchill, who noted: "The German prisoners liberated by the Treaty of Brest-Litovsk returned infected with the Lenin virus." *The World Crisis, 1916-1918* (New York, 1927), II, 218.

61. Lutz, *op. cit.*, p. 113.

62. Walter Nicolai, *"Die Gesamtlege,"* Süddeutsche Monatshefte, *April, 1924, p. 24;* The Times (London), November 7, 1918.

63. See Daniel Horn, *War, Mutiny and Revolution in the German Navy. The World War I Diary of Seaman Richard Strumpf* (New Brunswick, N.J., 1967); Charles Rubin, *The Log of Rubin the Sailor* (New York, 1973).

64. See Gisela Jähn and Hans-Werner Schaaf, "Die Unterstützung Sowjetrusslands durch das Proletariat in den Jahren der revolutionären Nachkriegkrise," *Die Grosse Sozialistische . . .*, pp. 117-147.

65. For a detailed account, see Otto-Ernst Schüddekopf, *Karl Radek in Berlin: Ein Kapitel deutsch-russischer Beziehungen im Jahre 1919* (Hannover, 1962); a summary article by the same author in *Archiv für Sozialgeschichte,* II (1962), 87-166; E.H. Carr, "Radek's Political Salon in Berlin 1919," *Soviet Studies,* III, No. 4 (1952), pp. 411-430; Warren Lerner, *Karl Radek: The Last Internationalist* (Stanford, Calif., 1970), Chapter 5; and for a wider though no less detailed account of this era, Seymour Rotter, "Soviet and Comintern Policy toward Germany, 1919-1923" (Ph.D. Dissertation, Columbia University, 1954).

66. For a detailed look at Reuter's experience as a POW in Russia, his attraction to the Revolution, and his leadership of the KPD, see Willy Brandt and Richard Löwenthal, *Ernst Reuter: Ein Leben für die Freiheit* (Munich, 1957), especially Chapters 2 ("Rebell im Weltkrieg"), 3 ("Volkskommissar an der Wolga"), and 4 ("Genosse Friesland"). Perhaps most important in Reuter's biography is a very useful 16-page list of friends, comrades and fellow prisoners of war in Russia (pp. 745-58). See also, the Ernst Reuter Archive Microfilm Collection at the Hoover Institution; Donald Blair Pryce, "German Government Policy Towards the Radical Left, 1918-1923" (Ph.D. Dissertation, Stanford University, 1969).

67. Hermann Weber, *Die Wandlung des deutschen Kommunismus: Die Stalinisierung der KPD in der Weimarer Republik,* II (Frankfurt a/M, 1969),

59, 99, 213, 241, 265; Ossip K. Flechtheim, *Die kommunistische Partei Deutshlands in der Weimarer Republik* (Offenbach a/M, 1948).

Ironically, the man who helped organize Lenin's transport from Switzerland, Philip Scheidemann, ruefully conceded that "Liebknecht [head of the *Spartakusbund*] has been carried high by the soldiers who have been decorated with the Iron Cross." "From Prussianism to Bolshevism," "*Independent*, XCVI, November 23, 1918.

68. Hereward T. Price, *Boche and Bolshevik: Experiences of an Englishman in the German Army and in Russian Prisons* (London, 1919), p. 224.

69. Branko M. Lazitch and Milorad M. Drachkovitch, *Biographical Dictionary of the Comintern* (Stanford, Calif., 1973), pp. 97, 195, 407. In at least on significant case, that of the well-known socialist statesman, Otto Bauer, imprisonment committed him to andt-Bolshevism.

70. Lazitch, *op. cit.*, pp. 205, 281, 286, 328, 350, and 393; István Deák, "Budapest and the Hungarian Revolutions of 1918-1919," *The Slavonic and East European Review*, XLVI, 106 (January 1968).

71. Tökés, *op. cit.*, p. 95-96.

72. Richard Georg Plaschka, et. al., *Innere Front: Militärassistenz, Widerstand und Umsturz in der Donaumonarchie 1918* (Vienna, 1974) I, 278-290.

73. Gerburg and Thunig-Nittner, *Die tschechoslowakische Legion in Russland: Ihre Geschichte und Bedeutung bei der Entstehung der 1. Tschechoslowakischen Republik* (Wiesbaden, 1970).

CONTRIBUTORS

Banac, Ivo; Associate Professor of History, Yale University

Davis, Gerald H.; Professor of History, Georgia State University

Fichtner, Paula S.; Professor of History, Brooklyn College and the Graduate School CUNY

Jannen, William, Jr.; Assistant Professor of History, Brooklyn College CUNY

Kalvoda, Josef; Professor of History and Political Science, St. Joseph College

Király, Béla K.; Professor of History, Brooklyn College and the Graduate School CUNY.

Krammer, Arnold; Professor of History, Texas A & M University

Palumbo, Michael; Graduate School and University Center CUNY

Pastor, Peter; Professor of History, Montclair State College of New Jersey

Williams, Rowan A.; Associate Professor of History, U.S. Naval Academy

Williamson, Samuel R., Jr.; Professor of History, Dean College of Arts and Sciences, University of North Carolina at Chapel Hill

BROOKLYN COLLEGE STUDIES
ON SOCIETY IN CHANGE

Distributed by Columbia University Press
(except No. 5)

Editor -in-Chief Béla K. Király

No. 1— *Tolerance and Movements of Religious Dissent in Eastern Europe.* Edited by B. K. Király, 1975. Second Printing, 1977.

No. 2 — *The Habsburg Empire in World War I.* Edited by R. A. Kann, B. K. Király, P. S. Fichtner, 1976. Second Printing, 1978.

No. 3 — *The Mutual Effects of the Islamic and the Judeo-Christian Worlds: The East European Pattern.* Edited by A. Ascher, T. Halasi-Kun, B. K. Király, 1979.

No. 4 — *Before Watergate: Problems of Corruption in American Society.* Edited by A. S. Eisenstadt, A. Hoogenboom, H. L. Trefousse, 1978.

No. 5 — *East Central European Perceptions of Early America.* Edited by B. K. Király and G. Barany. Lisse, The Netherlands: Peter de Ridder Press, 1977. Distributed by Humanities Press, Atlantic Highlands, N.J.

No. 6 – *The Hungarian Revolution of 1956 in Retrospect.* Edited by B.K. Király and P. Jonas, 1978. Second Printing, 1980.

No. 7 – *Brooklyn U.S.A.: Fourth Largest City in America.* Edited by R. S. Miller, 1979.

No. 8 – János Décsy. *Prime Minister Gyula Andrássy's Influence on Habsburg Foreign Policy during the Franco-German War of 1870-1871,* 1979.

No. 9 – Robert F. Horowitz. *The Great Impeacher: A Political Biography of James M. Ashley,* 1979.

* * * *

Subseries: War and Society in East Central Europe

No. 10 – Vol. I *Special Topics and Generalizations on the Eighteenth and Nineteenth Centuries.* Edited by B. K. Király and G. E. Rothenberg, 1979.

No. 11 – Vol. II *East Central European Society and War in the Pre-Revolutionary Eighteenth Century.* Edited by G. E. Rothenberg, B. K. Király and P. Sugar, 1982.

No. 12 – Vol. III *From Hunyadi to Rákóczi: War and Society in Late Medieval and Early Modern Hungary.* Edited by J. M. Bak and B. K. Király, 1982.

No. 13 – Vol. IV *East Central European Society and War in the Era of Revolutions, 1775-1856,* forthcoming.

No. 14 – Vol. V *Essays on World War I: Origins and Prisoners of War.* Edited by S. R. Williamson, Jr. and P. Pastor, 1982.

No. 15 – Vol. VI *Essays on World War I: Total War and Peacemaking, A Case Study on Trianon.* Edited by B. K. Király, P. Pastor and I. Sanders, forthcoming.

No. 16 – Vol. VII Thomas M. Barker. *Army, Aristocracy, Monarchy: War, Society and Government in Austria, 1618-1870,* forthcoming.

No. 17 – Vol. VIII *The First Serbian Uprising.* Edited by Wayne S. Vucinich, forthcoming.

No. 18 – Vol. IX Kálmán Janics. *Czechoslovak Policy and the Hungarian Minority, 1945-1948,* forthcoming.

No. 19 – Vol. X *At the Brink of War and Peace: The Tito-Stalin Split in Historic Perspective.* Edited by Wayne S. Vucinich, forthcoming.

* * * *

No. 20 – *Inflation through the Ages: Economic, Social, Psychological and Historical Aspects.* Edited by N. Schmukler and E. Marcus, 1982.

No. 21 *Germany and America: Essays on Problems of International Relations and Immigration.* Edited by H. L. Trefousse, 1980.

No. 22 Murray M. Horowitz. *Brooklyn College: The First Half Century,* 1981.

No. 23 – Jason Berger. *A New Deal for the World: Eleanor Roosevelt and American Foreign Policy,* 1981.

No. 24 – *The Legacy of Jewish Migration: 1881 and Its Impact.* Edited by D. Berger, forthcoming.